D1480453

TINBERGEN
LECTURES
ON ECONOMIC POLICY

TINBERGEN LECTURES
ON ECONOMIC POLICY

Edited by

A. KNOESTER
University of Nijmegen
Erasmus University Rotterdam
The Netherlands

A.H.E.M. WELLINK
De Nederlandsche Bank N.V.
Free University Amsterdam
The Netherlands

N·H

1993

NORTH-HOLLAND

AMSTERDAM - LONDON - NEW YORK - TOKYO

ELSEVIER SCIENCE PUBLISHERS B.V.
Sara Burgerhartstraat 25
P.O. Box 211, 1000 AE Amsterdam, The Netherlands

Library of Congress Cataloging-in-Publication Data

Tinbergen lectures on economic policy / edited by A. Knoester, A.H.E.M. Wellink.
   p.   cm.
   Includes bibliographical references and indexes.
   ISBN 0-444-81569-4 (alk. paper)
   1. Economic policy.   2. Economic development.   3. Welfare economics.
4. Macroeconomics.   I. Knoester, A.   II. Wellink, A.H.E.M.   III. Tinbergen,
Jan, 1903—
HD87.T56   1993
338.9–dc20   93-15948
                                                            CIP

ISBN: 0 444 81569 4

This book is printed on acid-free paper.

Printed in The Netherlands.

PREFACE

This book contains the six Tinbergen Lectures held since 1987, when the Royal Netherlands Economic Association established this annual cycle of lectures in honour of one of its greatest members, Jan Tinbergen, who (together with R. Frisch) was awarded the first Nobel Prize for Economics in 1969. These Tinbergen Lectures were held at the invitation of the association's board by prominent and distinguished economists of international standing, viz. Lawrence R. Klein, Edmond Malinvaud, James Tobin, János Kornai, Robert M. Solow and Martin Feldstein. The lectures are preceded by a brief outline of their content and a chapter dealing with Tinbergen's membership of the Royal Netherlands Economic Association, which now already spans a period of more than sixty years. Next, Kol and De Wolff discuss the change and continuity in Tinbergen's work on the basis of a selection of Tinbergen's scientific publications, which now number well over 900. We wish to thank all those who have made the publication of this book possible. We are especially indebted to the board of editors of De Economist for its permission to reprint the six Tinbergen Lectures and the contribution of Kol and De Wolff, all of which were published previously in this journal in its volumes 136-141. We also gratefully acknowledge the financial support received from the Netherlands Ministry of Economic Affairs, the Trust Fund of Erasmus University Rotterdam and the Royal Netherlands Economic Association. Without their help, this publication would not have been possible. Last but not least, we would like to thank Mrs Mieke Karemaker-Van Petten, Mrs Paula Hofkamp-Quint and Mrs Marianne Brans for their stimulating and buoyant help in completing the manuscript, Mr Coen Collee for his professional help in correcting the English of the editors' contribution and Mr Piet Mallekoote, Mr Diederick Nevenzeel, Mrs Renske Oort and Mrs Cora Zonderland for providing the relevant material on the addresses delivered by Tinbergen to the Royal Netherlands Economic Association.

The Hague/Wassenaar, November 1992   Anthonie Knoester
                                                      Arnout H.E.M. Wellink

NOTE ON THE CONTRIBUTORS

Martin Feldstein	Professor of Economics, Harvard University, and President of the National Bureau of Economic Research
Lawrence R. Klein	Benjamin Franklin Professor of Economics, University of Pennsylvania, and Nobel Prize Winner for Economics 1980
Anthonie Knoester	Professor of Economics, University of Nijmegen, Professor of Economic Policy, Erasmus University Rotterdam, and President of the Royal Netherlands Economic Association
Jacob Kol	Associate Professor of International Economics and Economic Integration, Erasmus University Rotterdam
János Kornai	Professor of Economics, Harvard University, and Professor of Economics, Hungarian Academy of Sciences
Edmond Malinvaud	Professor, Collège de France, former Director General of the Institut National de la Statistique et des Etudes Economiques
Robert M. Solow	Professor of Economics, Massachusetts Institute of Technology, and Nobel Prize Winner for Economics 1987
James Tobin	Sterling Professor Emeritus of Economics, Yale University, and Nobel Prize Winner for Economics 1981

Arnout H.E.M. Wellink   Executive Director of De Nederlandsche Bank
                         NV, Extraordinary Professor of Money and Banking,
                         Free University of Amsterdam, and Secretary-Treasurer
                         of the Royal Netherlands Economic Association

Pieter de Wolff   Emeritus Professor of Economics, University
                         of Amsterdam, and former Director of the Central
                         Planning Bureau

CONTENTS

SIX TINBERGEN LECTURES ON ECONOMIC POLICY

BY

ANTHONIE KNOESTER AND ARNOUT H.E.M. WELLINK

1 INTRODUCTION

The institute of annual Tinbergen Lectures was established by the Royal Netherlands Economic Association in 1987 in honour of one of its greatest members, Jan Tinbergen, who (together with R. Frisch) was awarded the first Nobel Prize for Economics in 1969. This book contains the lectures which have been delivered from 1987 onwards by distinguished economists of international standing, all of which were published afterwards in the association's quarterly journal De Economist.[1] By way of introduction, this chapter provides a brief outline of these lectures. Before the actual reprints in chapters 4 to 9 of the six Tinbergen Lectures delivered thus far, chapter 2 presents a brief description of the historical roots of the Royal Netherlands Economic Association and Tinbergen's role in it during his membership, now already spanning a period of more than sixty years. In addition, chapter 3 contains a survey of the change and continuity in Tinbergen's work by Kol and De Wolff.

2 ON MACROECONOMETRICS, PROFITABILITY AND MACROECONOMIC POLICY

On October 24, 1987 Lawrence R. Klein delivered the first Tinbergen Lecture in The Hague. Concerned with carrying forward the Tinbergen initiative in macroeconometrics, Klein reviewed highlights in macroeconometric modelling since the late 1930s, the period in which Tinbergen founded this nowadays well-established branch of economics. However, Kol and De Wolff rightly argue that in the late 1930s Tinbergen's work on economic modelling was seen as rather arbitrary, quoting for instance Keynes in saying: '... that there is anyone I would trust with it at the present stage or that this brand of statistical alchemy is ripe to become a branch of science, I am not yet persuaded'.[2] By referring, for example,

---

1   See Feldstein(1993), Klein(1988), Kornai(1992), Malinvaud(1989), Solow(1992), Tobin(1990), reprinted in this book with the kind permission of the editors of De Economist.
2   Compare Kol and De Wolff, chapter 3, and Keynes (1940).

to his conversation with Jacob Marschak towards the end of the war, when Marschak stated: '...what this country (the USA) needs is a new Tinbergen model'[3] Klein makes perfectly clear how at that time Keynes misjudged the importance of economic modelling.

Klein also notes the difficulties in economic modelling in those early years when no computers were yet available. According to him, the early models may look very simple from today's vantage point, but in those days it was an enormous task to build them without the help of the postwar electronic computer. The nucleus of Klein's lecture deals with the way in which Tinbergen's work is embedded in economics. Klein argues that it was built on Keynes' contributions to macroeconomic theory and on Kuznets' design of accounts to measure national income and product while Leontief's input-output models helped to extend this to many industrial sectors. Klein also stresses that Tinbergen developed macroeconomic models as a fundamental tool for economic analysis, viz. the formation of economic policy by using instruments and targets of economic policy. According to Klein, it is of the utmost importance that structural models - contrary to pure time series models such as those of the ARIMA or VAR type - should be available in order to use these concepts of Tinbergen to advantage in policy formation. Klein also deals with the extension of Tinbergen's original work on national models to world models capable of handling an entirely fresh class of problems such as international policy coordination, world crises, debt default and oil price rises, disarmament and protectionism and trade wars. Klein ends his lecture with a discussion of the new classical theory in which rational expectations are seen as extremely important. According to him '...This approach to expectations formation is said to be forward-looking, while the mainstream approach, initiated by Professor Tinbergen, is said to be backward-looking. This is, in my opinion, a very unfortunate and misleading way of presenting expectation behavior.' Klein argues that rational expectations constitute no more than a theoretical hypothesis for which sample surveys provide very weak support. Apart from this, Klein notes several more reasons why the claims made by the new classical economists should be taken with a grain of salt.

In the second Tinbergen Lecture on October 8, 1988, Edmond Malinvaud concentrates on the main question motivating his research in the past decade, viz. the medium-term relationship between wages and employment. Malinvaud rightly notes that this question also concerned Tinbergen as early as fifty years ago[4] and stresses that this question is still topical today. In his opinion, a precise analysis of the demand for labour and capital is a prerequisite for understanding this relationship. For this reason, Malinvaud scrutinizes two major propositions, viz. that, on the one hand, the productive capacity chosen by a firm mainly depends

---

3   See Klein, chapter 4.
4   In this respect Malinvaud refers to, among others, Tinbergen and De Wolff (1939).

on its expectations about future demand and on the profitability of production and that, on the other, the desired capital intensity mainly depends on the relative cost of capital with respect to labour. This analysis is preceded by an overview of the three conclusions to be drawn about the relationship between profitability and investment:

- caution is called for as regards the role of profitability because the value of Tobin's q is endogenous;
- the elasticity of productive capacity with respect to profitability varies a great deal, depending on the reference equilibrium, making its role strongly non-linear;
- production capacity depends not only on profitability and on the random distribution of demand, but also on relative factor costs. At the same time, capital intensity depends not only on relative factor costs but also on profitability and the distribution of demand.

Next, Malinvaud shows in formal derivations how to deal with the behaviour of firms and how to reach relevant statics properties. One of his concerns is that wage restraint, although conducive to profitability, is likely to depress demand. Whether or not it helps to stimulate the creation of new productive capacities depends on which one of two effects predominates. Similar conclusions can be drawn for other policy issues. Therefore, Malinvaud sees the model as developed by him as a major building block for larger equation systems. He also argues that it should be used in more embracing theories such as those studied by Tinbergen in the 1930s. Malinvaud ends his lecture by referring to two empirical tests which seem to support his theoretical model on profitability and factor demand under uncertainty.

In the third Tinbergen Lecture on October 20, 1989, James Tobin focuses on the theory of macroeconomic policy. According to Tobin, the two standard instruments of short-run demand management - viz. fiscal policy and monetary policy - cannot achieve the two usual targets, full employment and price stability. Instead, they should together be capable of hitting some other pair of targets. One member of the pair would be a real GNP and employment target, with whatever price outcome is connected to it. The second target might be a variable connected with the external balance, the exchange rate, international reserves or the current account, or it might be the composition of national output between consumption and investment, a variable important for long-run growth. According to Tobin, it is fundamental that the fiscal/monetary policy mix affects this composition. He also notes that monetary policy and fiscal policy each comprise numerous specific instruments. However, from a macroeconomic viewpoint, most of them are different ways of doing the same thing, Tobin says. Central banks choose among specific monetary tools on quite subsidiary considerations. And although the variety of fiscal instruments is even greater, Tobin emphasizes that their direct macroeconomic impacts on aggregate spending on goods and services are similar. Attention to incentive and substitution effects enriches the fiscal policy menu. One example is differentiation between public investment outlays and collective consumption.

In his lecture, Tobin also deals with the uncertainty about the effects of the instruments and with some pitfalls in the policy exploitations of observed empirical regularities. With regard to uncertainty, Tobin states that policy-makers are rightly reluctant to move into *terra incognita*, where they have few observations of policy impacts. But they can overdo conservatism about instruments when faced with new circumstances. In the Great Depression, for example, it was not really conservative of governments to try to keep their budgets balanced. As far as the pitfalls in policy exploitations are concerned, Tobin emphasizes that Lucas, Barro and other exponents of the New Classical Macroeconomics are guilty of the fallacy of misplaced concreteness. According to him, they apply to the hurly-burly of short-run adjustments and fluctuations theorems that might under ideal conditions hold good for long runs and long horizons. In Tobin's opinion, recent history has not been kind to these approaches whereas, relative to them, old-fashioned macroeconometric models have been doing well. Tobin ends his lecture with discussions of the relations between qualitative and quantitative policies and of the question what economists can say about policy objectives. Among other things, he suggests that policy plans should involve re-settings of the various instruments in order to achieve desirable future paths of the objective variables. In this respect, policy 'rules' should involve responses to new information and in practice allow 'discretion'. Tobin also suggests - in line with Klein's Tinbergen Lecture - that Tinbergen's theory of policy needs to be extended to policy coordination among nations.

3 ON PRIVATIZATION, ECONOMIC GROWTH AND MONETARY POLICY

The fourth Tinbergen Lecture, delivered by János Kornai on October 19, 1990, deals with the principles of privatization in Eastern Europe. In discussing the subject, Kornai does not use the word 'privatization' in its narrow sense (meaning the transfer of assets hitherto owned by the state into private hands), but in its broader sense with the share of the private sector growing until it ultimately becomes the dominant economic sector. Kornai starts his lecture with a discussion of the main aspects of privatization, viz.:
1) the sociological aspect with a longer time horizon, and in particular the objective to create a large class of business people;
2) economic aspects, notably the objective to increase efficiency and improve management;
3) political aspects, especially the problem of how popular, deservedly or undeservedly, any privatization programme will be;
4) distributional-ethical aspects, including considerations of restitution and compensation for the loss of confiscated property.

The value judgements on which Kornai's own view rests are primarily connected with aspects 1 and 2. With regard to aspect 1, Kornai stresses that ('even though I am an economist') he rates the long-term sociological angle as decisive and with regard to aspect 2 the need for privatization to be accomplished in a way providing the strongest incentive for efficient production.

Next, Kornai deals with the role of the state in the process of privatization. In this respect, he sounds a warning against the widely held view that state institutions should play a very large part in privatization as was the case in Hungary with the so-called State Property Agency and as could also be observed in Germany. According to Kornai, such approaches are artificially created, whereas the vitality of capitalist development is the result of the fact that its viable institutions arise naturally, without being forced. In this respect, he refers to the period of Stalinist collectivization in the Soviet Union, when it was possible to eliminate the class of well-to-do farmers, the *Kulaks*, by state decree. Kornai then states: '... But no state decree can create a class of well-to-do farmers; that will emerge only by a process of historical development. The state can decide to implement confiscation but no state resolution can appoint a Ford, a Rockefeller or a Du Pont .... Governments should not be expected to replace the spontaneous, decentralized, organic growth process of the private economy by a web of bureaucratic, excessively regulatory measures and a hive of zealous activity by state officials.'

Kornai continues his lecture with an extensive discussion of the types of owners, highlighting the significance of the evolution of personal owners as well as employee ownership, various forms of institutional ownership, give-away schemes of privatization and property rights of foreigners. He ends his lecture by presenting his personal view on the desired speed of privatization, stating that he is a believer in the process of privatization proceeding as fast as possible, but that at the same time he does not think that it can be accelerated by some artful trick. In Kornai's view, the key issue is not the pace at which the wealth hitherto owned by the state is transferred into private hands but the pace at which the private sector grows through newly established firms or through the transfer of state wealth.

In his Tinbergen Lecture delivered on October 4, 1991, Robert M. Solow focuses on policies for economic growth. He first notes that it is not a good idea to mix up economic growth and business-cycle upswings as tends to be done, for example, in journalistic writings and political debates. In Solow's terms, economic growth is the increase in the *capacity* to produce output, not in production itself. Hence, the story of growth is the story of the trend of potential output, and growth-oriented policy is policy aimed at affecting the potential trend. In his lecture, Solow distinguishes between the 'old' growth theory of the 1950s and the 'new' growth theory of the 1980s. The old growth theory differentiated sharply between policies that could *lift* the potential trend curve and those that could *tilt* the curve, i.e. change the rate of growth. The conclusion was that the conventional range of fiscal or regulatory policies, those aimed at increasing the rate of capital formation or even the rate of human capital formation, could lift the potential trend but not tilt it. A sustained increase in the share of GNP invested would create only a temporary episode of accelerated growth. According to Solow, in this view there are only two options for growth-oriented policies. One is to aim for temporary increases in the growth rate, accepting that lifting the potential trend is ambitious and important. The second option is to seek higher growth rates on a long-term basis. In this respect, Solow holds that the 'research-and-development-and-entrepreneurship' path is the only serious candidate.

Solow emphasizes that, in the modern world, problems arise which were not allowed for in the old growth theory, such as the fact that skilled people can emigrate and that new technology can do so even faster. As a result, investment paid for in one country may primarily benefit other countries (e.g. in the case of brain drain) or may benefit other countries as well as the originating country (e.g. in the case of technological imitation). This 'globalization of economic activity' means that even a whole nation may be too small to 'internalize the externality' in order to capture a large fraction of the return on its own investment. According to Solow, the real novelty in the new growth theory is that investment decisions have a very great leverage on growth rates. Almost always the key assumption suspends the operation of diminishing returns on some factor of production.

Solow concludes that from powerful assumptions come powerful conclusions. The new growth theory offers wide scope for growth-oriented policies. A sustained rise in, for example, the share of national income invested can thus create a permanent increase in the economy's growth rate - which is exactly what the old growth theory denied. A second striking policy implication is that even temporary shocks to investment (or human capital) - such as a temporary tax increase on the profits from capital - leave major scars that never heal and may even get worse. These models make - as Solow says - policy very powerful and very dangerous. But at the same time it should be noted that the forces governing the slope of the potential trend are complex, mostly technological, and even a little mysterious.

Martin Feldstein deals in his Tinbergen Lecture delivered in The Hague on October 2, 1992 with the failure of US monetary policy in the early 1990s. Feldstein starts his lecture with two observations. First, he notes that since the spring of 1990, the rates of growth of real income, of nominal income, and of the broad monetary aggregate have been substantially less than the Federal Reserve had set as targets and than most observers regarded as appropriate. Or as Feldstein says '... In the language that Professor Tinbergen taught the economics profession, the links between the instrument of economic policy (the Federal Reserve's open market operations) and these targets of economic policy have not operated recently in the way that they did in the past.' Secondly, Feldstein notes that the Federal Reserve did not respond by changing the instrument values (viz. the extent of open market operations) sufficiently to compensate for the decline in its potency to affect the monetary aggregates and GDP. In his analysis of these two observations, Feldstein stresses that the breakdown of what he calls the 'traditional economic relation' has not been between the broad money supply (M2) and nominal GDP but between the increase in reserves caused by open market operations and the subsequent change in the broad money supply. Changes in bank reserves by open market operations have had much less effect on the money supply than the Federal Reserve had anticipated. Feldstein mentions two fundamental reasons for this phenomenon, viz. the lack of reserve requirements on all but a small fraction of total M2, on the one hand, and the recent imposition of bank capital requirements that limit the banks' ability to lend, on the other. The Federal Reserve failed, so Feldstein notes, to appreciate the importance of these conditions and thus misjudged the strength of its monetary policy.

In his lecture, Feldstein discusses these issues in more detail by considering the question why the Fed did not react more aggressively when it became clear that the money supply and the economy were stagnating and by suggesting how the link between open market operations and the broad monetary aggregate could be re-established by a change in Federal Reserve rules. In doing so, Feldstein stresses the importance of monetary policy in the management of aggregate demand. According to him '... we have to recognize that fiscal policy is a very blunt tool to use for macroeconomic stabilization and that monetary policy should therefore bear primary responsibility, indeed generally sole responsibility, for guiding the level of aggregate demand. Particularly with the American Congressional form of government, changes in taxes and government spending take a long time to enact and are difficult to modify.' Feldstein also notes that *anno* 1992, the high level of the US government budget deficit relative to private saving is an extra reason for not using a stimulative fiscal policy so that American economists generally look to the Federal Reserve for managing short-run variations in nominal GDP.

With regard to monetary policy, Feldstein first discusses the targets of monetary policy, starting his analysis in 1987 when Alan Greenspan became chairman of the Federal Reserve. Greenspan's aim was to create 'virtual price stability', which was generally interpreted to be an inflation rate of about two percent. This Fed's goal of reducing inflation without an economic downturn was undermined, among other things, by Saddam Hussein's invasion of Kuwait in August 1990, which resulted in a jump in consumer prices and a decline in economic activity because of the rise in oil prices. However, after the quick repulse of the Iraqi invasion resulting in a sharp fall in oil prices, the Fed failed, so Feldstein holds, to increase M2 sufficiently rapidly thus frustrating a healthy recovery of the American economy. Feldstein notes more of these failures such as the monetary policy pursued in 1992 which was frustrated by an - in Feldstein's view - exaggerated fear of increased inflationary expectations. Next, Feldstein deals with the question why the Fed was not aggressive enough in managing short-term interest rates, followed by a discussion of the implications for US monetary policy of so-called new bank capital requirements. In his concluding thoughts Feldstein raises, among other things, the suggestion that in order to avoid future failings of US monetary policy more accurate indicators of the condition of monetary policy are needed as well as alternative reserve requirement rules that permit tighter links between open market operations and subsequent movements in the broad monetary aggregate.

REFERENCES

Feldstein, M., The Recent Failure of U.S. Monetary Policy, *De Economist*, vol. 141, no. 1, 1993, pp. 29-42 (reprinted in chapter 9).

Keynes, J.M., Comment, *Economic Journal*, vol. 50, 1940, pp. 154-156.

Klein, L.R., Carrying Forward the Tinbergen Initiative in Macroeconometrics, *De Economist*, vol. 136, no. 1, 1988, pp. 3-21 (reprinted in chapter 4).

Kornai, J., The Principles of Privatization in Eastern Europe, *De Economist*, vol. 140, no. 2, 1992, pp. 153-176 (reprinted in chapter 7).

Malinvaud, E., Profitability and Factor Demands under Uncertainty, *De Economist*, vol. 137, no. 1, 1989, pp. 2-15 (reprinted in chapter 5).

Solow, R.M., Policies for Economic Growth, *De Economist*, vol. 140, no. 1, 1992, pp. 1-15 (reprinted in chapter 8).

Tinbergen, J. and P. de Wolff, 'A Simplified Model of the Causation of Technological Unemployment', *Econometrica*, 1939.

Tobin, J., On the Theory of Macroeconomic Policy, *De Economist*, vol. 138, no. 1, 1990, pp. 1-14 (reprinted in chapter 6).

TINBERGEN AND
THE ROYAL NETHERLANDS ECONOMIC ASSOCIATION

BY

ANTHONIE KNOESTER AND ARNOUT H.E.M. WELLINK

1 THE ROYAL NETHERLANDS ECONOMIC ASSOCIATION

In 1987 Her Majesty the Queen awarded the Netherlands Economic Association the designation 'Royal' on the occasion of the association's 125th anniversary. The Royal Netherlands Economic Association is one of the oldest, and perhaps even the very oldest, economic association in the world. Its counterparts in other countries such as the United States, Germany and the United Kingdom were all founded later. The German association - Die Gesellschaft für Wirtschafts- und Sozialwissenschaften; Verein für Sozialpolitik - was established in 1872, the American Economic Association in 1885 and the Royal Economic Society in 1890. In 1987 the board of the Royal Netherlands Economic Association still thought that the association had been founded in 1862. This impression was based on historical research by Professor C.A. Verrijn Stuart, the association's secretary-treasurer in the period 1889-1930.[1] However, very recently it appeared that the Royal Netherlands Economic Association is even 14 years older than it was thought to be at its 125th anniversary in 1987. The immediate cause leading to this new insight was the institution of the 'Royal Netherlands Economic Association Prize', which will be awarded annually as from 1992 onwards for the best economic research of young Dutch researchers working on Ph.D. dissertations. Part of the prize consists of a medal with an engraving of the portrait of the first president of the Royal Netherlands Economic Association, Professor J. de Bosch Kemper. When the archives of the association were scanned in the search for a suitable portrait of this first president, it became evident that the association had been founded earlier than was supposed at the time. The actual year of establishment proved to be 1848 instead of 1862, four years before the

---

1 Verrijn Stuart (1940) and Knoester (1987).

association's quarterly review De Economist was founded in 1852[2]. The year 1848 also follows from Verrijn Stuart (1968), who refers to Vreede (1877) and Ambagtsheer (1959). The last two authors mention April 19, 1848 as the founding date because on April 19, 1873 De Bosch Kemper was honoured on the occasion of his silver jubilee as the association's president.

However that may be, on the occasion of its '125th anniversary' the Royal Netherlands Economic Association established the institute of annual Tinbergen Lectures in honour of one of its greatest members, Jan Tinbergen, who (together with R. Frisch) was awarded the first Nobel prize for Economics in 1969. The annual cycle of Tinbergen Lectures actually consists of two lectures, one given by a prominent foreign economist and one by a leading Dutch economist. In the period 1987-1992, the 'foreign' Tinbergen Lectures were delivered by Lawrence R. Klein, Edmond Malinvaud, James Tobin, János Kornai, Robert M. Solow and Martin Feldstein. The 'Dutch' Tinbergen Lecture is usually delivered by a politician and is published in Dutch. In the period 1987-1992, these lectures were held by R.F.M. Lubbers (Dutch Prime Minister), H.H.F. Wijffels (chairman of the board of the Dutch Rabobank), H.O.C.R. Ruding (Dutch Minister of Finance), J. Attali (President of the European Bank for Reconstruction and Development), J.E. Andriessen (Dutch Minister of Economic Affairs) and E. van Lennep (former Secretary-General of the OECD).

Of course, the Tinbergen Lectures do not constitute the sole activity of the Royal Netherlands Economic Association. In the Netherlands, the association has built up a long-standing tradition as *the* national forum for discussing major theoretical and practical policy issues. It should be noted, however, that in the early years of the association, emphasis was not so much on economics as on statistics. Originally, the Royal Netherlands Economic Association - like some of its foreign counterparts - was named the 'Association for Statistics'. In those days - from 1848 to 1892 - the association published quite innovating yearbooks containing statistical information. Gradually, its focus shifted from statistics towards economics, culminating in 1892 in a change of the association's name into 'Association for Economics and Statistics'.[3] From that time onwards, the main objective of the association has been to increase the economic knowledge of its members. The main vehicle for this purpose is an annual cycle of addresses - instituted in 1892 - on topical economic policy issues to be presented and defended by prominent members of the association at the association's annual meeting in December of each year. These addresses and meetings, rooted in a tradition of a hundred years, have evolved into an indispensable means of communication among

---

2   Although both De Economist and the Royal Netherlands Economic Association have a long tradition, it was only in 1989 that the two came together. In that year, De Economist officially became the association's journal to which all the members of the association (about 3500) have an automatic subscription.

3   See Verrijn Stuart (1940).

the association's members on the issues concerned.[4] One of the highlights of this cycle was the presentation in 1936 by Jan Tinbergen of the first macroeconomic model, an event which will be discussed in more detail in section 2.

In 1950 the association changed its name again, this time from 'Association for Economics and Statistics' into 'Netherlands Economic Association', reflecting the association's focus on economic rather than statistical problems. As noted above, this change of name was followed in 1987 by the addition of the designation 'Royal', thus leading to the present name: the Royal Netherlands Economic Association. In recent years, the association has substantially broadened its activities, not only by the institution of the Tinbergen Lectures but also by organizing on an *ad hoc* basis national and international conferences on topical economic policy problems. Thus, the association introduced an annual 'economists debate' in 1988 on practical and current Dutch policy issues held in the spring of each year.[5] It is also an active participant in the annual conferences organized by the Confederation of European Economic Associations (CEEA). In this context, the Royal Netherlands Economic Association organized the 1991 CEEA conference on 'Taxation in the United States and Europe: Theory and Practice' which was held at the Nederlandsche Bank in June 1991[6]. Concurrently with this broadening scope of activities, the number of members has increased substantially. Whereas in the early 1980s the association's membership had totalled about 1500 persons, this number had risen to about 3500 in the early 1990s. Obviously, the Royal Netherlands Economic Association appeals to the interests and imagination of Dutch economists.

2 TINBERGEN'S 1936 ADDRESS TO THE ROYAL NETHERLANDS ECONOMIC ASSOCIATION: THE WORLD'S FIRST EMPIRICAL MACROECONOMIC MODEL

In 1929 Tinbergen joined the Royal Netherlands Economic Association at the age of 26. From November 1935 to October 1938 he served on the board of the association and held the post of president in the period 1952-1953. In 1987 he was awarded honorary membership. During his membership of the association, now already spanning a period of more than sixty years, Tinbergen has proved himself an active and imaginative member, both as author of addresses and as discussant at the annual December meetings of the association. In all, Tinbergen wrote five addresses for these annual meetings, viz. in 1932, 1936, 1947, 1949 and in 1959.[7]

---

4   For a survey of the topics discussed, see Knoester (1987).
5   In the annual economists debate, Dutch politicians and economists discuss a highly topical issue in Dutch economic policy making.
6   See Knoester (1993).
7   In addition, Tinbergen contributed to the volume on the occasion of the association's '125th' anniversary in 1987. See Tinbergen (1987).

Up to the early 1960s - thus during the period in which Tinbergen delivered his addresses - the association's board used to invite a limited number of members (three to five) each to deliver an address on a specific question raised.[8] In 1936 Tinbergen was invited to answer the following question:

> 'Is a recovery in domestic economic activity in this country possible, whether or not aided by government intervention, even without an improvement in our export position? What can be learned about this problem from the experience of other countries?'

Tinbergen provided, at the age of 33, a very original and seminal answer to this question. It should be noted that the addresses presented to the Royal Netherlands Economic Association in 1936 were concerned with the depression in the Netherlands, which, contrary to the situation in other countries, was not yet showing any signs of abatement. Foreign trade had fallen to a third of the level which had been recorded in 1929. The government held on to the gold standard, causing the guilder to be heavily overvalued. In his 1936 address, Tinbergen discussed a number of policy measures which could help reinvigorate the economy so as to achieve lasting increases in employment and, hence, prosperity. As requested by the association, Tinbergen assumed that the export position would show no improvement. In order to gain an insight into the effects which the prospective measure(s) would have on the economy, with movements in one variable influencing others and contrary effects having to be balanced, Tinbergen considered that a quantitative approach was called for, stating[9]:

> 'What we want to find out is the result of the complicated economic process. In order to obtain this general view, stylization is indispensable. The numerous phenomena have to be grouped in such a way that a view is gained of the overall picture without obscuring its characteristic features. The so-called macroeconomic approach must be introduced where, for example, we consider each article not individually but in groups such as raw materials, finished products, etc. Any attempt at stylization is, of course, a risky undertaking. The artistry in the work of the social economist lies in this stylization. Some attempts have been made which have proved impracticable. Some have proved unrealistic. We have to steer clear of these rocks. Stylization is necessary, however. The alternative is sterility. It almost goes

8   After the early 1960s the addresses invited by the board have been subject to a less specific mandate. They are now meant to focus on a fairly broad topical issue in economic theory and policy. Each addresser is expected to deal with the selected issue from his own specific economic expertise. For a list of the authors and addresses in the period 1893-1987, see Knoester (1987), pp. 517-526.
9   See Tinbergen (1936), pp. 67-68 and for an English translation Tinbergen (1959), pp. 41-42.

without saying that the identity of those elements which play a major part in current discussions should be preserved as much as possible. Qualitative stylization, i.e. the classification of people, goods, etc. into large groups, is not sufficient. We also have to work with figures and stylize quantitatively. We must know by how many percentage points wages will go up as the price of consumer goods rises by one per cent. We have to know this if only because, otherwise, evaluating contrary influences would not be possible. An example is the price increase argument referred to before. Undoubtedly, certain prices will go up as a result of domestic cyclical conditions. Consequently, the export industries will indubitably be confronted with difficulties. The question is whether these difficulties will lead to a reduction in total employment, immediately and later on, exceeding the increase resulting from the other causes. An evaluation of these contrary effects is necessary. In this connection, a rough figure is better than no figure at all. We must note that the figure is rough, for that leaves uncertainty. But merely pointing out the uncertainties does not bring the resolution of the problem any nearer. The latter is regrettably the customary manner of discussing this subject. I therefore conclude that it is necessary to come to a quantitative stylization of the economic process. An initial attempt in this direction is presented in the following section.'

This attempt on the part of Tinbergen took the form of the design of a model expressing the relationships between a number of economic variables in 24 equations. The result was the world's first empirically tested, dynamic macroeconomic model of an open economy, which is reprinted in the appendix of this chapter. More than half a century later, Dhaene and Barten (1989, p.204) would say: 'The idea of building a model and using it for policy analysis was without precedent. The Great Depression was the Great Boom for business cycle theory, but there was little in its mainstream that suggested anything like a model'. Against this background, it is understandable that De Wolff (1987, p. 245), a contemporary of Tinbergen as a member of the association, notes that at the 1936 annual meeting of the Royal Netherlands Economic Association in Amsterdam, Tinbergen's model was received not so much with pertinent comments as with a mixture of suspicion and astonishment. Even so, its publication marked the start of a period in which the design and use of macroeconomic models would show a spectacular development.

Tinbergen's model described the principal relationships underlying the cyclical fluctuations in the Netherlands real economic sector. Various distinctions were made, such as between consumer goods and capital goods, consumption and saving, the moment of earning and that of receiving income, final goods and raw materials, and between the Netherlands and the rest of the world. The international variables (import prices, world prices, the volume of world exports, and income from abroad), like the long-run trend, were taken to be exogenous by

Tinbergen. Variables relating to the government sector and monetary and financial variables were not included in individual equations; according to Tinbergen, the effect of interest rates was very small. Tinbergen estimated the coefficients of the equations on the basis of annual figures for the period 1923-1933; in respect of the exogenous variables, he assumed certain values.[10] Using a reduced model consisting of five equations, he calculated the effects of economic policy alternatives on the values of the endogenous variables in the future, comparing the results with the course of the Netherlands economy in the case of unchanged policy. It should be noted that, in his address, Tinbergen pointed out that his method might have shortcomings and that the results might not be accurate.

However that may be, Tinbergen dealt with six measures of economic policy:
1) additional public investment for a period of three years (denoted in the report as alternative P);
2) trade protection by limiting imports of consumer goods (Q);
3) enhancement of efficiency by additional increases in productivity, combined with a reduction in prices (R);
4) a reduction in prices alone (R');
5) a non-recurrent decrease in remuneration per employee (S);
6) a devaluation by lowering the gold value of the guilder (T).
For the purposes of each of these scenarios, (positive or negative) terms were added to one or more equations. With these scenarios, Tinbergen answered the first question - as to the possibility of an improvement in domestic economic activity - in the affirmative. A 20% devaluation (scenario 6) could bring about a major increase in employment. This would, however, be attended by a measure of deterioration of the balance of payments, so that it might have to be considered to combine this measure with certain curbs on imports (scenario 2). Furthermore, in line with the proposals made in the Socialist Netherlands Labour Plan of 1935 (of which he was one of the authors), Tinbergen recommended a number of measures based on scenarios 1 and 4, although such a course of action was not directly prompted by the results produced by the model.

Apart from these specific policy recommendations, the model-based approach employed by Tinbergen in his 1936 address constituted a major innovation in economic science and in policy planning. In his address he showed that the use of a macroeconomic model allowed a better-founded choice between alternative forms of economic policy than had hitherto been possible on the basis of verbal reasoning and discussion. Although Tinbergen's later work on economic modelling attracted more attention internationally - such as his work for the League of Nations which was published in 1939 - Tinbergen's 1936 address should be seen

---

10   Although, when measured by present criteria, the figures were of low quality, later re-estimations have not led to significantly different results. See, for instance, Dhaene and Barten (1989).

as the very beginning of economic modelling.[11] As noted by Barten (1991, p. 167):

> 'One cannot help but be deeply impressed by the enormous step forward that the Tinbergen 1936 model constituted. With virtually no antecedents, Tinbergen produced a model of no less than 24 equations, justified on the basis of economic reasoning and empirical experience, fitting well the scarcely available data. It made it possible to answer questions of great practical importance with an exceptional degree of consistency .... Going over the old text, trying to derive again the published results, one finds out over and over again that every detail is justified, that little or nothing is left to luck, but almost all is consciously selected.'

3 REACTIONS TO TINBERGEN'S MODEL AT THE 1936 ANNUAL MEETING OF THE ROYAL NETHERLANDS ECONOMIC ASSOCIATION

Each year, one year after the presentation of the addresses at the annual meeting of the Royal Netherlands Economic Association, a report is published reflecting the discussions following the addresses. This was also the case for the discussions with respect to the addresses presented at the association's 1936 meeting.[12] From a historical viewpoint, the report on the 1936 annual meeting provides an unique document permitting a reconstruction of the initial reactions to Tinbergen's presentation of the world's first empirical macroeconomic model. This section contains a selection from these reactions; when assessing them, readers should be wary of making the mistake of judging them from present knowledge. More than fifty years after the presentation of Tinbergen's 1936 address, it is easy to say that the discussants on Tinbergen's 1936 address failed to appreciate the importance of his contribution to economic analysis. As quoted before, Dhaene and Barten (1989, p. 204) quite rightly state that in 1936 the idea of building a model and using it for policy analysis was without precedent and that at that time there was little in the mainstream of economic literature that suggested anything like a model.

With this in mind, a first impression of the reactions to Tinbergen's 1936 address can be obtained by simply looking at the number of pages in the report on the association's 1936 annual meeting dealing with Tinbergen's address. About 25 pages of the total of 120 of the report are concerned with Tinbergen's address; the remaining pages regard the three other addresses, presented by H.A. Kaag, S. Posthuma and H.M.H.A. van der Valk, and 'other business'. This suggests that Tinbergen's 1936 address certainly did not attract more than moderate attention compared to the other three addresses. It is only on page 32 of the total of 120

---

11 See Tinbergen (1939a, 1939b).
12 See Vereeniging voor de Staathuishoudkunde en de Statistiek (1936).

pages of the 1936 report that we find the first, not very flattering reaction, from Dr L.G. Kortenhorst who - after a nine-page reaction to the other addresses - commented in a mere two pages on Tinbergen's address by stating, among other things:[13] 'With regard to Professor Tinbergen's address, I must say - and this may be a self-accusation - that I have great respect for the learning incorporated in it, but also that, after repeatedly reading and studying it, I have not fully understood it. I hope, yes I am convinced that in this respect I am the only one among those present here, and that the others have indeed understood it. However this may be, using highly complex and impressive formulas - it is reassuring that I have at least admired their complexity - Tinbergen arrives at fairly simple and obvious conclusions. I once heard an anecdote about a man with a beard who was asked: When you go to sleep, do you put your beard on or under the blankets? The man had never been aware that this might be a problem, but now that he did he began to suffer from insomnia as he found it impossible to fall asleep before having ascertained scientifically just where to put his beard! That is exactly what some economists do, starting off by representing simple matters in a highly complex way and ending by drawing a conclusion reached long before by people possessing very much less expertise.'

The second reaction to Tinbergen's address, from the then secretary-treasurer of the association, Professor C.A. Verrijn Stuart, also struck a fairly critical note. According to Verrijn Stuart, Tinbergen reversed the causality between wages and prices in a questionable way. In his model, Tinbergen had assumed that price increases would induce wage increases whereas Verrijn Stuart argued that - given the mechanism that prices also depend to a considerable extent on wage increases - this relationship led to the well-known circular argument for which the classical economists had been rightly blamed. In this respect Verrijn Stuart said:[14] 'I am all the more doubtful as this postulate plays a role in the mathematical machine,[15] which Professor Tinbergen has indubitably manipulated in a highly proper way. I am convinced that his calculations are correct, but if one proceeds from postulates which are so disputable from an economic viewpoint, I believe that the conclusions are in some way vitiated. In what way is difficult to ascertain for me. By what is known as 'verbal economics', I could easily show to which wrong conclusion the incorrectly established relationship must lead. If Professor Tinbergen can demonstrate the plausibility of his postulate, then let him maintain his calculations, but if he cannot, then I am most sceptical towards the set of results attained by him.'

---

13   Vereeniging voor de Staathuishoudkunde en de Statistiek (1936), pp. 32-33.
14   Vereeniging voor de Staathuishoudkunde en de Statistiek (1936), p. 38.
15   Tinbergen himself called his first model a *mathematical machine*. See Tinbergen (1936, p. 75) and Tinbergen (1959, p. 51).

However, the next commentator on Tinbergen's address, Mr J.G. Koopmans, was very positive, stating:[16] 'My admiration for this address is twofold: first, it concerns the technique with which the addresser has constructed and handled his mathematical machine, but in addition I have equal admiration - although the addresser may consider this somewhat ambiguous - for the daring with which, at this early stage, he already uses this machine to draw conclusions and make recommendations for measures of practical policy.' On the other hand, Koopmans questioned the conclusive force of the correlations made by Tinbergen, especially as some coefficients in the model, so Tinbergen had said, had been chosen because they provided the best fit.

Dr W.L. Valk's criticism of Tinbergen's model mainly concerned its potential function as a vehicle for economic forecasts.[17] In addition, Dr Valk was critical of the fact that in Tinbergen's model interest rates and cost-effectiveness did not play any significant role. Mrs. E.C. van Dorp was also critical, because the effects of wage moderation suggested by Tinbergen's model - being based on estimated relationships in the past - need not be automatically valid for the future to the same degree (circumstances may change, in the past exceptional relationships might have been valid, etc.).[18] Professor J. Goudriaan, in turn, stated that Tinbergen's method deserved full praise and support. Contrary to Mrs. Van Dorp, Professor Goudriaan held that it was only experience from the past which could serve as a guideline for extrapolations to the future.[19] He also inserted a critical note, stating that, because of the use of algebra instead of verbal reasoning, Tinbergen's model should be seen as a night train instead of the day train he preferred. Finally, Dr J.H. van Zanten stated, before asking some informative questions, that he was convinced that Tinbergen's address had opened up a new and broad field of research, which was bound to yield many benefits in future years.

Having heard all this, Tinbergen himself reacted pointedly to these comments, noting among other things:[20] 'Allow me to begin by saying a few words about the method which I used. Mr Kortenhorst has said that, to him, the method seemed overly learned, especially in view of the relatively measly conclusions which followed but, to my satisfaction, he has not hesitated to endorse these conclusions. I regret that the method may look a bit unfriendly but yet I hold that it is simple, much more simple perhaps than the mere verbal consideration of an issue; in much the same way, no-one would consider keeping the accounts of a large enterprise in a verbal manner. But that may be a matter of habit, and some may keep their accounts in a different way from others. Faced with these complex

16   Vereeniging voor de Staathuishoudkunde en de Statistiek (1936), p. 51.
17   Vereeniging voor de Staathuishoudkunde en de Statistiek (1936), pp. 58-59.
18   Vereeniging voor de Staathuishoudkunde en de Statistiek (1936), pp. 61-62.
19   Vereeniging voor de Staathuishoudkunde en de Statistiek (1936), pp. 67-71.
20   Vereeniging voor de Staathuishoudkunde en de Statistiek (1936), pp. 101-113.

economic problems, one must invariably weigh different influences, one positive and the other negative, and one cannot make progress unless one knows which of the two is the greater. The only option is to compute. Some use a chart, others a slide rule and yet others their intuition. The only thing that I have tried to do is to be systematic, and I am grateful for the kind words bestowed upon the method by Mr Goudriaan and Mr Van Zanten, among others, albeit that the latter has done so in a different manner from the former. I fully agree with Mr Goudriaan that I have taken the night train whereas the day train would have been preferable. I have not, however, succeeded yet in transforming everything into a readable novel, but I hope that once I will be able to do so. I can, of course, fully endorse Mr Van Zanten's remark. It stands to reason that those peculiar people who wish to introduce this semi-mathematical method are under an obligation to make it comprehensible; this will take some time, but we are working on it. Mr Valk has said that it is dangerous to make forecasts. I do not believe that what I do is make forecasts; I have extrapolated what we know from past experience, and what practical human being does things differently? Anyone knows that, if one extrapolates from the past, unexpected elements may turn up. In the final analysis, my curves are, therefore, not more than tendencies. Mrs Van Dorp has gone into this more deeply, expressing surprise at how the method which I used made it at all possible to consider the autonomous wage decrease. She held that, in my system of equations, wages were always dependent, considering their very formula. That is not so. The trick is that, in that wage equation, the relationship which is assumed for wages is, for one moment, made inoperative and that, instead, it is assumed that wages show a decrease, independently of the forces acting on them.'

In this vein, Tinbergen went on, explaining and parring the criticism levelled at his model. For instance, to Professor Verrijn Stuart's allegation as to the circular argument on wages and prices, Tinbergen reacted: 'Hence, there is no question of a circular argument here. If wages were to depend on prices and prices themselves on wages, that does not constitute a circular argument. If there are two relationships between two variables, that in itself is not a circular argument. It only becomes so if, on closer inspection, these two relationships were to prove identical. If there are two relationships, this may mean that the two variables are determined by it, and that is the case here.'

In retrospect, it may be concluded that De Wolff, quoted earlier, was right in saying that Tinbergen's 1936 model was received with a mixture of suspicion and astonishment.[21] De Wolff's opinion, however, that the comments induced by the model were not very much to the point is not borne out by the actual discussion at the association's 1936 annual meeting. It is even amazing that, more than fifty years ago, various members of the association, giving their initial reactions to the world's first empirical macroeconomic model, perhaps doing so more or less

---

21   See De Wolff (1987), p. 245.

intuitively, already pointed to pitfalls in economic modelling and to the limitations of economic models. Verrijn Stuart's comment on a possible circular argument with regard to Tinbergen's relationship between wages and prices - incidentally quite adequately refuted by Tinbergen - pointed directly to the nowadays well-known causality problems in economic modelling, which have led, among other things, to simultaneous estimation techniques. Also, Valk's criticism on the use of a model for economic forecasts is still highly topical today, while Van Dorp's doubts about the validity of estimated models for future relationships may, with a measure of good will, be interpreted as being in line with the present so-called Lucas critique on economic models. At the same time, it must be noted that, in spite of their criticism, some of the association's members also recognized the true merits of Tinbergen's model.

4   TINBERGEN'S FOUR OTHER ADDRESSES TO THE ROYAL NETHERLANDS ECONOMIC ASSOCIATION

As noted before, not only in 1936, but also in 1932, 1947, 1949 and 1959 Tinbergen presented an address to the association's annual meeting. Like his 1936 address, these addresses, too, were highly relevant from a policy standpoint. In his 1932 address, Tinbergen answered the question raised to what extent the regulation of production by producers could enhance prosperity and whether or not the government should intervene. His answer was written from a socialist view of economic activity. It should be borne in mind that the time when the address was written was one of deep economic crisis, a condition which played a major role in Tinbergen's analysis. In the socialist view, Tinbergen noted, the level of prosperity achieved under conditions of free competition was less than the maximum attainable with the available technical and natural resources. According to Tinbergen, optimum economic results required government intervention, because:
- ultimately, the higher level of organization would pose a threat to consumers(higher prices, lower supply);
- it was questionable whether, after a disturbance of equilibrium (with the recession at the time serving as a case in point), the economy would automatically return to an equilibrium state which would not differ unduly from the initial situation; at the time, examples were provided both by theory and by practice.
Regulation of production by private agents could be effected in various ways. Tinbergen focused notably on the regulation of the manner of production. This could be achieved by horizontal and vertical coordination as well as by coordination over time.

The various forms of coordination by private agents could thus lead to a more efficient manner of production and, hence, to an increase in prosperity. However, cartels and trusts also exerted adverse effects on prosperity. Profits being maximized, the volume of production would be lower than under conditions of full competition. In order to retain the advantages of cartels and trusts while eliminating their drawbacks, the government would have to control price determination. The principal conclusion drawn by Tinbergen in his 1932 address was that regulation of production by private agents could have positive effects on prosperity, but that the government was to exercise control over prices so as to prevent rising prices and dwindling supply. According to Tinbergen, the economic crisis prevailing at the time would prove prolonged if governments refrained from active intervention.

Tinbergen's 1947 address answered the question about the conditions to be fulfilled and the measures to be taken or abolished in the event that, in due course, the current planned economic system was to be replaced, in full or in part, by a free economic system. For a proper understanding of this answer, it should be noted that, after the Second World War, the Netherlands allowed no free price determination, no free movement of goods and capital and no free foreign exchange dealings. According to Tinbergen, there were four grounds for the government regulation of the economy as it was conducted in 1947:
1) scarcity;
2) cyclical movements abroad;
3) domestic disequilibria, and
4) general development tendencies and views held in society.
This enumeration showed that not all forms of regulation were connected with the war, although the scarcity was, of course, one of its direct consequences. Hence, it was this aspect which received most attention in his address. Tinbergen reviewed the conditions for a return to greater freedom in the economy, differentiating between the various markets, and concluded that the following conditions would have to be fulfilled for a return to free, or freer, markets:
- supply would have to be increased so as to satisfy normal pre-war demand; to that end, productivity was to be raised to the level prevailing before the war;
- personal wealth would have to be brought into line with national prosperity, the tax system having been adjusted;
- the war psychosis would have to be over and pent-up demand satisfied.

He also suggested that exchange rate adjustment was not the proper instrument to alleviate the post-war Netherlands scarcity of foreign exchange. In the short run, appreciation (to combat inflation) and, in the longer run, depreciation (to restore a healthy balance-of-payments position) would be desirable. However, with a view to international cooperation, he considered this option unacceptable. More freedom as regards foreign exchange dealings would not be possible until equilibrium had been restored to the balance of payments. To that end, the price level in the Netherlands had to be decreased relative to other countries. In addition, production should have recovered to the extent permitting imports to be reduced and exports to be raised. On balance, Tinbergen drew the conclusion that the conditions for a return from a planned economy to a free (or freer) economy would be fulfilled at different points in time, depending on the market and the type of goods concerned. For most markets, however, he held that the conditions could indeed be fulfilled in the longer run. The labour market, where government regulation would remain necessary, constituted an exception.

In his 1949 address, Tinbergen attempted to answer the question how to restore balance-of-payments equilibrium in the Netherlands after the termination of Marshall aid. Whereas before the Second World War, the Netherlands balance of payments had not given cause for concern, it showed considerable deficits after the war, which, in Tinbergen's view, were caused by a sharp rise in demand. This increased demand arose from the need to repair the damage inflicted by the war and the wish to restore pre-war living standards, and was made possible by an increased money supply and by running down capital assets. Furthermore, the deficit on the balance of payments was also due to the changed position in respect of Indonesia, which had as one of its consequences that the flow of income from enterprises in that former colony dried up. In addition, a role was played by the devastation in Germany, which curtailed the possibilities of selling part of production abroad. In Tinbergen's view, restoring balance-of-payments equilibrium after the termination of Marshall aid required an increase in exports relative to imports. The best remedy was to step up production, especially of export goods and import substitutes.

However, overall equilibrium on the Netherlands balance of payments would not be sufficient. According to Tinbergen, it was also required that the currencies in which the Netherlands would record surpluses were convertible into the currencies in which it would incur deficits, that is, notably dollars. For 1952/53, the first year without Marshall aid, Tinbergen attempted to predict the pattern of the balance of payments. He held that exports of goods depended on the development of incomes in the countries where Netherlands products were sold. Whether the Netherlands would be able to share proportionally in that demand would to a major extent depend on the prices of Netherlands products relative to those of competitor countries.

A model-based forecast showed that the balance of payments in 1952/53 would be in near-equilibrium. The principal assumptions underlying Tinbergen's forecast were success in restoring the competitive position of 1938, achievement of the necessary level of investment and a limitation of per capita consumption at the level of 1949. Tinbergen held that the competitive position could be restored in three ways: through an increase in productivity in excess of that recorded abroad, through a reduction in the level of wages (and profits) - or at least an increase below that in other countries - and through devaluation of the guilder unattended by full adjustment of domestic incomes. If the growth of productivity would be insufficient, a decrease in the level of wages and, possibly, a devaluation would be required. To the extent that the recommended measures would not be taken or would prove insufficiently effective, qualitative curbs on import might be called for.

In his 1959 address, Tinbergen focused on the question as to the policy to be pursued with regard to the relations between the Western world and the underdeveloped countries. In doing so, he dealt with the theoretical backgrounds to the question how the widened gap in prosperity between the West and the underdeveloped countries could be narrowed. In order to be able to answer this question, Tinbergen first explained why major differences in prosperity may exist. He pointed out that national economies may differ in terms of the available per capita amounts of land and capital. Furthermore, he referred to differences in economic and technological skills. He noted that all these differences may lead to discrepancies in prosperity, arguing that the level of incomes, and more in particular of wages, tended to be in line with average productivity in a country as a result of the available per capita amounts of capital and the technological and other skills of the population.

According to Tinbergen, the aim should be to encourage a development towards increasing prosperity in the underdeveloped countries, while avoiding excessive fluctuations, and towards narrowing the prosperity gap with the West. Tinbergen preferred assigning a certain quantitative substance to the objective of increasing prosperity. In the absence of such quantification, no professional set-up and control would be possible. Tinbergen was of the opinion that international economic policy should focus on narrowing the very large differences in prosperity between the Western world and the low-wage countries. The principal instruments would have to be constituted by income transfers and technical assistance in the broadest sense of the word; thus, Tinbergen was among the very first advocates of development aid. Development aid would help to increase investment in the developing countries, step up the growth of production and raise income towards the levels enjoyed in the rich countries.

APPENDIX: TINBERGEN'S 1936 MODEL

This appendix contains the 24 equations and the list of symbols of Tinbergen's 1936 model. Today, with our present knowledge, the model may look quite simple, but it should be stressed that what Lawrence Klein said in his Tinbergen Lecture is entirely true: 'Many of Professor Tinbergen's approximations and linearizations would not have been made in the computer age ... It all looks very simple now, in comparison with the average national model of some hundreds of equations, but it was an enormous task without the help of the postwar electronic computer.' A complete translation of Tinbergen's address, including his 1936 model, can be found in Klaassen, Koyck and Witteveen (1959), and a discussion of its major characteristics, dynamic properties and use for policy analysis in Dhaene and Barten (1989). Following De Wolff (1987, p.245), the model can be described in a nutshell as follows. Tinbergen's 1936 model is in essence a Keynesian model, focusing on the modelling of the most important expenditure categories. Tinbergen composed his model around four markets, viz. those for consumption, investment, exports and labour. For each of these markets, Tinbergen developed a demand and a price equation. Total wage income - which was supposed to be wholly consumed - followed from the demand for labour (employment) and the wage rate. The remaining income (mainly profits) was determined as a residual of total income and wage income. It was supposed that this income was used for both consumption and investment. Exogenous variables are world trade and foreign prices. De Wolff also notes that the model has an interesting characteristic in that, in the wage equation, wages were also dependent on employment which he held could be interpreted as a Phillips curve *avant la lettre*. In addition, Dhaene and Barten (1989, p. 210) note that one of the striking features of Tinbergen's 1936 model is the care with which the open nature of the Dutch economy has been modelled. In their opinion, the theoretical coherence of Tinbergen's 1936 model is well ahead of that of the models of the late 1950s.

THE MODEL[22]

1. $1 - l_{-1} = 0.27\,(p_{-1} - p_{-2}) + 0.16a$

2. $p = 0.04\,p'_A + 0.15\,(r'_A + 2\,l - 6\,t) + 0.08\,u$

3. $q = 0.74\,q'_A + 0.16\,(s'_A + 2\,l - 6\,t)$

4. $p_A = 1.28\,p_w - 0.04\,(r'_A + 2\,l - 6\,t)$

5. $u = u_A + u'$

6. $u_A = z + 2.23\,(p_w)_{-0.25} - 1.26\,p_A$

7. $u' = L + E' - 2.49\,p$

8. $v_A' + 3\,y'_A = 0.51\,Z_{-1}$

9. $a = b + 0.20\,u'_A + 0.98\,x'_A$

10. $y'_A = 0.69\,b$

11. $u = 1.72\,u'_A + 4.35\,x'_A$

12. $x'_A - 0.71\,u'_A = -0.42p + 0.39\,p'_A$

13. $y'_A - v'_A = 0.86\,(q'_A - q)$

14. $L = a + l$

15. $Z = I + U' + U_A + 3b + 0.71q - L - X'_A - U'_A - Y'_A + 0.24\,[s'_A - (s'_A)_{-1}]$
    $+ 0.38\,[r'_A - (r'_A)_{-1}] + 0.47[p'_A - (p'_A)_{-1}] + 0.3\,(Z - Z_{-1})$

16. $E = 0.48\,Z + 0.20\,Z_{-1}$

---

22   See Tinbergen (1936), p. 91.

17. $E' + E'_{-1} = 0.26\, E_{-1}$

18. $E'' + E''_{-1} = 1.74\, E_{-1}$

19. $U_A = u_A + 0.88\, p_A$

20. $U' = L + E'$

21. $U'_A = u'_A + 0.58\, p'_A$

22. $V'_A = v'_A + 0.13\, q'_A$

23. $X'_A = x'_A + 0.41\, r'_A$

24. $Y'_A = y'_A + 0.13\, s'_A$

LIST OF SYMBOLS[23]

Prices

l = wages

p = cost of living

q = prices of production equipment

p_A = export prices

p_A' = import prices : finished consumer goods

q_A' = import prices : finished production equipment

r_A' = import prices : raw materials for consumer goods

s_A' = import prices : raw materials for production equipment

Physical quantities

a = total employment

b = total employment in investment work

u = total production

u_A = export quantity

u' = consumption quantity

u_A' = import quantity : finished consumer goods

v_A' = import quantity : finished production equipment

x_A' = import quantity : raw materials for consumer goods

23 See Tinbergen (1936, p. 70) and Klaassen, Koyck and Witteveen (1959, pp. 46-47).

y_A' = import quantity : raw materials for production equipment

z = volume of world exports

Value figures

L = wage sum

Z = all other income, at the moment of earning, incl. non-distributed profits

E = all other income, at the moment of payment, incl. non-distributed profits

E' = part of aforementioned income spent

E" = part saved (incl. part put by)

U_A = value of exports

U' = value of consumption

U_A' = value of imports of finished consumer goods

V_A' = value of imports of finished production equipment

X_A' = value of imports of raw materials for consumer goods

Y_A' = value of imports of raw materials for production equipment

L = income from enterprises operating abroad

REFERENCES

Ambagtsheer, H. Th., *Jhr. Mr. Jeronimo De Bosch Kemper: behoudend maatschappijhervormer* (Jeronimo de Bosch Kemper: Conservative Social Reformer), Amsterdam, 1959.

Barten, A.P., The History of Dutch Macroeconomic Modelling, 1936-86, in R.G. Bodkin, L.R. Klein, K. Marwah, *A History of Macroeconomic Model-Building*, Edward Elgar Publishing Company, Aldershot/Hants/Vermont, 1991.

Dhaene, G, and A.P. Barten, When it all began: The 1936 Tinbergen model revisited, *Economic Modelling*, vol. 6, no. 2, April 1989, pp. 203-219.

Keynes, J.M., 'Comment', *Economic Journal*, vol. 50, 1940, pp. 154-156.

Klaassen, L.H. L.M. Koyck and H.J. Witteveen (eds.), *Jan Tinbergen: Selected Papers*, North-Holland Publishing Company, Amsterdam, 1959.

Knoester, A. (ed.), *Lessen uit het verleden: 125 jaar Vereniging voor de Staathuishoudkunde* (Lessons from the Past: 125 Years Netherlands Economic Association), H.E. Stenfert Kroese BV, Leiden/Antwerp, 1987.

Knoester, A. (ed.), *Taxation in the United States and Europe: Theory and Practice*, Macmillan, London/New York, 1993.

Tinbergen, J., Address to the Royal Netherlands Economic Association on the question: '*To what extent can the regulation, whether or not through the government, of the volume of the supply of certain goods by producers be considered to be conducive to prosperity?*', Martinus Nijhoff, The Hague, 1932 (in Dutch).

Tinbergen, J., Address to the Royal Netherlands Economic Association on the question: '*Is a recovery in domestic economic activity in this country possible, whether or not aided by government intervention, even without an improvement in our export position? What can be learned about this problem from the experience of other countries?*', Martinus Nijhoff, The Hague, 1936 (in Dutch). A translation of this address was published in: Klaassen, L.H., L.M. Koyck and H.J. Witteveen (eds.), *Jan Tinbergen: Selected Papers*, North-Holland Publishing Company, Amsterdam, 1959.

Tinbergen, J., *Statistical Testing of Business Cycle Theories, vol. I, A Method and its Application to Investment Activity*, League of Nations, Geneva, 1939a.

Tinbergen, J., *Statistical Testing of Business Cycle Theories, vol. II, Business Cycles in the United States of America, 1919-1932*, League of Nations, Geneva, 1939b.

Tinbergen, J., Address to the Royal Netherlands Economic Association on the question: '*If, in due course, the current planned economic system should be replaced, in full or in part, by a free economic system, what conditions should be fulfilled and what measures should be taken or abolished?*', Martinus Nijhoff, The Hague, 1947 (in Dutch).

Tinbergen, J., Address to the Royal Netherlands Economic Association on the question: '*What ways and means are possible to restore equilibrium to the Netherlands balance of payments after the termination of Marshall aid, while at the same time pursuing a predominantly greater freedom in international trade and capital flows?*', Martinus Nijhoff, The Hague, 1949 (in Dutch).

Tinbergen, J., Address to the Royal Netherlands Economic Association on 'Economic equilibrium between areas with unequal levels of prosperity', actuated by the question:'*What economic policy should be pursued in the relationship between the Western world and the low-wage countries?*', Martinus Nijhoff, The Hague, 1959 (in Dutch).

Tinbergen, J., Over Modellen (On Models), in: A. Knoester (ed.), *Lessen uit het verleden: 125 jaar Vereniging voor de Staathuishoudkunde* (Lessons from the Past: 125 Years Netherlands Economic Association), H.E. Stenfert Kroese BV, Leiden/Antwerp, 1987.

Tinbergen, J. and P. de Wolff, 'A Simplified Model of the Causation of Technological Unemployment', *Econometrica*, 1939.

Vereeniging voor de Staathuishoudkunde en de Statistiek, *Verslag van de algemene vergadering gehouden te Amsterdam op zaterdag 24 october 1936* (Report of the General Meeting held in Amsterdam on Saturday, October 24, 1936), Martinus Nijhoff, The Hague, 1936.

VerrijnStuart, C.A., *Schets ener geschiedenis van de Vereeniging voor de Staathuishoudkunde en de Statistiek* (Outline of a History of the Association for Economics and Statistics), The Hague, 1940.

Verrijn Stuart, G.M., *Uit de geschiedenis van de vereniging* (From the History of the Association), unpublished manuscript (probably dated 1968).

Vreede, G.W., *Jhr. Jeronimo De Bosch Kemper als staatsburger en geleerde herdacht* (Jeronimo de Bosch Kemper Commemorated as a Citizen and a Scientist), Utrecht, 1877.

Wolff, P. de, Jan Tinbergen: kwantitatief econoom (Jan Tinbergen: Quantitative Economist), in: A.J. Vermaat, J.J. Klant and J.R. Zuidema (eds.), *Van liberalisten tot instrumentalisten* (From Liberalists to Instrumentalists), H.E. Stenfert Kroese BV, Leiden/Antwerp, 1987.

TINBERGEN'S WORK: CHANGE AND CONTINUITY

BY

J. KOL AND P. DE WOLFF*

1 INTRODUCTION

Tinbergen's economic writings started being published in 1927 and have continued till the present day, thus spanning a period of more than 65 years. The number of scientific publications is now well over 900.

In order to present an overview of such a vast body of work, a selection is needed as well as a classification.

With respect to the classification this overview follows Tinbergen's own interest which is 'in economic substance rather than in methodological econometric issues' (Tinbergen 1979). Six broad areas of Tinbergen's economic work have thus been distinguished:

I   Economic Dynamics and Business Cycles
II   Economic Policy: Theory and Models
III International Economics and Economic Integration
IV   Economic Development
V   Income Distribution
VI   The Economic Order

The six areas of work mentioned allow for the classification of much of Tinbergen's economic writings.[1] But obviously, some of Tinbergen's work falls out-

---

*   J. Kol is Associate Professor of International Economics and Economic Integration at the Faculty of Economics of the Erasmus University in Rotterdam; P. de Wolff is Emeritus Professor at the University of Amsterdam and was Director of the Central Planning Bureau in The Hague as successor of J. Tinbergen. The authors are grateful to Mrs. I.M. Lageweg and Mr C.J. van Opijnen for their assistance with references.

1   This classification is more extensive and comprehensive than those in Klaassen, Koyck and Witteveen (1959), Bos (1984) and Chakravarty (1988), but is congenial to these in nature. The present deviates, however, from such as in Hansen (1969) with its stronger focus on methods.

side the areas indicated. Examples are professional recollections such as in Tinbergen (1970-3, 1979, 1984 and 1991-3). These publications have been used as a framework for this overview. They further served as a first indicator for the selection of publications to be dealt with under the various headings in this overview. A second criterion was whether a publication's content could be considered to be of major scientific importance for a specific area of work. A third criterion was whether a publication could be considered as typical for any of the headings in this overview.

Some commentators on Tinbergen's work, such as Hansen (1969), concluded that the areas of research could be regarded as stages in Tinbergen's development, marked more or less clearly by specific time periods. It is true that Tinbergen's work on Business Cycles was mainly done in the 1930s, that Economic Policy was the main subject of the late 1940s and early 1950s, followed by some 15 years when his work concentrated on Economic Development. A too strict periodization would, however, obscure the continuity in Tinbergen's work. For instance, Tinbergen (1928 and 1989-2) mark the period of his intermittent writing on Unemployment. The writings on Economic Integration cover a period of 46 years (Tinbergen 1945 and 1991-1), while Tinbergen (1934) marks the beginning of his writing on Economic Planning. Moreover, recently Tinbergen (1991-4, 1991-5, and 1992) addressed anew the measurement of welfare and the Optimum Economic Order.

There is a further, and more important element of continuity in Tinbergen's work, which relates to its nature. To underline this aspect of continuity four characteristics have been selected, which are constant marks of Tinbergen's work. These four main characteristics are adopted from Tinbergen's own guidelines for scientific work given in his professional recollections (Tinbergen 1979, 1991-3):

1. Policy Relevance
2. Measurement
3. Balance
4. Learning from Experience

The six areas mentioned above embody the change in Tinbergen's work, whereas the four characteristics mark its continuity. These are the subjects of sections 2 and 3 in this study, respectively. Section 4 concludes with some of Tinbergen's observations on the motivations and tasks of an economist's work and the achievements to be expected from scientific research.

Making an overview such as this poses various options. The procedure adopted here is that Tinbergen's work should speak for itself. Also regarding comments on Tinbergen's work, this overview derives most from Tinbergen's own recollections. And, as has been said above, even the classification and selection of the publications is in line with Tinbergen's own priorities.

2 AREAS OF TINBERGEN'S WORK: CHANGE

2.1 *Introduction*
In the years 1921–1925 Tinbergen studied physics at the University of Leiden. Professor Paul Ehrenfest was his most influential teacher, with his brilliant didactic capabilities (Tinbergen 1979). Later, working with Ehrenfest as a member of staff, Tinbergen prepared the thesis for his doctorate in physics; the title of his thesis was (translated from Dutch): 'Minimum Problems in Physics and Economics.' This thesis, published in 1929, marked the shift in discipline of Tinbergen's work from physics to economics. Naturally, this shift in interest had not come about suddenly but had been inspired in previous years by a growing awareness of unemployment and poverty. Already in 1928 Tinbergen had addressed the measurement of unemployment, in particular the distribution of the duration of unemployment, first at the moment of the unemployment count and, derived from that, at the start of re-employment (Tinbergen 1928). In his doctoral thesis, Tinbergen (1929-2) presents an overview of results in physics that can be explained by the assumption that certain central phenomena, such as energy and time, have a tendency towards an extreme, mostly minimum, value. In this respect, some striking analogies are demonstrated to exist with economic phenomena, such as production, stocks and business cycles.

In retrospect, Tinbergen (1970-3) explains his shift towards economics as follows: 'I felt the existing inequalities among people as an injustice but was told it to be something that could not be removed without a better knowledge of the structure of society ... The Great Depression, some years after, reinforced my conviction that economic research might be more useful than physical research.'

More generally, a sense of responsibility for society was one of the powerful motives for Tinbergen's transition from physics to economics and the same explanation can be applied to 'the changes in emphasis on the main subjects that I tackled' (Tinbergen 1970-3). These are the topics of the remainder of this section.

2.2 *Economic Dynamics and Business Cycles*
In 1929 Tinbergen joined the Central Bureau of Statistics in The Netherlands and concentrated his research on dynamic phenomena in economics.[2] Economic theory at the time ran almost exclusively in static terms (Hansen 1969). Tinbergen's work on economic dynamics arose from his interest in business cycles, an essentially dynamic phenomenon. Tinbergen started his work at a

---

2   In fact, Tinbergen rejoined the Central Bureau of Statistics, having worked there shortly – after finishing his study in physics in 1926 – in fulfillment of his duties as a conscientious objector. As a result, a study was published on the mathematical-statistical methods for business cycle research. (Tinbergen 1927).

time when little empirical information was available. Statistical data were collected and a series of studies was made by Tinbergen, later joined by various
colleagues at the Central Bureau of Statistics, on the behaviour of demand as
well as supply on markets mostly of individual products such as potato flour,
ship building and the stock exchange (Tinbergen 1930, 1931, 1932).

Tinbergen (1979) recalls the example of the Dutch anchovy market, for
which data were available over the period from 1855 to 1930, when the closing
of the Zuiderzee disturbed the functioning of the mechanism. Annual catches
had varied in the ratio 200 to 1, for which a biological explanation was known;
the main factor involved was the temperature in March in the sea around Den
Helder, the nursery of the anchovies. Another interesting feature of the market
was that the fish, after being salted, had to be stocked for four years to reach
top quality and be fit for canning. As a consequence prices clearly varied
negatively with the total of the last four years' catches.[3]

A somewhat different example of a supply lag Tinbergen (1979) recalls, was
implied by the analysis of the pork market in Hanau (1928). Farmers need time
to react to price changes and raising pigs also requires time. The result is a
roughly 3-year cycle in the pork market. Because of its graphical presentation
this mechanism became known as the cobweb theorem, which constitutes the
simplest example of a family of explanations of cycles in individual markets.

These studies on demand and supply were therefore of great importance for
the empirical knowledge of the business cycle. Invariably, a large part of the
fluctuations of the turnover in the different markets could be explained by the
cyclical movements of either income or production (De Wolff 1970).

Tinbergen's pioneering work drew attention both in The Netherlands and
abroad. In 1931 the University of Amsterdam appointed him part-time as a
private university teacher. Later, the Netherlands School of Economics in
Rotterdam offered him a part-time professorship. Tinbergen accepted; his
inaugural lecture was on statistics and mathematics in the use of business cycle
research (Tinbergen 1933). Tinbergen kept his chair in Rotterdam (full-time
since 1955), till his retirement in 1973 from the – then – Erasmus University.

International recognition was apparent from the invitation by the League of
Nations in 1936 to subject the various theories on business cycles to statistical
analysis as far as possible. A survey of these theories had been made by G. von
Haberler (1936), also on request of the League of Nations which was interested
in the subject because of the Great Depression. The first results were published
in 1939 in a volume containing an outline on the method of correlation analysis, and applications to fluctuations in investment, in general, and in residential
building and in railway rolling-stock, in particular. Data of varying quality
were used for the UK, the USA and other industrial countries (Tinbergen
1939-1). The main result was, that the method of correlation allowed to dis-

3   These findings were never published (Tinbergen 1979).

criminate on an empirical basis between the various factors theoretically conceived to influence fluctuations in investment.

Tinbergen's methodology was exceptional at that time and was received
sometimes with scepticism. In particular J.M. Keynes (1939), at the time editor
of the *Economic Journal*, reviewed 'Professor Tinbergen's Method' quite critically, raising as one of the fundamental points that 'The method is neither of
discovery nor of criticism. It is a means of giving quantitative precision to
what, in qualitative terms, we know already as the result of a complete theoretical analysis.' Of course the latter criticism illustrates precisely Tinbergen's
conviction that knowledge relevant for policy making should preferably be
quantitative in nature. As to 'discovery,' Tinbergen (1940) in his 'Reply' indicated that 'it sometimes happens that the course of the curves itself suggests that
some factor not mentioned in most economic textbooks must be of great
importance,' and he mentioned some examples. 'As to the possibility of 'criticism,' it seems to me,' Tinbergen (1940) argued, 'that the value found for one
or more of the regression coefficients may imply a criticism on one or more of
the theories that have been used.'

In a 'Comment' to Tinbergen's 'Reply,' Keynes (1940) still held some
doubts: 'that there is anyone I would trust with it at the present stage or that
this brand of statistical alchemy is ripe to become a branch of science, I am not
yet persuaded.' But Keynes concluded: 'No one could be more frank, more
painstaking, more free from subjective bias or *parti pris* than professor Tinbergen... But Newton, Boyle and Locke all played with alchemy. So let him
continue.' And so Tinbergen did.

2.3 *Economic Policy: Theory and Models*
The main problem of the business cycle, however, was not connected with a
single market, but with the complete process of investment, production and
consumption, and price and income formation. Keynes' model leading to the
famous multiplier concept did not try to explain the period of the main cycle.
Consequently, the two main features of testing business cycle theory were
considered to be (Tinbergen 1979):
  (i) formulating and testing statistically a whole system of relations;
  (ii) finding out which of the elements in these relations could explain the
       relative constancy of the cycle's period.
Such a system of relations was developed in Tinbergen (1936), containing a
model for the economy of The Netherlands as a whole. This first macro
country model has 24 equations and can be regarded as an extension of the
Keynesian equations of income formation and consumption expenditure. Ad-
ditions were made by splitting up money flows into a price and a quantity
component, and by the introduction of imports, exports, employment and
wage rates (Tinbergen 1979). In a number of equations, lags were introduced.
Consumption and investment were assumed to lag behind their explanatory

variables such as income and profits. The model was constructed partly to discover the dynamic properties of The Netherlands' economy.

The model, however, could not give a full explanation of the business cycle fluctuations in The Netherland's economy, because some of the main influences in such an open economy, like world exports and foreign price levels, were exogeneous to the model. The aim of the 1936 model, however, was first and foremost to evaluate the various policies considered to remedy the depressed economy: wage cuts, public works, increased trade protection and devaluation, the latter turning out to be the preferred policy. For the first time there was a possibility to make quantitative assessments about policy implications (De Wolff 1970).

Subsequently, a similar model was made for the USA which was published as part II of Tinbergen's study for the League of Nations on Statistical Testing of Business Cycle Theories (Tinbergen 1939-2). With its foreign trade being relatively unimportant in relation to its national product, the USA presented a better case for explaining business cycle fluctuations than the open economy of The Netherlands could provide. The USA model had 48 equations and was estimated for the period 1919–1932. Tinbergen (1979) highlights a main finding on fluctuations in investments. The principle of rigid acceleration with its assumed full capacity production was rejected on the basis of the empirical estimates, and the flexible accelerator was developed instead. The new principle implied investments to be equal to a fixed portion of the deviation between required and actual production capacity, with required capacity equal to the demand for the consumer good concerned. Regarding the short cyclical movements, the mechanism for the USA shows that an automatic revival is to be expected, but for the movements of longer duration a definite statement could not be made. The results further indicated several possible policies that would prevent a depression from developing (Tinbergen 1939-2).

During the early years of World War II, Tinbergen built a similar model for the economy of the UK covering the period 1870–1914. This study was published some years after the war (Tinbergen 1951). An unsatisfactory property of the models developed thusfar was the extreme sensitivity of the cycle period to changes in the lags and to the coefficients appearing in the equations (Tinbergen 1979).

In 1945, Tinbergen left the Central Bureau of Statistics of The Netherlands to become Director of the Central Planning Bureau. This Bureau was a new institution in The Netherlands, established in September 1945 on initiative of the Minister of Trade and Industry at the time, Mr H. Vos.[4] The Planning Bureau was given the task to produce a Central Economic Plan containing a balanced set of estimates and directives for the economy of The Netherlands.

---

4 Ten years before, during the Great Depression, Tinbergen and Vos had cooperated in designing a Plan for Employment offering a socialist alternative to the government policy at the time.

The Central Economic Plans are produced annually (De Wolff and Van der Linden 1988).

During his directorship at the Central Planning Bureau (1945–1955) Tinbergen's insight and experience resulted in three monographs on economic policy (Tinbergen 1952-1, 1954-2, 1956-2).

On the Theory of Economic Policy (Tinbergen 1952-1) presents a brief description of the issues involved; qualitative and quantitative policies are distinguished, variables are divided into targets, instruments, data and irrelevant variables,[5] static and dynamic processes are distinguished and the equality and implications of inequality between the number of targets and instruments are discussed. In addition, *Economic Policy: Principles and Design* (Tinbergen 1956-2) explains the use of models for economic analysis and for economic policy in which variables switch their position between being exogeneous and endogenous. Moreover, 21 examples of models are presented varying in being closed or open, static or dynamic and macro or micro, each model designed to deal with a specific set of policy issues. This monograph also contains chapters on changes in the foundations of society, utopist ideas regarding complete freedom or complete state regulation, and on the organisation of economic policy, discussing national and international agencies and their tasks.

Within the framework of Tinbergen (1952-1 and 1956-2), Tinbergen (1954-2) discusses Centralization and Decentralization in Economic Policy, stating among others the need for centralization in the case of supporting and conflicting instruments, with decentralization possible or warranted in the case of neutral instruments. This discussion also appears in Tinbergen (1954-1) on International Economic Integration.

Mainly in view of this work on economic modelling and in particular for his pathbreaking work for the League of Nations, Tinbergen, together with Ragnar Frisch, was awarded in 1969 the First Nobel Prize in Economics. In his Lecture to the Memory of Alfred Nobel on 12 December 1969 Tinbergen summarized once again the advantages of models: on the one hand, 'they force us to present a "complete" theory by which I mean a theory taking into account all relevant phenomena and relations, and, on the other hand, the confrontation with observation, that is, reality.'

2.4 *International Economics and Economic Integration*
In Tinbergen (1979) it is recalled that Keynes (1919) tried to show that the war indemnity required from Germany by the Allied Nations after the First World War was unrealistic, given Germany's limited export possibilities. Keynes' argument would have been weakened considerably had the value of the price elasticity of demand for exports been taken equal to the theoretical value of minus infinity and not to –2 as Keynes had assumed. Econometric studies

---

5   According to Tinbergen (1973-3, 1979) the distinction of these four types of variables was due to Frisch (1949).

carried out by Tinbergen and his colleagues found, however, values around −2 indeed and Tinbergen told Keynes so. Keynes' reaction was surprising: 'how nice for you to have found the correct figure!' Tinbergen (1979) admits that sometimes intuition indeed constitutes a basis for new scientific results, but adds that it should be the intuition of a genius. Simpler souls have to rely on measurement.

Tinbergen (1949) presents a study on long-term price elasticities of foreign trade; the measurement of these elasticities was important because at that time Western European countries were considering devaluation as one of the means to balance their foreign accounts. Estimates of short-term elasticities had resulted in rather low values rendering the success of a devaluation policy doubtful. Tinbergen (1949) put forward some reasons why long-run elasticities would probably be significantly higher than short-run elasticities: the empirical estimates showed such a difference indeed.

In Appendix VI to Tinbergen (1962-2) the *gravitation model* was developed. This model assumes that bilateral trade flows depend positively on the GNP of the exporting country and on that of the importing country, and negatively on their physical distance.[6] The model and its estimation were meant to establish a normal or standard pattern of bilateral trade; observed deviations from this pattern would be indicative of the existence of trade barriers or preferences. Although the gravitation model's simplicity renders it somewhat restrictive, its empirical applications turned out to be very successful.

Written during World War II and published shortly after, Tinbergen (1945) described the essence of international economic relations and outlined the desirable extent of their regulation. This study was inspired by the observation 'that lack of international cooperation ... has played an important part in causing many of the controversies of an intricate nature from which ... war arose.' Although Tinbergen (1984), in retrospect, considered this *International Economic Co-operation* as amateurish, it already contained proposals for international policy coordination regarding trade, investment, finance, the business cycle and competition, as well as a proposal for supranational institutions designing and executing such coordinated policies.

Nine years later the study *International Economic Integration* was published (Tinbergen 1954-1).[7] In his preface Tinbergen said the study was, in a way, a second edition of *International Economic Co-operation*, completely rewritten, however, to take into account the rapid development in thinking as well as in international economic co-operation itself. The study defines the concepts of *negative and positive economic integration*; the former would be merely the reduction of barriers to trade,[8] while the creation of new institutions for policy

---

6   The model and its mathematical formulation closely resemble Newton's Law put forward in 1687, describing the attraction between any two particles of matter. In his well-known study Linnemann (1966) elaborated the model.

7   A second edition was published in 1964.

8   This therefore represents only the removal of distortions previously introduced.

co-ordination and centralization would represent positive integration. The *optimal level of decision making* was discussed. *Decentralization* is desirable in view of the maximum participation in the decision making and its low cost of implementation. *Centralization* or at least co-ordination is necessary in view of external effects. Such external effects can be positive when the policy instruments used by individual countries are supporting each other, negative when conflicting. In both cases co-ordination or centralization of the use of policy instruments would be welfare improving. Earlier, Tinbergen (1952-2) had already advocated that the choice between economic freedom and economic planning depends on the specific circumstances and should be made on rational grounds.

The equalization of factor prices between free-trade areas was studied in Tinbergen (1949). It was concluded that under a number of specific conditions, equalization of factor prices will occur, even if factors cannot move across countries. In the likely case however, that the number of factors is smaller than the number of products, the equality of factor prices is no longer warranted.[9]

With foresight, Tinbergen (1957-2) studied the effects on welfare of increased membership of a customs union. It is shown that with increased membership total production rises in an accelerated way, in proportion to the number of tariff walls eliminated. Upon entrance, a previously non-member country jumps to the posititon of shared welfare increases among member states.

Recently, Tinbergen (1991-1) presented a method to measure the velocity of integration. This velocity is measured for several processes of economic integration in history, such as in Switzerland in the period 1291–1978, in France from 1205 to 1919 and in Europe as a whole from 1500 onwards. The velocities of integration arrived at are then used to estimate the time needed for the completion of integration in Europe and the world as a whole.

2.5 *Economic Development*

In 1955 Tinbergen resigned his post as Director of the Central Planning Bureau of The Netherlands and accepted a full-time professorship at the Netherlands School of Economics.[10] From then on most of his work would be connected with the unequal distribution of welfare among countries. In retrospect, Tinbergen (1984) explained that contributing to the economic development of the underdeveloped continents seemed to have the highest priority from a humanitarian standpoint.

---

9   In fact, Tinbergen (1949) investigated the viability of the conditions and the evidence provided by empirical facts regarding the theoretical formulation of the factor price equalization theorem by Samuelson, which formulation was later mentioned as an example of the irrelevance of some purely theoretical work in Tinbergen (1979).

10   Previous academic appointments had been part-time in combination with positions at the Central Bureau of Statistics and the Central Planning Bureau.

Tinbergen's interest in economic development, however, was already present in the 1930s. With the study of economic dynamics came the desire to break down time series into a number of components; namely, the trend and cyclical, seasonal and random components. The trend component reflected *long-term developments* and was given a mathematical form, which varied from a straight line and a parabola to exponential and logistic functions. The choice was determined by statistical fit rather than on theoretical grounds, a comprehensive theory of economic development not being available. Elements of such a theory were to be found in theories of population and its growth and theories on the growth of capital and savings. A first attempt to combine these elements can be found in Tinbergen (1942).[11] This was a theory of economic development 'in an embryonic state' (Tinbergen 1984). It distinguished between periods in which production is determined by the supply side and those in which it is determined by demand. For long-term movements the supply side was considered more relevant. The analysis was meant as a supplement to business cycle theory and was typically inspired by the situation in developed countries (Tinbergen 1984).

The focus on developing countries grew from a visit to India in 1951. Poverty prevailing as a normal situation in a country was such a contrast to the situation in the industrialized countries that Tinbergen's thinking and main activities were redirected (Tinbergen 1984).

Upon invitation from the World Bank Tinbergen wrote a general guide on development policy in 1955: *The Design of Development*. This study discussed some of the techniques available and in use for setting realistic targets and deriving appropriate policy instruments; it dealt with the evaluation of public investment projects and the choice of appropriate industries; it also discussed the means to stimulate private initiatives (Tinbergen 1958).[12]

Limited data availability and uncertainty about the efficiency of public and private economic agents called for a simple but nonetheless consistent framework for economic development. This led to the concept of *planning in stages* (Bos 1970). Three stages were distinguished (Tinbergen 1956-1, 1957-1, 1968-1).

1) *The macro-stage*, where for the economy as a whole the desired rate of growth and the required savings and investments are determined.
2) *The middle-stage*, where total investments are distributed over economic sectors, according to their contribution to the development aims while avoiding bottlenecks and overcapacities.

---

11 Tinbergen (1984) adds that as a check on the non-Nazi attitude of the editors of the *Weltwirtschaftliches Archiv* – in which the study was published in 1942 – a considerable number of Jewish authors were quoted. The editors accepted the text as it stood. A translation in English can be found in Tinbergen (1959-1).

12 The World Bank delayed publication for three years probably because of the author's view on the role of the public sector in development (Tinbergen 1984).

3) *The micro-stage*, where concrete projects are chosen on the basis of their contributions and costs in terms of the targets of development.[13]

To establish overall consistency, the models and methods used in the three phases may have to be employed iteratively. Apart from its practical structure, the method of planning in stages can also be justified theoretically (Tinbergen 1962-1).

Gradually it became clear, that apart from the scarcity of physical capital, the lack of human skills was also a bottleneck for economic development. Consequently, the planning of education became part of the planning procedure (Tinbergen *et al.* 1965-1).

Finally, the element of space was introduced in development planning. Commodities and industries were classified according to four degrees of transportability and shiftability: international, national, regional and local (Tinbergen 1965-2). Furthermore, differences in economies of scale between industries and hence in their optimum size gave rise to the so-called hierarchy model. This model enables the determination of the number of economic centres for a country and its regions and the spread in industries over these centres given demand (Tinbergen 1961-1).

In this work on economic development, Professor Tinbergen contributed also to the activities of international organizations such as the OECD and UNESCO, and he was chairman of the UN Committee for Development Planning (1965–1972). Furthermore his advice was sought by the governments of many developing countries, of which Egypt, Indonesia and Turkey are mentioned in particular by Tinbergen (1984).

2.6 *Income Distribution*

In 1973, after 40 years, Tinbergen retired from his chair at the Netherlands School of Economics, which in the same year ceased to be an independent institution and became the Faculty of Economics of the Erasmus University in Rotterdam. With Tinbergen's valedictory lecture on November 8th, 1973 both occasions were combined; H.M. the Queen of The Netherlands bestowed upon him the Order of the House of Orange, a distinction granted only very rarely.[14]

Tinbergen now returned to the university where his academic life had begun: Leiden, where he became a visiting professor for two years. During these years Tinbergen concentrated his research activities on income distribution issues.

Studies on income distribution deal with such distribution between produc-

---

13   Project evaluation was also applied by Tinbergen to the Delta Works in The Netherlands, a large public investment project in an industrialized country (Tinbergen 1961-4).

14   Queen Juliana declared (translated from Dutch): '... to Professor Tinbergen who represents this university in such a unique way, I wish to present the Medal for Drive and Ingenuity, a distinction from the Order of Orange, established by my mother (Queen Wilhelmina) for great Dutch citizens'; and, after handing over the order to Professor Tinbergen: 'With this I declare the Erasmus University open.'

tion factors, or, going a step further (Tinbergen 1979) between individuals. Regarding the factoral distribution, Tinbergen (1979) observed that nature had been often neglected as a production factor since the countries for which figures were available were industrialized countries, where the role of primary production had become small. In traditional analysis, capital and labour are being paid their marginal product; since the marginal product can be derived from the production function, the analysis of the distribution of factor income and the estimation of production functions are closely connected subjects.

With respect to the distribution of personal income Tinbergen (1979), in retrospect, observes that existing approaches in the 1950s lacked an economic interpretation for individuals or occupational groups of individuals and, as a consequence, lacked the possibility of giving rise to an economic policy directed at reducing income inequality – a generally accepted aim of economic policy.

This induced Tinbergen to design a theory in which the homogeneity of labour as a factor of production is replaced by the introduction of a considerable number of types of labour, characterized by a number of relevant qualities. Moreover, a distinction was made between the demand side and the supply side of each of the many compartments into which the labour market is then subdivided.

Until the time Tinbergen (1956-3) developed this line of thought income distribution studies had concentrated on the supply side. Inequality in incomes was then seen as a result of diversity in income earning capabilities. The neglect of the demand side of the labour market renders a policy on income distribution difficult to design (Hartog 1970). Tinbergen (1970-1) indeed distinguishes between a positive and a normative theory of income distribution.

On the Theory of Income Distribution (Tinbergen 1956-3) already contains the main elements of Tinbergen's work on income distribution. The supply side of the labour market consists of individuals with productive capabilities, possessed by them in varying degrees. These productive capabilities relate to cognitive capabilities, such as intelligence, and other capabilities such as leadership, willingness to co-operate, and persistence. Likewise, the demand side of the labour market consists of available jobs, characterized by the same attributes as the productive capabilities mentioned above, but now labelled as productive requirements, again in varying degrees. Demand and supply on the labour market can therefore be represented by multidimensional frequency distributions, specifying for each relevant combination of degrees of attributes the number of jobs and individuals available. Normally, the two frequency distributions will not be equal; income differences emerge because of the differences between productive requirements demanded and productive capabilities supplied. Income differences thus play an allocative role, establishing equilibrium on the labour market.

This approach has important implications for income distribution policy (Hartog 1981). Only when from the outset the frequency distributions on both sides of the markets are the same, will equality of income follow as a result. Otherwise, income differences have to play the allocative role mentioned above and are for that reason efficient. Moreover, the productive value of an individual does not depend exclusively on his productive capabilities but also on circumstances of demand. The non-homogeneity of labour as a factor of production was again underlined in Tinbergen (1973-1).

In his *Income Distribution: Analysis and Policies* Tinbergen (1975) brought the various elements of his previous publications on the subject together, presenting empirical estimates of important parameters for Canada, The Netherlands and the USA, and discussing proposals for income distribution policies. Part of the empirical verification made use of the assumption that utility can be measured, an assumption not very popular among economists as Tinbergen (1984) recalls. In this respect the material collected by Van Praag (1971) proved to be useful. The measurability of utility or welfare has subsequently been studied in Tinbergen (1985-2, 1987-1).

One of the chapters in Tinbergen (1975) deals with the race between technological development and education. Having dealt with the relationship between education and income distribution in a more general way in Tinbergen (1972-2), Tinbergen (1975) addresses more specifically the popular notion that the educational system in the industrialized countries has produced 'too many' university graduates whereas at the other end of the market unskilled labour is said to be in serious shortage and foreign workers have to be attracted. In the short run such statements can be more or less correct but for long-term developments these statements are irrelevant, because the price mechanism is neglected. Empirical evidence corroborates this assertion. Tinbergen (1975) concludes that there is no pre-ordained wage ratio between skilled and unskilled workers or any other type of labour, a point too often overlooked in public discussions on income and education policies.

Tinbergen (1975) also advocates a search for entirely different types of taxation, closer to lump-sum taxes and possibly based on human capabilities rather than on the results of their use. The feasibility of lump-sum taxes would require more refinement in psycho-technical testing, but the need for this type of tax derives from welfare economics and was already mentioned in Tinbergen (1959-2) within the framework of the optimal economic order.

Within the same framework, Tinbergen (1985-1) addresses income distribution issues again, partly in response to criticism on Tinbergen (1975). The 1985 publication consists of 19 chapters, based on earlier publications, and classified under four categories. The first three of these: Production, Income, and Welfare, are considered to be building blocks for the subject of the fourth category: The Optimal Social Order, to be dealt with in the next section.

2.7 *The Economic Order*

Tinbergen's work on income distribution – reviewed in the previous section –appeared to fit in with the search for the optimal economic order. In this perspective, Tinbergen's work on business cycles, economic policy models, economic integration and economic development was also directed towards the improved functioning of the economic system.

This subject was dealt with specifically in *The Theory of the Optimum Regime* (Tinbergen 1959-2). The optimum regime was defined as the set of institutions which in their common operation would lead to maximum welfare. This is the efficiency condition for optimality. The distribution of income is another aspect of the optimum regime. Since efficiency and distribution are characteristics of the optimum regime, the terms optimal economic order and optimal social order have been used as alternatives (Tinbergen 1985-1). In his acceptance speech of the Nobel Prize, Tinbergen (1969-2) again underlined the role of institutions: 'The true unknowns of the problem are not so much the quantities of consumption and productive effort to be made ... but rather the set of institutions which, taken as a set, are able to approach the welfare economic optimum as well as possible.'

As a start to the problem of finding the characteristics of the social welfare optimum, Tinbergen (1972-4) distinguishes:

1) the choice of the social welfare function.

2) the choice of the restrictions under which the optimum can be attained.

Five approaches are considered regarding the choice of the welfare function, differing predominantly in the method of aggregating from individual to social welfare. The choice of restrictions involves four possible approaches, differing, among others, with respect to the presence of external effects of production.

The theory of the optimal economic and social order furthermore deals with the desirable degree of centralization in decision-making, the desirable degree of market regulation, and the desirable extent of the public sector. With respect to the need of a public sector, Tinbergen (1984) recalls that around 1900 the State Mines were created in The Netherlands because private initiative and capital were insufficient to exploit the national coal deposits. A few decades later state ownership was temporarily established for farms on recently reclaimed land in order to prevent the first generation of settlers from going bankrupt, as had happened on previous occasions. It turned out that state farms were slightly less efficient than comparable private farms, whereas for the mines the opposite was true.

A well-known derivative of the theory of the optimal economic order is the *convergence theory*. Tinbergen (1961-2) developed this theory mainly to lead the discussion on the optimal order in East and West away from hostile dogmatism towards scientific analysis (Tinbergen 1969-1). The convergence theory has an analytical and a normative component. Analytically, Tinbergen describes the main differences between the economic systems of East and West. These relate to the size of the public sector, and the degree of freedom regarding price movements and economic decision-making. Secondly, Tinbergen argued that the impression given in ideological statements that the economic systems in East and West are not subject to change is contradicted by the facts.

The changes in the West in the last century, for instance in the extent of planning and the size of the public sector, and more recently, changes towards more freedom and centralization in the Soviet economy, testify to that. These changes represent movements away from the extremes of unrestricted capitalism and complete central planning. Convergence, however, does not imply complete equality as the end result, as Tinbergen (1972-3) argued in answer to criticism.

The main component of the convergence theory is however normative in nature, in line with the theory of the optimal economic order (Tinbergen 1959-2). The main objective is the search for a synthesis of elements in the order of East and West that have proven their merit; no blue print is available however, the optimal economic order will differ according to time and other circumstances (Tinbergen 1970-2).

Tinbergen also considered the question of the optimum regime or the optimal economic order in an international context.

In a report to UNESCO Tinbergen (1961-3) discussed the economic criteria underlying the international division of labour. It formulated three main criteria: a) the international division of labour should be based on differences among countries in comparative costs, b) the international trade system should be open without discrimination and with protection as low as possible, and c) the balancing of a country's trade should not be aimed for in each bilateral trade relation but should be considered multilaterally. In this perspective, Tinbergen (1968-2) dealt with the optimal distribution of industries across countries, while Tinbergen (1968-3) addressed the problem of risk connected with a too narrow specialization. It was concluded that the need for diversification becomes less to the extent that undesirable fluctuations in prices and proceeds can be controlled.

In 1974 the Club of Rome suggested that professor Tinbergen should form and coordinate a group of specialists to report on the question what new international order should be recommended to meet – to the extent possible –the needs of present and future generations. The report *Reshaping the International Order* was published in 1976 and contains proposals regarding the international monetary order and development funds, the international division of labour and technological development.

Revitalizing the United Nations System is the subject studied in Tinbergen (1987-2). It is submitted that the essential task of the UN is managing our planet. A source of inspiration for reform is therefore good management, that is of large well-run enterprises or of a successful national government. Learning from well-organized large enterprises means that business-like approaches deserve attention, that staff forms a well-defined hierarchy and that for the resolution of each problem an optimal level of decision-making exists. Among the many concrete proposals, one relates to a new system of representation in the General Assembly; the present system of one nation one vote reduces credibility and impact to a very low level. Representation must reflect more clearly the significance of member nations to world affairs, in terms of money contributions to the UN, or of real national income or of population size. For each of these variants a concrete proposal is made. A World Treasury is an example of the new institutions needed, representing at the world level a treasury so important in a well-run nation state.

In *Warfare and Welfare* Fischer and Tinbergen (1987-3) argued that security policy affects welfare, the conventional objective of socioeconomic policy, to such an extent that the two policies had better be integrated. This integration would imply that the aim of such a generalized economic policy becomes 'welfare in security' or 'generalized welfare.' The main conclusions and propositions of *Warfare and Welfare* are given in qualitative and verbal form, dealing mainly with the optimal world decision-making structure.

With *World Security and Equity* Tinbergen (1990) provided a quantitative foundation to the findings arrived at earlier with Fischer. A range of macro-models is designed, representing the world economy in two or three main regions – West, East and South – or more; in each model welfare in security is optimized under restrictions on expenditure, with transfers of assistance payments and development aid providing links between the regions.

The main conclusion of Tinbergen (1990) is that the aims of military policy (security) and development co-operation (equity) cannot be pursued independently. In order to maximize world welfare in security, reductions in military expenditure of the same order as the increase in development assistance are necessary. The UN norm of 0.7 percent of GNP for development assistance should be replaced by more sophisticated norms, the percentage rising with income per capita of the donor countries.

3 CHARACTERISTICS OF TINBERGEN'S WORK: CONTINUITY

3.1 *Introduction*

In 1923 Tinbergen, while studying at Leiden University, joined the Labour Party and its Youth Organization. Tinbergen (1991-3) recalls: 'I came in contact with the poorer part of Leiden, not usually known by students. Even before the Great Depression, conditions among the working classes in Leiden were about the most abominable in Holland. Unemployment was high, public assistance minimal. Many people were living in slums in utmost poverty. A postman I met and frequently talked with offered to show me the inside of this town with its famous history. I was horrified, and this certainly influenced my ultimate choice to focus on economics rather than continue in physics.'

A sense of responsibility for society has already been indicated in section 2.1 as one of the powerful motives for Tinbergen's transition from physics to economics. Specifically Tinbergen (1979) mentions strengthening solidarity with those living in poverty, organizing a peaceful world, and providing for the interests of future generations, as the three areas of research that have highest priority.

For scientific work, Tinbergen (1979) gives four guidelines: to minimize dogmatism and subjectivity, to remain as close to empirical data as possible, to work in interdisciplinary teams and to address the most pressing problems, as mentioned above.

Tinbergen's work itself has not predominantly been carried out in interdisciplinary teams. For that reason, another aspect is added, namely that of 'learning from experience,' so characteristic of Tinbergen's approach to scientific work (Tinbergen 1991-3).

The four characteristics thus arrived at testify to the continuity in Tinbergen's work, and are taken up in the subsequent sections.

3.2 *Policy Relevance*

In principle, research has to go through the basic, fundamental stage in order to reach that of application, a process Tinbergen (1972-1) compares to the production of commodities, starting with raw materials and continuing, through processed primary materials and semi-finished products to finished goods. Tinbergen (1972-1) adds however that concerning final products a choice has to be made and that this determines to a certain extent the corresponding fundamental research required.

The distinction between two phases in research, namely a fundamental one on the basis of which a stage of application can be reached, corresponds to the objectives of scientific work formulated by Tinbergen (1979) in his *Recollection of Professional Experiences.* The first is to analyze the operation of an economic system in an impartial, unbiased way. The second is the construction of an ideal economy. These two objectives are formulated in the following way by Tinbergen (1991-2) when discussing the Functioning of Economic Research:

a) to attempt to explain an economic phenomenon;

b) to recommend an economic policy or structure.

There is no doubt that Tinbergen considers the first and analytical objective as a first though indispensable step in pursuit of the second and normative objective of economic research, which in Tinbergen (1979) is described as its final goal.

With respect to the first element, Tinbergen (1950-1) underlines objectivity in the analysis as a task for all sciences, so that existing differences of opinion can be dealt with in an unbiased way. Similarly, Tinbergen (1979) recalls his physics teacher, P. Ehrenfest, saying that the objective of scientific work should generally be to formulate differences of opinion in a more noble way than merely as conflicts. This way, scientific research also leads to a better understanding of other views, in general, and to a greater tolerance, also in general, towards differences in economic attitudes and institutions; this in turn counteracts the powerful but dangerous and irrational forces of nationalism (Tinbergen 1968-4). Scientific research may contribute therefore to the solution of conflicts through reasoning rather than through violence, although science may meet its limits here.

In relation to policy recommendations, the second and ultimate goal of scientific research, Tinbergen (1950-2) expands on the role of planning in economic activities. In principle, planning in economics is superior to the blind working of free market forces. The reason is that planning involves more choice. Free competition precludes the setting of prices differently among countries, which may be desirable in specific circumstances. Complete free trade does not allow the introduction of selective import restrictions. When market forces bring about a change in the structure of the economy, the resulting unemployment may turn out to be a crude and wasteful way. Well-designed re-schooling and unemployment benefits are to be preferred.

Of course – Tinbergen (1950-2) adds – practice has shown that planning may lead to inefficiencies. With planning, incentives may be reduced to engage in adaptations, innovation, schooling and economic efforts in general.

A final point is the relation between preparing economic policy recommendations and economic forecasting. Forecasting is not a strong side of economics (Tinbergen 1988). Yet, in general, economic forecasts are very useful, especially when phenomena are involved with a long time horizon (Tinbergen 1962-3). The question has been posed whether the relative lack of success of economic forecasts may be due to the fact that – otherwise than in physics – economic behaviour is not independent of forecasts published. On this point Tinbergen (1962-3) observes that the form in which the forecasts are presented can make a difference.

As the future is a *terra incognita*, forecasts inevitably are based on assumptions. Basically, these assumptions come down to the supposed constancy of certain phenomena, be it their level, their growth rate or other characteristics. With increased knowledge of economic mechanisms, which represents the first goal of economic research, the quality of forecasts will improve. This is important especially with respect to economic activities, which have a long-lasting effect. Examples are the design, construction and implementation of infrastructural facilities, large capital intensive production sites, the use of exhaustible natural resources, and the educational system. It is there that economic forecasting and economic policy preparation are intertwined. (Tinbergen 1962-3).

3.3 *Measurement*

It is generally realized, Tinbergen (1979) in his *Recollections*, that the amazing progress made in the natural sciences is due in no small degree to the continual confrontation of thinking and measuring.

Economic theory, however, in order to be suitable for statistical testing must be expressed in quantitative – *i.e.* mathematical – form, explains Tinbergen (1939-1) in his introduction to his *Statistical Testing of Business-Cycle Theories*; it is added however, that many of the theories on cyclical fluctuation in business activity do not exist in a form immediately appropriate for statistical testing. That is not to say that non-measurable phenomena may, of course, at times, exercise an important influence on the course of events, and the results of quantitative analysis must therefore be supplemented by such information about the extent of the influence of non-measurable phenomena as can be obtained (Tinbergen 1939-1). On the other hand, qualitatively interesting phenomena lose their importance as soon as it can be established that they are not of quantitative importance, and the phenomena that are of quantitative importance will usually also be of qualitative interest (Tinbergen 1950-1).[15]

In this sense, 'econometrics – a combination of economics, mathematics and statistics – lifted economics to the level of a fullfledged science' (Tinbergen 1989-1). Before the time econometrics was established as a discipline, in 1930 in the United States and in 1931 in Europe, economics was formulated mostly in verbal terms with a small part formulated with the aid of mathematical symbols. Empirical measurement was largely absent. As regards economic science however Tinbergen (1979) underlines that his interest is in economic substance rather than in methodological econometric issues.[16]

As a general argument in favour of the numerical measurement of economic concepts, Tinbergen (1989-1) puts forward that the qualitative solution of a number of economic problems can be different for different numerical values of the mathematical shape and the coefficients of the functions used. Firstly, the number of solutions depends on the shape of the functions used. Secondly, a market equilibrium may be stable or unstable, depending on the slopes of the demand and supply curves near the point of intersection. Thirdly, movements over time may be cyclical or unilateral, and both may be unlimited or approach some limit.

Addressing specifically the question of measurement in human sciences Tinbergen (1971) acknowledges that a description of economic phenomena should start with a qualitative description of these phenomena. After that, measurement of the phenomena can take place. Tinbergen (1971) explains the importance of measurement. First of all, measurement opens the possibility of testing theories. If the measurement result does not correspond to the theory, then the theory is rejected on that basis. In the case of correspondence, the theory may be accepted, but since more than one theory may fit the empirical facts, a choice can be made with simplicity as criterion. The testing of theories and through that their improvement is however not the only purpose of measurement. Secondly, and more importantly, it enhances the possibility of influencing society in pursuit of human welfare. In this perspective Tinbergen (1971)

---

15   Tinbergen (1950-1) recognizes of course that qualitative phenomena and quantitative problems cannot always be separated completely.

16   Hansen (1969) on this point observes that Tinbergen's preoccupation has always been with quantification and empirical application, and as soon as a method proves useful empirically 'he does not waste time on further theoretical refinements, obviously believing that marginal returns are rapidly falling.'

formulates as one of the ultimate aims of measurement in human sciences the design of an optimal social order.

Measurement is defined by Tinbergen (1971) as representation by numbers. Numbers can be cardinal or ordinal. The measurement of temperature in physics shows the development of an ordinal classification in cold, cool, luke-warm, warm and hot, based on subjective sense perceptions towards the use of thermodynamical changes in substances embodied in a thermometer leading to a cardinal classification. This historical development around the measurement of temperature illustrates the vocation of science: the retreat of subjectivity and the simultaneous advance of objectivity.[17]

In *The Necessity of Quantitative Social Research* Tinbergen (1973-2) ex-presses his plea for measurement in this intriguing way: 'For some queer and deplorable reason most human beings are more impressed by words than by figures, to the great disadvantage of mankind.'

3.4 *Balance*

Polarization in ideas is useful sometimes in order to demonstrate the existence of a problem, Tinbergen (1984) observed, when reviewing the changes over time in development economics. On the other hand, it is argued, polarization implies reinforcement of extremist political forces both within and between nations. This testifies to the fact that polarization is an incomplete process which must be supplemented by a synthesis. This is the well-known method of dialectic philosophy dealing with the consecutive phases of thesis – antithesis – synthesis.

Tinbergen (1984) adds the following example. Some politicians hold that markets are self-regulatory and can solve many problems without intervention by the public authorities. Others are in favour of market regulation with the aid of buffer stocks, minimum and maximum prices, and quotas. So far this is a polarized situation. The synthesis can be created from the moment we under-stand that there are essentially two types of markets, stable and unstable. Stable markets can indeed be left to themselves, but unstable markets need regulation.

The same search for synthesis is applied regarding other aspects of the optimal economic order (Tinbergen 1959-2) and the convergence theory (Tin-bergen 1961-2), namely, the size and tasks of the public sector in relation to the private sector, the degree of free competition, and more generally than in the example above, the relative position of market forces and planning, also with respect to the future course of the economy. Planning the main elements of the economy does not necessarily imply the need for detailed planning (Tinbergen 1961-2).

In answering criticism on the convergence theory Tinbergen (1972-3) makes it very clear that the search for a synthesis is something very different from

17   In one of his early publications Tinbergen (1929-1) had expressed the same thought.

seeking a compromise. Compromising is horse-trading or even jobbery, whereas the search for a synthesis involves the weighing of various points of view and diverse proposals until they integrate (Tinbergen 1950-2).

With respect to the optimal economic order Tinbergen's balance in analysis is also clear from the observation that no blue print is available and that 'the optimum organization of the economy will differ from country to country and from period to period' (Tinbergen 1961-2).

In the introduction to *Statistical Testing of Business-Cycle Theories*, Tinbergen (1939-1) mentions that many of these theories do not exist in a form immediately appropriate for statistical testing, while, on the other hand, most of the theories take account of the same body of economic phenomena -*viz.* the behaviour of investment, consumption, income, prices *etc*. Accordingly, the procedure adopted by Tinbergen (1939-1) is not to test the various theories one by one, which would involve much repetition, but to examine in succession, in the light of the various explanations which have been offered, the relation between certain groups of economic phenomena.

This modesty in wording of a researcher in his mid-30s has vanished 43 years later when Tinbergen (1982) more explicitly calls for a synthesis among modern economic views and their advocates, so that economics does not lose its credibility. Tinbergen (1982) wrote his plea for synthesis in view of the economic stagnation persisting in the industrialized economies. Monetarism and supply-side economics were sometimes advocated by economists believing that they represent the whole truth. It would be more mature, Tinbergen (1982) argued, to acknowledge that the various approaches offered contain part of the truth. The essence of scientific work is to forge a thesis (for example the work of Keynes) with one or more antitheses (for instance the work of Friedman) into a synthesis. The criterion for such a synthesis is that a better explanation for economic developments of the time emerges.

It is added, that politicians and citizens have the right to ask for such a synthesis; Tinbergen (1982) warned that if 'we as economists continue to oppose each other, we forsake our duty as scientists.'

3.5 *Learning from Experience*

'Trial and error' might characterize my way of working Tinbergen (1991-3) concludes and adds that this might be considered one of his shortcomings. However, this engineering approach to economic research has been advocated by Tinbergen in many instances.

Tinbergen (1940) in his 'Reply to Keynes' suggests that dealing with the 'supposed omissions' in estimating the influence of the rate of interest on railway investments in rolling-stock would be 'an invitation to try it out.'

Tinbergen (1950-2) discusses markets for agricultural products and investment goods in connection to market regulation. It is concluded that the markets for these products and goods differ in important aspects requiring, as a consequence, different types of regulation. It is advocated that such different regulation regimes are installed and that experience is obtained regarding their effectiveness.

Regarding the measurement of welfare, Tinbergen (1989-1) concludes that it remains an open question among economists whether such measurement is possible. On this point Tinbergen also advocates a process of measurement in various steps. One could start with a questionnaire allowing for ten qualifications ranging from excellent, very good down to bad and very bad as in school reports, to express the respondent's degree of satisfaction with his real income. Next, each qualification is given a numerical score, for instance from 10 down to 2 and 1. By experience, the techniques of interviewing and the procedure for quantification of the material could be gradually improved. Such a procedure is advocated because 'In the practice of socio-economic policy, decisions are taken that are implicitly based on a scale; this scale is applied by politicians and, in serious cases, may be checked by ethical experts. As an economist I claim that such a check had better be made by economists, because the measurement of welfare affects economic policy and this connection is part of the economists' expertise' (Tinbergen 1989-1).

Tinbergen (1984) concludes that 'during its short history the development strategy for underdeveloped countries has been subject to an intensive learning process.' It was attempted to avoid repeating previous mistakes by shifts from less to more satisfactory approaches: for instance from capital to more appropriate labour-intensive technologies, from employment creation in cities to that in villages, from external, intergovernmental to internal policies. Such experience-induced shifts in priorities were also meant to combat negative forces blocking the road to further development: shortsightedness (e.g. too narrow nationalism), polarization (with its waste of energy) and cynicism (which discourages action).

Learning from experience is also advocated by Tinbergen (1961-2) in connection to the construction of an optimal economic order; it is thought 'hardly conceivable that we will soon be able to indicate precisely where the optimum lies.' It is added that conditions in developing countries seem favourable to try to combine the best elements from communism and free enterprise. 'These countries therefore may become the experimental ground for economic regimes' (Tinbergen 1961-2).

A second way of learning from experience is through finding parallels and exploiting similarities between various areas within one discipline or between various disciplines.

In his doctoral thesis Tinbergen (1929-2) indicated parallels regarding the formulation of the central problems in both physics and economics as minimum problems. And Tinbergen (1970-3) recalls that in his work on business cycle models several mathematical methods were used that were inspired by models used in physics.

In this perspective Tinbergen (1968-4) analyzed the similarities and differences between the social problem and the development problem, that is the problems of income distribution within and among nations. A series of parallels is found regarding institutions and policies relevant to the development problem and the social problem: privileges of rich classes, taxes and social security, and education on the side of the social problem have their parallel for the development problem in protection by rich nations, financial transfers, and technical assistance. Such parallels are searched for and analyzed as a matter of efficiency: the possible transfer of experience from one field to another.

In this perspective Tinbergen (1987-2) advocates that in restructuring the United Nations likely benefits are to be derived from studying the experience of the management of well-run large companies and well-governed countries.

Tinbergen (1970-3, 1979) warns however against pushing the desire to see parallels too far; this may distort the nature of the problem.

A third way of learning from experience is followed in Tinbergen (1944, 1965-3). Thirty years after the beginning of the First World War Tinbergen published *The Lesson of Thirty Years*. It has three parts: a chronicle of the bitter experience of those thirty years, an analysis of the economic events and policies of that time, and a design for the future including improved policies to deal with business cycles, structural problems and international relations. Twenty years later Tinbergen (1965-3) wrote *The Lesson of Fifty Years*, focussing on developments in and prospects for East, West and South. The lesson of these fifty years is that in these three main areas of the world more or less serious forms of stagnation can be found; breakthroughs are formulated in terms of aims and policies.

Reported lessons from experience should however be taken with caution. Tinbergen (1950-1) mentions the example of the interest rate for decades reported in the literature as the main factor in explaining demand for investment goods. This however was true only for specific capital goods with a declining share in total investment, with, as a consequence, a declining relevance of the interest rate as explanatory variable in general. Tinbergen (1950-1) warns that the literature has a tendency to build on previous experience without checking its present day relevance.

And Tinbergen (1983) added – one day after his 80th birthday – that one is never too old to learn.

4 CONCLUDING REMARKS

In his inaugural lecture at the Netherlands School of Economics in 1933 Tinbergen expressed the wish: 'I hope to be able to contribute in due course to the solution of some of the main economic problems of this time' (Tinbergen 1933). No doubt, he had in mind the pressing problems of unemployment and economic stagnation of the 1930s. From the survey in this article the reader can judge whether Tinbergen has succeeded in that task and has continued to do so.

In general, Tinbergen (1963) argued, an economist has two main responsibilities: a scientific responsibility and a social responsibility. Economics being a science, the economist as a rule will act as an adviser. Tinbergen mentions the example that he had to explain to the government of The Netherlands that a considerable increase in labour productivity overall – while maintaining the balance of payments – would lead to unemployment; and that it would be more desirable to promote productivity in a selective way, for instance in industries with a labour shortage. In order to be an objective adviser to governments, firms and institutions, the economist first of all should be a competent professional. He should also have the ability to communicate with politicians and others (Nobel Memorial Lecture, Tinbergen 1969-2).

Secondly, the social responsibility would imply that the economist has to consider the wider implications of actions undertaken by the firm or other institutions on his advice. Such implications may relate to negative effects on other firms and institutions or on the environment but, above all, to the distribution of income, which presently has assumed an international dimension.

Finally, the economist should be economical with his time and energy and also with those of others (Tinbergen 1963).

In Tinbergen (1972-1) the question is asked 'Does science, on balance, advance overall human happiness?' Reviewing examples of medical, chemical and nuclear research with their positive, negative and mixed effects on society, it is concluded that 'important misallocations still exist because of traditional thinking and the large amounts spent on gainful but not-essential activities.' Only when some co-ordination and organization of research can be obtained by a conscious policy of subvention on the basis of an agenda or priorities for research the answer could be more positive. As coordination and setting of priorities should include the international level, a world government is needed with authority in areas where national governments are bound to take the wrong decisions. Tinbergen (1972-1) concludes: 'As long as we have not achieved this decision structure, I fear that I must remain uncertain about the real contribution of science to human happiness.'

REFERENCES

Tinbergen, J. (1927), 'Over de mathematies-statistiese methoden voor konjunktuuronderzoek' (On the Mathematical-statistical Methods for Business-cycle Research), *De Economist*, 76, pp. 711–723 (in Dutch).

Tinbergen, J. (1928), 'De roulering in het werklozenleger' (The Circulation Among the Unemployed), *De Economist*, 77, pp. 772–782 (in Dutch).

Tinbergen, J. (1929-1), 'Het ekonomiese getij' (The Economic Tide), *De Socialistische Gids*, XIV, pp. 849–858 (in Dutch).

Tinbergen, J. (1929-2), *Minimumproblemen in de natuurkunde en de ekonomie* (Minimum Problems in Physics and Economics), Amsterdam (in Dutch).

Tinbergen, J. (1930), 'Het verband tusschen den aardappeloogst en den prijs en den uitvoer van aardappelmeel' (The Relation between Potato Crop and the Price and Export of Potato Flour), *De Nederlandsche Conjunctuur*, 1, pp. 18–26 (in Dutch).

Tinbergen, J. (1931), 'Ein Schiffbauzyklus?' (A Cycle in Shipbuilding?), *Weltwirtschaftliches Archiv*, 34, pp. 152–164 (in German).

Tinbergen, J. (1932), 'Prijsvorming op de aandeelenmarkt' (Price Formation on the Stock Exchange), *De Nederlandsche Conjunctuur*, 4, pp. 12–23 (in Dutch).

Tinbergen, J. (1933), *Statistiek en wiskunde in dienst van het konjunktuuronderzoek* (The Use of Statistics and Mathematics in Business Cycle Research), Inaugural Lecture, Netherlands School of Economics, Rotterdam, October 4, 1933 (in Dutch).

Tinbergen, J. (1934), 'De economische zijde van het ordeningsvraagstuk' (The Economic Side of the Planning Problem), *Ordening*, pp. 17–28 (in Dutch).

Tinbergen, J. (1936), *An Economic Policy for 1936*, ook opgenomen in: L.H. Klaassen, L.M. Koyck and H.J. Witteveen (eds.), *Jan Tinbergen, Selected Papers'*, Amsterdam, 1959 pp. 37–84 (original in Dutch).

Tinbergen, J. (1939-1), *Statistical Testing of Business Cycle Theories, I, A Method and Its Application to Investment Activity*, League of Nations, Geneva.

Tinbergen, J. (1939-2), *Statistical Testing of Business Cycle Theories, II, Business Cycles in the United States of America, 1919–1932*, League of Nations, Geneva.

Tinbergen, J. (1940), 'On a Method of Statistical Business Cycle Research. A Reply,' *Economic Journal*, L, pp. 141–154.

Tinbergen, J. (1942), 'Zur Theorie der langfristigen Wirtschaftsentwicklung' (On the Theory of Long-term Development), *Weltwirtschaftliches Archiv*, 55, pp. 511–549 (in German).

Tinbergen, J. (1944), *De les van dertig jaar* (The Lesson of Thirty Years), Amsterdam, (in Dutch).

Tinbergen, J. (1945), *International Economic Co-operation*, Amsterdam.

Tinbergen, J. (1949), 'The Equalisation of Factor Prices between Free-Trade Areas,' *Metroeconomica*, 1, pp. 39–47.

Tinbergen, J. (1950-1), 'Wesen und Bedeutung der Oekonometrie' (Nature and Importance of Econometrics), *Zeitschrift für Oekonometrie*, 1, pp. 5–13 (in German).

Tinbergen, J. (1950-2), 'De Grenzen der Ordening' (The Limits of Planning), in the series: *Vraagstukken van heden en morgen* (16), (Problems of Today and Tomorrow), Comité ter Bestudering van Ordeningsvraagstukken, Voorburg, The Netherlands, (in Dutch).

Tinbergen, J. (1951), *Business Cycles in the United Kingdom, 1870–1914*, Amsterdam.

Tinbergen, J. (1952-1), *On the Theory of Economic Policy*, Amsterdam.

Tinbergen, J. (1952-2), 'Dirigisme et liberté dans le cadre de l'intégration économique de l'Europe' (Planning and Freedom and Economic Integration in Europe), *Anais do Instituto Superior de Ciências Económicas e Financeiras*, Lisbon, 1952 (in French).

Tinbergen, J. (1954-1) (2nd ed. 1964), *International Economic Integration*, Amsterdam.

Tinbergen, J. (1954-2), *Centralization and Decentralization in Economic Policy*, Amsterdam.

Tinbergen, J. (1956-1), 'The Optimum Rate of Savings,' *Economic Journal*, LXVI, pp. 603–609.

Tinbergen, J. (1956-2), *Economic Policy: Principles and Design*, Amsterdam.

Tinbergen, J. (1956-3), 'On the Theory of Income Distribution,' *Weltwirtschaftliches Archiv*, 77, pp. 155–175.

Tinbergen, J. (1957-1), 'The Appraisal of Road Construction: Two Calculation Schemes,' *Review of Economics and Statistics*, 39, pp. 241–249.

Tinbergen, J. (1957-2), 'Customs Unions: Influence of their Size on their Effect,' *Zeitschrift für die Gesamte Staatswissenschaft*, 113, pp. 404–414.

Tinbergen, J. (1958) *The Design of Development*, World Bank, Baltimore, USA, 1958.

Tinbergen, J. (1959-1), 'On the Theory of Trend Movements,' in: L.H. Klaassen, L.M. Koyck and H.J. Witteveen (eds.), *Jan Tinbergen: Selected Papers*, Amsterdam, 1959, pp. 182–221.

Tinbergen, J. (1959-2), 'The Theory of the Optimum Regime,' in: L.H. Klaassen, L.M. Koyck and H.J. Witteveen (eds.), *Jan Tinbergen: Selected Papers*, Amsterdam, pp. 264–304.

Tinbergen, J. (1961-1), 'The Spatial Dispersion of Production: A Hypothesis,' *Schweizerische Zeitschrift für Volkswirtschaft und Statistik*, 97, pp. 1–8.

Tinbergen, J. (1961-2), 'Do Communist and Free Economies Show a Converging Pattern?,' *Soviet Studies*, XII, pp. 333–341.

Tinbergen, J. (1961-3) 'Stuctures générales du problème de l'optimum du bien-être d'un groupe de nations' (General Stuctures of the Problem of the Optimum Welfare in a Group of Countries), in: *Les critères économiques de la division internationale du travail*, (Economic Criteria for the International Division of Labour), Report to UNESCO, Université Libre de Bruxelles, Brussels, (in French).

Tinbergen, J. (1961-4), 'De economische balans van het Deltaplan' (The Economic Balance of the Delta Plan), in: *Rapport Deltacommissie*, Den Haag, 1961.

Tinbergen, J. (1962-1), 'Planning in Stages,' *Statskonomisk Tidsskrift*, 1, pp. 1–20.

Tinbergen, J. *et al.* (1962-2), *Shaping the World Economy: Suggestions for an International Economic Policy*, New York, 1962.

Tinbergen, J. (1962-3), 'Voorspellingen in politiek, economie en sociologie' (Forecasts in Politics, Economics and Sociology), *Nederlands Tijdschrift voor de Psychologie en haar Grensgebieden*, XVII, pp. 193–197 (in Dutch).

Tinbergen, J. (1963), 'De sociale verantwoordelijkheid van de economist' (The Social Responsibility of the Economist), *Universiteit en Hogeschool*, 10, pp. 21–28 (in Dutch).

Tinbergen, J. and H.C. Bos (1965-1), 'A Planning Model for the Educational Requirements of Economic Development', in: *Economic Models of Education* OECD, Paris, pp. 9–31.

Tinbergen, J. (1965-2), 'International, National, Regional and Local Industries,' in: R.E. Caves, H.G. Johnson and P.B. Kenen (eds.) *Trade, Growth, and the Balance of Payments*, Essays in Honour of Gottfried Haberler, Amsterdam.

Tinbergen, J. (1965-3) *De les van vijftig jaar*, (The Lesson of Fifty Years), Amsterdam, (in Dutch).

Tinbergen, J. (1968-1), *Development Planning*, London.

Tinbergen, J. (1968-2), 'The Optimal International Division of Labour,' *Acta Oeconomica Academiae Scientiarum Hungaricae*, 3, pp. 257–282.

Tinbergen, J. (1968-3), *Over de optimale internationale arbeidsverdeling* (On the Optimal International Division of Labour), Speech for the Royal Academy of Sciences in The Netherlands, Amsterdam (in Dutch).

Tinbergen, J. (1968-4), 'Similarities and Differences between the Social Problem and the Development Problem,' *Mens en Maatschappij*, pp. 120–127.

Tinbergen, J. (1969-1), 'Ideology and Coexistence,' *Review of International Affairs*, XX, pp. 1–2.

Tinbergen, J. (1969-2), 'The Use of Models: Experience and Prospects', Lecture in Memory of Alfred Nobel, December 12th, 1969, in: *Les Prix Nobel en 1969*, Stockholm, 1970, pp. 244–252.

Tinbergen, J. (1970-1), 'A Positive and a Normative Theory of Income Distribution,' *Review of Income and Wealth*, 16.

Tinbergen, J. (1970-2), 'Was spricht für die Konvergenztheorie?' (What Speaks for the Convergence Theory?), *Wirtschaftswoche der Volkswirtschaft*, 23 December 1970 (in German).

Tinbergen, J. (1970-3), 'Some Work Experiences,' in: T. Dalenius, G. Karlsson and S. Malmquist (eds.), *Scientists at Work*, Festschrift in honour of Herman Wold, Uppsala.

Tinbergen, J. (1971), 'Over meten in de menswetenschappen' (On Measuring in the Human Sciences), *Jaarboek Maatschappij der Nederlandse Letterkunde*, 1970–1971, Leiden, pp. 11–26 (in Dutch).

Tinbergen, J. (1972-1), 'Society Needs to Organize the Structures and Uses of Science,' *Impact of Science on Society*, XXII, pp. 289–297.

Tinbergen, J. (1972-2), 'The Impact of Education on Income Distribution,' *Review of Income and Wealth*, 18, 3.

Tinbergen, J. (1972-3), 'De convergentietheorie: antikritiek' (The Convergence Theory: Anti-Criticism), in: *Mens en Keuze* (Man and Choice), Amsterdam pp. 1–11 (in Dutch).

Tinbergen, J. (1972-4), 'Some Features of the Optimum Regime,' in: *Optimum Social Welfare and Productivity*, The Charles C. Moskowitz Lectures, New York University, New York.

Tinbergen, J. (1973-1), 'Labour with Different Types of Skills and Jobs as Production Factors,' *De Economist*, 121 pp. 213–224.

Tinbergen, J. (1973-2), 'The Necessity of Quantitative Social Research,' *Indian Journal of Statistics*, Series B, 35.

Tinbergen, J. (1973-3), 'Ragnar Frisch's Role In Econometrics: A Sketch,' *mimeo*.

Tinbergen, J. (1975), *Income Distribution; Analysis and Policies*, Amsterdam.

Tinbergen, J. (1979), 'Recollections of Professional Experiences,' *Banca Nazionale del Lavoro Quarterly Review*, 131, pp. 331–360.

Tinbergen, J. (1982), 'De noodzaak van een synthese' (The Need for Synthesis), *Economisch-Statistische Berichten*, 67, pp. 1284–1285 (in Dutch).

Tinbergen, J. (1983), 'Enkele ervaringen' (Some Experiences), *Economisch-Statistische Berichten* 68, p. 307.

Tinbergen, J. (1984), 'Development Cooperation as a Learning Process,' in: Gerald M. Meier and Dudley Seers (eds.), *Pioneers in Development*, New York pp. 315–331.

Tinbergen, J. (1985-1), *Production, Income and Welfare, The Search for an Optimal Social Order*, Brighton, UK.

Tinbergen, J. (1985-2), 'Measurability of Utility (or Welfare),' *De Economist*, 133, pp. 411–414.

Tinbergen, J. (1987-1), 'Measuring Welfare of Productive Consumers,' *De Economist*, 135, pp. 231–236.

Tinbergen, J. (1987-2), *Revitalizing the United Nations System*, Nuclear Age Peace Foundation, Santa Barbara, Ca.

Tinbergen, J. (1987-3) (with D. Fischer), *Warfare and Welfare*, Brighton.

Tinbergen, J. (1988), 'The Role of Errors in Scientific Development,' *Review of Social Economy*, XLVI, pp. 225–230.

Tinbergen, J. (1989-1), 'The Birth of New Disciplines and its Role in Teaching Science,' *Universiteit en Hogeschool*, 36, pp. 44–53.

Tinbergen, J. (1989-2), 'How to Reduce Unemployment,' *Review of Political Economy*, 1, pp. 1–6.

Tinbergen, J. (1990), *World Security and Equity*, Aldershot, UK.

Tinbergen, J. (1991-1), 'The Velocity of Integration,' *De Economist*, 139, pp. 1–11.

Tinbergen, J. (1991-2), 'The Functioning of Economic Research,' *Journal of Economic Issues*, XXV, pp. 33–38.

Tinbergen, J. (1991-3), 'Solving the Most Urgent Problems First,' in: Michael Szenberg (ed.), *Eminent Economists; Their Life Philosophies*, Cambridge, pp. 275–281.

Tinbergen, J. (1991-4), 'On the Measurement of Welfare,' *Journal of Econometrics*, 50, pp. 7–13.

Tinbergen, J. (1991-5), 'The Optimum Economic and Security Order,' in: T.K. Kaul and J.K. Sengupta (eds.), *Essays in Honor of Karl A. Fox*, Amsterdam.

Tinbergen, J. (1992), 'The Optimal Economic Order: The Simplest Model,' *De Economist*, 140, pp. 253–257.

BACKGROUND PUBLICATIONS

Bos, H.C. (1970), 'Tinbergen's Scientific Contribution to Development Planning,' *De Economist*, 118, pp. 141–154.

Bos, H.C. (1984), 'Jan Tinbergen: A Profile,' *Journal of Policy Modelling*, 6, pp. 151–158.

Chakravarty, S. (1988), 'Jan Tinbergen,' in: *The New Palgrave, A Dictionary of Economics*, Macmillan, London.

Frisch, R. (1949), *A Memorandum on Price-Wage-Tax-Subsidy Policies as Instruments in Maintaining Optimal Employment*, UN Document, E/CN 1/Sub 2/13.

Haberler, G. von, (1936), *Prosperity and Depression, A Theoretical Analysis of Cyclical Fluctuations*, League of Nations, Geneva.

Hanau, A. (1928), 'Die Prognose der Schweinepreise' (Forecasting the Price of Pork), *Vierteljahreshefte zur Konjunkturforschung*, Sonderheft 18, Institut für Konjunkturforschung, Berlin, 1930.

Hansen, Bent (1969), 'An Appraisal of His Contributions to Economics,' *Swedish Journal of Economics*, LXXI, pp. 325–336.

Hartog, F. (1970), 'Tinbergen on Prices, Incomes and Welfare,' *De Economist*, 118, pp. 126–140.

Hartog, J. (1981), *Personal Income Distribution, A Multicapability Theory*, Boston.

Keynes, J.M. (1919), *The Economic Consequences of the Peace*, London.

Keynes, J.M. (1939), 'Professor Tinbergen's Method,' *Economic Journal*, XLIX, pp. 558–568.

Keynes, J.M. (1940), 'Comment,' *Economic Journal*, L, pp. 154–156.

Klaassen, L.H., L.M. Koyck and H.J. Witteveen (eds.) (1959), *Jan Tinbergen: Selected Papers*, Amsterdam.

Linnemann, H. (1966), *An Econometric Analysis of International Trade Flows*, Amsterdam.

Praag, B.M.S. van (1971), 'The Welfare Function of Income in Belgium: An Empirical Investigation,' *European Economic Review*, 2.

Wolff, P. de (1970), 'Tinbergen's Contribution to Business-cycle Theory and Policy,' *De Economist*, 118, pp. 113–125.

Wolff, P. de and J.T.J.M. van der Linden (1988), 'Jan Tinbergen: A Quantitative Economist,' *Review of Social Economy*, XLVI, pp. 312–325.

Summary

TINBERGEN'S WORK: CHANGE AND CONTINUITY

This article provides an overview of Tinbergen's economic writings, comprising well over 900 publications. Six broad areas have been distinguished to allow for the classification and discussion of Tinbergen's economic work. These six areas embody the change in Tinbergen's areas of interest apart from the shift from physics to economics early in his career. Tinbergen's work, however, is not only characterised by change of areas but also by continuity in approach. To mark this continuity four main characteristics of Tinbergen's work have been elaborated. The article concludes with Tinbergen's observations on the achievements to be expected from scientific research.

CARRYING FORWARD THE TINBERGEN INITIATIVE IN MACROECONOMETRICS**

BY

L.R. KLEIN*

In the half century that has elapsed since Jan Tinbergen first prepared national econometric models, thereby establishing a whole methodology within economics, there have been significant consolidations of thinking about the subject, countless efforts in replicating his work for different economies, and many new lines of development. In this presentation, I shall review some of the highlights of the last 50 years in macroeconometric modeling and try to point out where these efforts seem to be leading us at the present time.

It is fully understandable that in the beginning there was preoccupation with the problems caused by the Great Depression and a concentrated effort to explain 'the business cycle.' J.M. Keynes provided, in the *General Theory* and its aftermath, a framework for macroeconomic analysis. This obviously had profound influence on model design and anticipated use by Professor Tinbergen. A second stream of effort centered around the work of Simon Kuznets in national income accounting. These two streams of thought, plus the data availability that emanated, gave great impetus to the entire effort. These were certainly the things that primarily guided and motivated me when I took up the thread of the research effort (1944) that had been interrupted by the War. Towards the close of the War, Jacob Marschak invited me to my first professional position with the irresistible enticement, 'What this country (the USA) needs is a new Tinbergen model.' He wanted to be ready at the Cowles Commission for the first postwar economic assessments, and, indeed, that was the first application of the Tinbergen approach in the United States in 1946 on behalf of the Committee for Economic Development.

Jan Tinbergen, to use common language, put it all together, but many other great figures besides Keynes and Kuznets influenced the outcome by their contributions. Theoretical specification was enhanced by the work of Frisch, Hicks, Kaldor, Kalecki, and Lange. With respect to statistical method, again Frisch was instrumental, but Anderson, Haavelmo, Koopmans, Marschak, Rubin, Stone, Wald and Wold also made fundamental contributions, some

---

* Benjamin Franklin Professor of Economics, University of Pennsylvania.
** Final draft of the first Tinbergen Lecture delivered on October 24th in The Hague on the occasion of the 125th anniversary of the Royal Netherlands Economic Association.

during the 1930's and some during the 1940's, when work began in earnest in the United States (at the Cowles Commission). From my own point of view, I would include Wassily Leontief's input-output analysis as a strong factor in both model specification and in national accounting. Some would characterize his efforts as microeconomic, but I find the Keynes-Leontief model a natural combination that is needed to produce both the demand and supply sides of the macroeconomy.

In the beginning, the necessary ingredients were people and statistical data, but for the past 25 years (or so) there has been a major technological development that changed the face of econometric research, namely, the arrival of the electronic computer. Many of Professor Tinbergen's approximations and linearizations would not have been made in the computer age. Of course, searching, testing, experimenting, and repetitive policy analysis would have been much richer and more informative had we not had the computational obstacle to overcome. I, personally, tried to start my own analysis with simple prototype models and aimed for something much more compact than the celebrated League of Nations Model of the economy of the United States. I admired then, and still do, the daring of the pioneers of the 1930's who undertook larger scale system construction with elaborate data bases. It all looks very simple now, in comparison with the average national model of some hundreds of equations, but it was an enormous task without the help of the postwar electronic computer. I can only say that the research team assembled by Professor Tinbergen, many members of which have been distinguished products of this country's educational system, were extremely talented. My knowledge of the workings of that group comes mainly from extensive discussions about the subject that I had with Tjalling Koopmans at the Cowles Commission.

A model, by nature, is only an approximation of reality; therefore we shall never have the definitive system. With much more data, more thinking about the functioning of the economy, and improved statistical method, we should be able to come closer to reality. The computational difficulty has not, so far, been an obstacle, and I do not foresee an obstacle in the near future, but it is conceivable that specifications can become so complicated that the computing burden outruns the speed of development of efficient CPU delivery.

It would be an achievement for our subject if we were able to narrow the field to one best specification either at the partial or total system level, but that stage has not been reached. Generally speaking, more than one hypothesis is consistent with the same body of economic data. That reflects the nonexperimental nature of econometric methodology, speaking of experimentation strictly in terms of scientific control. Our lack of control, the sparseness of our samples, and the comparatively high noise-to-signal ratio preclude our selecting the *best* specification, but we can eliminate unsatisfactory hypotheses. Professor Tinbergen was able to reject the crude or gross accelerator model of investment behavior, but it probably would not be possible to reject, outright, the generalized or relaxed acceleration principle.

Similarly, the crude quantity theory in which velocity is a fixed parameter or even a smooth trend does not stand up against sample based statistical tests. In general, my view, which was inspired by the work of Professor Tinbergen and also Trygve Haavelmo, is that the economic universe is very complicated. We need large, detailed complicated systems to interpret this universe, even in approximation, and simple formulas, particularly bivariate and linear ones, will not work. If they appear to do so in some fairly small samples, they are bound to fail at some critical point of extrapolation beyond sample limits. That is why the Tinbergen approach to macroeconometric model building appealed so much to me.

A primary objective of Keynesian economics was to explain the main economic magnitudes in the near term for use in contemporary policy formation. That objective makes really heavy demands on forecasting, although this may be denied by many Keynesian economists, mistakenly, I believe. Professor Tinbergen obviously had policy applications in mind, as well, but there was very serious preoccupation with explanations of the business cycle.

Over the years I have come to appreciate this problem more and more. While the approach of the pre-computer age focused more on the characteristic roots of linear systems – the propagation problem in Frisch's terminology – I have personally been more interested in the stochastic aspect of cycles. The theoretical work was laid out by Yule, Slutzky, Frisch, and Kalecki, but statistical investigations became possible during the computer age, under the heading of stochastic simulation. Some cycle properties that are peculiar to economics need a nonlinear explanation, but I believe that a damped system, or a stable nonlinear limit cycle, with random disturbance, gives an excellent approximation of reality. Again, we cannot rule out all competitive views, but some simple deterministic models of the cycle do seem to be inferior to those associated with stochastic simulation of large scale macro models.

The issue of linearity is troubling. Contributions of Kaldor, Goodwin, Hicks, Kalecki and others are all constructive and very good idea generators, but they fail to deal with one important problem, namely at what point does a dynamic system move from nonaccelerating into accelerating inflation? The modelers of nonlinear business cycles had little to say about the dynamics of inflation; they contributed most to understanding of real output cycles.

A great deal of the inflation that occurred in the 1970's was associated with unusual increments in the world prices of food and fuel. A good case can be made for treating these events as changes in exogenous variables, but forecasters using models, primarily of successor generations to Tinbergen models, underestimated the degree of inflation that ensued. Even if the large exogenous changes are introduced in the appropriately observed amounts, after the fact, the models will probably underestimate the degree of inflation. The real output recession was not badly forecast, but the increase in inflation was missed, not in direction but in magnitude.

The fault could lie with the expectations mechanism, but I believe that such a subjective explanation is simply an easy way out and does not face up to the underlying issues. But a search for more appropriate nonlinear responses to large exogenous impulses or to other changes, perhaps induced changes, would be a better way to approach the problem. This is where the research effort should focus. Disequilibrium models, asymmetric response models, deeper treatment of expectations are all suggestive leads, but they have been pursued and to this date yield no demonstrable improvement over what I call mainstream models developed as successive generations of Tinbergen models.

The price mechanism in such models follows generalizations and extensions of the Phillips curve. To put the history of doctrine straight, I would say that at an early stage, Professor Tinbergen recognized the relationship between unemployment and wage rates. He then carried wage and other costs forward into price formation relationships, essentially versions of mark-ups on cost. Inspired by this line of reasoning, I developed and published in the late 1940's a conventional market clearing process (without necessarily implying that full equilibrium would be attained) between wage change and unemployment, followed by the usual mark-up of prices over costs. These equations, as in Professor Tinbergen's case, were built into complete models. Some years later, William Phillips established a long term inverse correlation between wage change and unemployment. The profession carelessly transformed Phillips' relation into one between inflation and unemployment. This carelessness would not have mattered very much in trying to interpret inflation during the 1970's if productivity had remained constant or steady in a trend sense, but productivity fell drastically, under the influence of adjustment to the oil shocks, and the distinction between the choice of wage change or price change (inflation) became critical.

If one remains pure, in the Phillips tradition, and associates wage change with unemployment but also extends the concept to allow for dynamic adjustments of lag distributions in both wages and unemployment, demographic variation in labor force and unemployment, and inter-industry shifts associated with industrial restructuring, then I believe that we can get a better explanation of inflation in the 1970's within the context of a full model of the economy. I find that the industrial shifts that are so well recognized now in the United States (from goods to services and from traditional to new technology lines of activity) actually started in the 1950's and were an on-going process in the 1970's.

To look for the explanation of accelerating inflation in terms of nonlinearities, productivity shifts, demographic changes, and industrial transition is necessarily going to involve large, detailed, complicated model building. That is why I am so attached to the Keynes-Leontief specification, with appropriate neo-classical optimizing behavior and aggregation. This approach is data intensive and computer intensive. It is less clever than the appeal to expectations formation within the context of a simple model, but I am confident that it will prove to provide more accurate results. In many respects the original

Phillips curve formulation, at the hands of William Phillips, is a simple bivariate relationship like the crude quantity theory and the crude accelerator hypothesis. The crude Phillips curve will break down just as the other two have already done. Generalized accelerators and generalized liquidity preference (portfolio decision) equations for money will stand up better than the crude versions of each, and the generalized Phillips curve will do so, as well. Within our profession, people are looking at wrong data sets and specifications to handle the inflation problem of the 1970's.

The role of forecasting is partly to help in policy formation or, more generally, in economic decision making, as for business enterprise, but forecasting also provides a severe testing ground for models and their uses. I remain a firm believer that the forecast test is the ultimate test for our subject; it is our 'bottom line.' I think that if one looks at all the evidence that has become available, one will find that the best (most accurate) economic forecasts are made with models built in the Tinbergen tradition. Until the challengers – the exponents of rational expectations, the monetarists, the time series analysts, the consensus surveyers – can produce a better record under replicated conditions, I believe that the objective verdict will be on the side of the mainstream model. That is not to say that the mainstream modeler gains no benefit from the other approaches. There are possibilities of improving forecasts – forecasts that are basically made by using mainstream models – by drawing upon results from other approaches, but the model approach is central and the other approaches make peripheral contributions.

In an interesting tabulation of forecast performance during the first half of this present decade, Charles Wolf scores two mainstream American models that could surely trace their roots to Professor Tinbergen – the models of Data Resources, Inc. and of Wharton Econometrics – very high, almost the same, and far above repetitive forecasts that use other approaches such as personal judgment or consensus among many independent forecasters.[1] Both of these outstanding forecasts were produced by commercially oriented organizations which used Tinbergen-type models as carefully and intensively as possible, combining the formal models with latest information that becomes available almost daily.

The most extensive studies of American forecast performance covering econometric models, consensus views, and pure time series relationships are those reported by Stephen McNees of the Federal Reserve Bank of Boston.[2] Dr. McNees finds that model based forecasts are mixed in comparison with

1 Some complaints have been raised against Charles Wolf's accuracy and weighting system. Corrections of his published numbers re-scramble some of the forecasters below the top two, but they do not show that non-model approaches do as well as the careful model based forecasts. Cf. Charles Wolf, 'Scoring the Economic Forecasters,' *The Public Interest,* Summer, 1987, p. 52.

2 Stephen K. McNees, 'The Accuracy of Two Forecasting Techniques: Some Evidence and an Interpretation,' *New England Economic Review,* March/April 1986, pp. 20-31.

consensus forecasts, but certainly not worse. He also finds that the time series forecasts by either single equation ARIMA methods or multivariate autoregression (VAR) methods both have mixed forecast performance records against those of structural models. After a brief early history of comparatively favorable results, time series methods have more recently had much more difficulty in keeping up with reality. These methods have been particularly weak in forecasting inflation and interest rate movements. And the lack of structure in the system has stood in the way of their improving inflation and interest rate forecasts because when they build systems that try to correct for the defects in handling these variables, they bring down the effectiveness of their dealing with the real variables.

In earlier studies of a leading monetarist inspired model, McNees found that its forecasts were clearly inferior to those of mainstream econometric models, and the Federal Reserve Bank of St. Louis withdrew from the practice of issuing forecasts of one or two years' horizon. In general, monetarist based models have a problem in coping with fluctuations in velocity, particularly with its recent sharp fall in the United States. In contrast with the more complex, interrelated models that were inspired by Professor Tinbergen, the monetarist approach is so simply structured at its apex that it runs into trouble when velocity becomes unpredictable, and that happens all too frequently.

Naturally, the consensus method of forecasting has no flexible facility for responding to latest information or to the evaluation of alternatives. Even if it had a forecasting performance that was as good as that of mainstream models, it would not be as useful in other applications that round out the forecasting exercise.

As for pure time series models, whether of the ARIMA or VAR type, it may be the case that they contain some useful short term information, up to 3–6 months' reliability, because of the inherent serial correlation in quantitative economic life, but they deny the use of information to be gained from accepted economic theory and analysis. Tjalling Koopmans put an unforgettable title to his review of the time series method of the National Bureau of Economic Research when he labeled it as 'Measurement without Theory.' As far as *economic* theory is concerned, that is the way that I would characterize the ARIMA-VAR techniques.

Perhaps Tjalling Koopmans was overly harsh about the National Bureau effort as a whole, but he made a fundamental point. I do not want to reject ARIMA-VAR methods entirely from use in econometric research because I shall outline procedures below for combining time series and econometric model applications, both in forecasting and simulation analysis, but these particular uses are quite different from those that motivate the bulk of time-series analysts in their efforts at economic analysis.

After Professor Tinbergen developed the macroeconometric model as a fundamental tool for economic analysis, he turned to a particular aspect of model use, namely, the formation of policy. In this effort he introduced an important pair of concepts–instruments and targets. In order to make use of these concepts in policy formation, it is of utmost importance to have structural models for application. VAR models try in an indirect way to interpret policy changes, but their scope is very limited in this respect; only certain simple policies can be simulated, and I find many of the results that have been generated to be strongly counterintuitive.

I always detected a strong economic theoretical content in Professor Tinbergen's models. He examined Slutzky demand conditions; neoclassical expressions for elasticity of substitution, and many of the theoretical properties of Keynesian macroeconomics. The theoretical underpinning that is found in structural models is essential in applying his policy formation approach. This is the crucial point in distinguishing between mainstream models and either consensus or time series methods of forecasting. It is my view that this property is decisive in showing the superiority of the structural model in this field of methodological competition.

Large systems of up to 1000 equations or even more are now in existence around the world. Practically every OECD country has one or more models; the more important centrally planned economies have models, as do many developing countries. They were spawned by Professor Tinbergen's work for the Dutch economy, the USA and the UK. They have become intricate systems with large data bases that are greatly enhanced in use by modern hard- and software, but they do things that the pioneer master laid out years ago. They provide forecasts, estimates of cyclical properties, simulations of policies, and search for optimal policies. They also create scenarios, which are, in a sense, extensions of policy analysis.

Two other approaches to econometric model building, different but not necessarily inconsistent with the mainstream model, are the use of Bayesian estimation techniques and the use of computable general equilibrium (CGE) models. The Bayesian approach is largely based on a particular way of using *a priori* information in model estimation. It differs from the mainstream approach in that it is more tractable for small models, and this may take one far from the complicated reality of the economic world that we are trying to analyze. Also, the method depends on subjective decisions by the model builder, while mainstream model building is moving in a direction that is as completely objective as possible.

As for the CGE models, they tend to be less data intensive than the mainstream macro models and rely more on *a priori* judgments about parameter values or on relatively freer use of data to determine coefficient estimates. These techniques need not be used, but they often are in the construction of CGE models. Also, such models place even greater reliance on *a priori* economic theory than do mainstream models, too much reliance in many cases, by imposing the conditions of optimal behavior in fully competitive markets and market clearing. The CGE models serve as a useful complement for long range analysis. They are less useful for short term forecasting and study of the business cycle. It is, however, important to impose many of their long run properties on mainstream models, and they can certainly be used to good advantage in combination with mainstream models.

The great bulk of macroeconometric modelling was for many years confined to individual national economies, but it is no surprise that the next major thrust has been towards world modelling, which is presently flourishing. There was an early attempt to build an interrelated model of many countries simultaneously by Professor Tinbergen's associate, J.J. Polak. Ultimately his efforts resulted in a book. There was a great deal of formative thinking about the concept of a world model based on the contributions of Lloyd Metzler, Folke Hilgerdt, and Ragnar Frisch, but a full scale modeling effort known as LINK was launched, as a cooperative project, bringing together model builders, all in the Tinbergen tradition. This project was conceived in 1968 and is still active, becoming more comprehensive and more inclusive, both in terms of geography and economic processes. It is truly a world system because no significant area of the globe is excluded. Now, in addition to the LINK project, we find world models at OECD, the Federal Reserve Board, the Japanese Economic Planning Agency, and other research centers around the world. Also, there are commercially available world models, such as that of Wharton Econometrics.

These are all worthy and interesting efforts, but it is easiest to appreciate the LINK system in the present context because it is comprised of a systematic collection of models from all parts of the world that could easily have been conceived by Professor Tinbergen, one of his students, or one of his associates. They were all inspired by his work. The trick is to relate them in a mutually consistent way, and this is done, in the LINK case, through particular use of the world trade matrix, which is deployed in an analogous way to the use of input-output systems to relate sectors within a national economy.

Where does world modeling take us? In the first place it enables us to look at an entire new class of applications. World forecasts of macroeconomic tendencies is, of course, an obvious use. Not only are we able to prepare a whole set of world forecasts, as in the LINK case, for 80 models simultaneously, but we can also think about the world as a whole in macro magnitudes such as world GDP, world trade volume, world inflation, world unemployment, world capital formation, etc. Regional totals, also, for organizational groupings (NATO, OECD, EEC, CMEA, OPEC) or geographical entities are regularly reported. This provides the economist with a global view. From the *World Economic Survey* of the United Nations we find a comprehensive table which is heavily based on LINK projections. In Table 1, we can see one of the results of macroeconometric model building at the world level.

It is evident that econometric work of this scope is only possible in the computer era. The system consists of 80 models (some annual and some quarterly), nearly 20,000 equations and more than 100,000 lines of computer code and can be simulated (solved) for five annual periods in fewer than 5 minutes, after set-up with model inputs is complete. These are big numbers, but bigness is not the

TABLE 1 – GROWTH OF WORLD OUTPUT[1] AND TRADE, 1971–1988

	Level in 1980[2] (billions of dollars)	Average		1984	1985	1986[3]	1987[4]	1988[4]
		1971–1980	1981–1986					
		Percentage change						
Output								
World	..	3.9	2.7	4.5	3.4	3.0	3.2	3.7
Developing countries	2.085	5.6	1.5	2.2	2.0	2.5	2.7	3.8
Net energy importers	1.160	5.0	2.8	3.8	3.4	5.5	4.3	4.5
Net energy exporters	925	6.4	– 0.3	0.0	0.0	– 1.6	0.5	2.7
Developed market economies	7.640	3.1	2.2	4.7	2.9	2.4	2.6	3.0
North America	2.866	2.9	2.4	6.4	2.8	2.6	2.7	3.4
Western Europe	3.467	2.9	1.5	2.4	2.3	2.4	2.4	2.4
Japan	1.060	4.7	3.6	5.1	4.5	2.5	2.6	3.0
Centrally planned economies of Europe[5]	..	5.2	3.3	3.8	3.6	4.3	4.1	4.5
China[5]	..	5.7	8.8	12.0	12.3	7.0	7.0	7.0
Trade								
World trade volume[6]	1.990	5.0	2.7	8.9	3.2	3.5	3.0	4.0
Memorandum items:								
Per capita output								
Developing countries	900.0[7]	3.4	– 0.9	– 0.1	– 0.3	0.3	0.5	1.6
Developed market economies	10,296.2[7]	2.3	1.6	4.1	2.2	1.7	1.9	2.3

Source: Department of International Economic and Social Affairs of the United Nations Secretariat.

1 Real gross domestic product. The classification of countries into the various analytical groups is shown in the explanatory notes to the present survey. Output data for these country groups and for each member country are aggregated with weights estimated on the basis of 1980 prices and dollar exchange rates. Developed market economies are aggregated with weights based on 1982 prices and dollar exchange rates.
2 GNP or GDP level in 1980 based on 1980 prices and dollar exchange rates.
3 Preliminary estimates.
4 Forecasts (based on Project LINK and other institutional forecasts). Projections for 1987–1988 are based on an average crude oil export price of $17 a barrel.
5 Net material product.
6 Arithmetic average of the growth rates of world volume of exports and imports.
7 In United States dollars; 1980 prices and exchange rates.

objective; it is the inevitable consequence of world economic interdependence, which is a fact. There are no longer any closed economies. No part of the world economy can be neglected in trying to reach meaningful conclusions.

At a recent assembly of international model builders at the Brookings Institution, many serious scholars attempted to analyze monetary and exchange rate effects on the United States and other OECD countries, but they completely neglected the developing countries and the socialist countries. All their findings were flawed because capital flows, debt negotiations, and trade flows from the neglected areas were having significant effects on the very magnitudes that they were investigating. There simply is no easy way out if one is trying to be a careful economic analyst in this highly interdependent world.

An entirely fresh class of problems can be investigated through the medium of international models. Among those issues that have been studied with the LINK system, I list the following.

Arms race
Disarmament
Protectionism and trade wars
North-South capital transfers
Commodity price stabilization
Interdiction of shipping
Policy coordination among cooperating countries
World crises, debt default and oil price rises
Cross country multipliers
Crop failures

These are all world problems of obvious importance, but what light can be shed upon them through the deployment of a world econometric model? Most economic variables have a dual nature; they are somebody's credit and another person's debit. Oil exporters gain when oil prices go up, but oil importers lose. It is worthwhile looking at world magnitudes, and their distribution, to see if we can determine whether there are gains or losses, on balance, and how these gains and losses are distributed across countries.

To give an example, we notice in medium term projections of the LINK system that the developing world, at least significant parts of it, have poor economic growth and improvement prospects. This is particularly true of Africa, parts of the Middle East, and parts of Latin America. North-South capital transfers could be of assistance in bringing a better life to the Third World. In a simulation, we can target each industrial country for international development aid that would bring each closer to the widely accepted target of 0.7 percent of GDP. But many industrial countries have significant budgetary deficits and, for one reason or another, are reluctant to try to attain the target values of development assistance. An attractive way to try to persuade potential donors to increase such assistance is to seek to create a world fund through multilateral disarmament among both East and West countries. If the military cutbacks were to release sufficient funds to reach the assistance goal cited above, an annual pool of more than $50 billion could be created. This amount is distributed through simulation exercises from North to South in proportion, at the receiving end, to present shares of development assistance. Other formulas for giving and receiving could be tried, but this one appears to work well. The LINK system provides estimates of the prospective gains accruing to various developing regions. They are highest for Africa and the Middle East (non-oil exporters). And the donor countries do not suffer, although their gains are modest in percentage terms, but they benefit through better export sales to the developing countries even though they scale back domestic military outlays.

The world is ripe for major disarmament negotiations now, and LINK simulations can throw light on the process, just as it can be used, in a creative way, for the other policy issues listed above. The changes are rarely dramatic, but they are realistically modest and broad in their delivery of improvement.

World modelling has gone far on the merchandise trade side. This development followed obvious data availability on bilateral movements of goods and extensive statistics of world trade in primary commodities. A start has been made in handling trade in invisibles, but the data base is vastly inferior to that which exists for merchandise. After trade in services, the next step, which is already being taken, is to model capital flows. This is important simply for completing coverage of the items in the total balance of international payments, but it is of extreme importance now for use in the determination of international exchange rates and for studying the impact on the world economy of financial innovation. The technical changes that are taking place in telecommunications and computer use in international financial markets pose interesting challenges for econometricians. This, in itself, calls for new econometric work at the international level because the instruments have such a high degree of substitutability that what happens in any one market quickly spreads to others. The problem and its manifestations in the form of capital flows are truly global; so they must be modeled on a global (*i.e.,* international) basis.

To some extent, the Federal Reserve World Model treats financial problems in some detail, but its scope is severely limited to the G-5, while capital flows are important, both as cause and effect, on a much wider basis. Some success has been attained in modeling capital flows for the summit nations, and first considerations are being given to study of financial flows in models of centrally planned economies, the Polish one in particular. These are all recent LINK activities but must command the attention of international model builders everywhere.

Some other methodological directions for international model building concern the use of optimization techniques in new applications. Extensive simulations have been made of macro policy coordination, but only a few studies have examined such joint policies in an optimization framework. A natural approach is through the technique of dynamic games. This can pose difficult problems of computation, especially for very large models, but the new generation of computers – the supercomputer with parallel architecture – is making the effort possible. Within the context of the LINK system, dynamic optimization has been achieved and is being studied in applications of protectionist policies that lead to trade wars.

A second area of great interest for international modelling is stochastic simulation on a simultaneous cross country basis. In this problem, covariances of error across countries makes the calculations difficult but highly realistic. In small simplified systems, stochastic simulation of internationally linked models has been carried out, but it requires the power of new large computer facilities to do it for full size world models.

Finally, the power of telecommunications facilities is being brought to bear on international model applications. In project LINK, we have assembled groups of model operators, accompanied by general economists and journalists, in different areas of the world simultaneously (Tokyo; Bedminster, New Jersey; and Zurich). With audio-visual connections via satellite, the parties discussed a baseline LINK projection and reached conclusions about a desirable policy of international coordination. Fresh exogenous inputs were quickly read into the LINK system in Philadelphia; a simulation was executed; and transmitted trans Pacific/trans Atlantic for further discussion. A refinement was called for and similarly executed. All this took place in a single morning (evening Tokyo, afternoon Zurich) session. Apart from the substance of the exercise, it demonstrated how econometric technicians with models, common data files, high powered computers, and latest telecommunications facilities can stay in touch around the world. This could have enormous implications for handling economic policy controversies, trade wars, arms races, and even military confrontations. This is only the beginning of use of an entirely new medium for economic decision making, and model building is central to the exercise.

The international dimension is important and will surely occupy a great deal of econometric attention, but there are very important matters to be followed up at the national level too. Given that forecast performance is important, is there any prospect of our making a significant improvement in our ability to forecast the macro economy in the near future?

There is no method that has been shown to dominate the use of structural models for purposes of forecasting; therefore the question actually concerns the possibility of our improving models so that they produce better forecasts. Over the years, better samples of data, better quality of data, better use of economic theory, and better use of statistical estimation techniques have all been tried.

If we look back to our earliest attempts at forecasting from models (for me that would date from 1946), then I believe that we can cite a clear improvement in ability, not only with respect to annual estimates of aggregate output and employment, but also in the various dimensions of forecasting – using shorter intervals (say, quarters), expanding the range of variables being forecasted, hitting turning points, providing confidence intervals, *etc.*

There are accuracy statistics provided by Stephen McNees in the American case that show a deterioration of accuracy during the 1970's, but results for the 1980's are decidedly better. The improvement brings us back to the records established in the 1960's but not yet to a clear improvement over these.

Paul Samuelson once remarked that we may have reached an asymptotic level of accuracy. The inherent noise in our subject and the impossibility of making precise measurement, after the fact, of quantitative magnitudes in macroeconomics, are reasons why he may be right, but an interesting new line of approach is being investigated in order to try to bring up forecast accuracy. This approach is based on the idea of combining forecasts from different sources of information.

It has long been known that a user, by combining forecasts, can reduce the risk of error. The *variance* of forecasts can be reduced in this way. It is very much like the investment principle of using portfolio diversification in order to reduce the risk of return. In addition to the reduction of risk, there is reason to believe that absolute levels of accuracy can be improved.

I am suggesting the combination of forecasts for high frequency (say monthly or even weekly or daily) intervals from time series models with quarterly forecasts from structural econometric models. The time series models could be either VAR or single-equation ARIMA types. Various research centers are pursuing this path in particular ways, but my suggestion is to use time series methods for very short run forecasts, up to six months duration. It has been noted that ARIMA methods, by capturing the details of serial dependence inherent in the economy, do well in forecasting for very short periods ahead. They do not do uniformly better than structural models, but they do approximately as well, and for selected variables do better.

An advantage of using ARIMA methods is that they can capture the very latest pieces of information as they become available in reports that are released daily. One day it is orders, then inventories, then prices, then foreign trade, then employment, then retail sales and so on. Of course, there are daily financial reports. These high frequency data are published rapidly, often with little more than 30 days delay for reporting time. Early in a quarter, the overall patterns of economic activity begin to build up, on the basis of these daily reports.

This 'latest news' is not neglected by forecasters using models, but it is unsystematically assimilated. Forecasters use adjustments to the statistical equations of a model in order to bring the solutions in line, in a general way, with this unfolding flow of economic information. An equation of a model may be written as

$$y_{it} = f_i(y_{i,t-1}, y_{jt}, y_{jt-1}, \dots, x_{kt}, \dots, \theta_i, \dots) + e_{it}$$

where y_{it} is the ith endogenous variable
        x_{kt} is the kth exogenous variable
        θ_i is a parameter in the ith equation
        e_{it} is an additive random error

It is understood that the ith equation generally has many y variables, many x variables, and many parameters on the right-hand side.

In forecasting, *initial* lag values and exogenous variables are assigned values; parameters are replaced by their statistical estimates, $\hat{\theta}_i$; and the random errors are put at population mean values of zero.

$$\hat{y}_{it} = f_i(y_{i,t-1}, \hat{y}_{jt}, y_{jt-1}, \ldots, x_{kt}, \ldots, \hat{\theta}_i, \ldots) + 0$$

On the basis of latest information the error term may be assigned a non-zero value a_{it}. This is done subjectively and approximately. In fact this practice is severely criticized by non-model-builders.

Instead of assigning values to e_{it} in the usual way, we may choose adjustments (as few as possible) in order to force the model solution to agree with the ARIMA estimates from high frequency data over the coming 3 or 6 months, *i.e.*, for the current quarter and one more ahead. These adjustments are then left in the equation system for the operation of the model over the entire forecast horizon.

This procedure has the advantage of making the adjustments purely objective and scientifically replicable. If more and better high frequency data are studied carefully, we may incorporate so much more new information that forecast accuracy is improved. This is one promising line of attack on forecast error that is appropriate to the information age in which data are available with greater speed and wider coverage. Computer and telecommunications facilities enable us to process and use this information to advantage; herein lie the potential gains to be realized.

As far as accuracy is concerned, the record is there. In the United States, documentation is elaborate and in many other countries where accuracy has been studied – mainly in major OECD countries but also in some developing countries such as Mexico – the results are similar. No other method is demonstrably superior, and in many comparative tabulations, model based forecasts are definitely superior. Nevertheless, the noise factor is large, and users are understandably dissatisfied.

But a school has come into prominence in recent years arguing against the use of mainstream macroeconometric models. The central argument of this school is that expectations are extremely important and should be consistent with the model mechanism. The underlying hypothesis is that ordinary citizens in the economy have the same information as everyone else – the same as public authorities, as professional model builders, as large decision makers in enterprises or trade unions etc. If the macro model is correct, then it should be known to all, either implicitly or explicitly, and the expected values for prices, incomes, credit market rates, or other market determined variables should be the same as those generated by the model. The model should be used simultaneously to generate the expectations *and* to estimate the parameters on the basis of these same expectations. Such models, with 'own' expectations, are then deemed to be superior.

In particular, this approach to expectations formation is said to be forward-looking, while the mainstream approach, initiated by Professor Tinbergen, is said to be backward-looking. This is, in my opinion, a very unfortunate and misleading way of presenting expectations behavior.

It is misleading because the conventional technique, now labeled as backward-looking, is usually represented by general lag distributions, which make expected values of an economic variable functions of their history, and, as everyone knows, *forward solutions* to distributed lag relationships can be generated from initial conditions. This method simply says that people look forward by studying history and everything observable, as initial conditions, up to the present. It is not appropriate to call this backward-looking. It is simply a matter of determining, in a plausible way, how people actually do form expectations. Economic theory tells us something about equilibrium or steady state behavior on the basis of optimization theory; it does not tell us how expectations are formed. That involves the joint study of economic, social, political and psychological processes, out of which a definitive theory of expectations has not yet evolved.

Extreme arguments of monetarists have been shown to be unsubstantiated by manifest data, but money *is* important. Similarly, extreme arguments of this new school of expectations theorists do not stand up to the facts of life, but expectations *are* important. The present school is putting forward its ideas as innovational, at least dating from the well known article of John Muth, but expectations have always been prominent in specification of macroeconometric models. In fact, Keynes devoted an entire chapter to expectations in the *General Theory,* and expectations formation has always been on the mind of model builders in trying to specify Keynesian, neoclassical, or other structural models.

What is the evidence for different methods of expectations formation? The new school, labeled in almost a pejorative way as *rational expectations*, is only a theoretical hypothesis. Some statistical studies of expectations formation confirm this hypothesis during restricted sample periods, but much more often the statistical findings reject the validity of this hypothesis. The nearest approaches to expectations formation that are based on social psychological analysis are those in sample surveys of the people who actually formulate expectations. Results from sample surveys show very weak support of so-called rational expectations. For example, a Norwegian study of individual household expectations finds that the procedure of adaptive expectations, which has been prominently used in mainstream macroeconometric models, strongly dominates the rational expectations hypothesis. Many model builders, in fact, use sample survey expectations for prices, general market conditions and capital formation as direct variables. These observed expectations are then generated as endogenous variables in models, just as other economic variables are generated. This is as direct and forward looking as one can get in model building and goes directly to the atomistic source of expectations formation, not relying on hypotheses to generate expectations indirectly. In my opinion, the direct use of survey information is the most promising way of treating expectations in economic models, and has been used for more than 25 years in econometric practice.

Another piece of statistical evidence is associated with the 'cobweb' theory of demand and supply interaction in individual commodity markets. This evidence is interesting because Muth based his original development of expectations behavior by considering the cobweb hypothesis. Broadly and generally speaking, this hypothesis asserts that supply of a commodity depends on historical (lagged) prices that are known up to the time of making a supply commitment, such as planting a crop. It then asserts that actual market price is set at a level that clears the market so that demand and supply are brought into balance.

Simple mathematical models of this supply-demand, *cum* market clearing, process generate time paths of prices and quantities with distinctive oscillatory patterns. Theorists argue that this model cannot prevail because people will be able to work out in advance such price-quantity movements and will take profitable action that will iron out the oscillations. This is one aspect of an efficient-market hypothesis.

If one stands strictly by the crude cobweb hypothesis, one will find little statistical support, although there are a few unusual markets where crude cobweb phenomena do appear to exist. It is very much like the study of the crude acceleration principle or the crude monetarist model. Observable data reject these versions. If, however, the crude models are generalized to such elaborations as the flexible accelerator or the liquidity preferences hypothesis, then much more statistical support can be found. In the same sense, an extended cobweb system in which a general lag distribution of prices appears in the supply equation, other supply factors are also included (costs, subsidies, natural conditions), other demand factors besides current prices are used in the demand equation (income, taxes), and inventory accumulation is introduced so that markets are not always cleared provides the structure of a more elaborate system which does fit the facts quite well. An extended cobweb in which these other aspects are introduced and in which no trace of the rational expectations hypothesis enters cannot be shown to be dominated by the new approach. If a serious forecaster were to keep an ear to the ground, always using latest information, combine an extended cobweb model with a high frequency ARIMA system as outlined previously, and make repetitive predictions, I believe that he or she will do at least as well in accuracy terms as any so-called rational expectations model, and probably will do even better if the alternative investigator insists on standing by the new approach in a strict and rigid way.

It is well known that there are identification and uniqueness problems with rational expectations. As noted above, it is asking a great deal of a model and sample to provide a basis for determining both how expectations are formed and for determining the parameters associated with this expectations process. There is, in general, a multiplicity of estimated models that have this consistency property. The *models* may not be unique (identification), and the estimates may not be unique (estimation). In another connection, statisticians have eschewed the approach of using a model and sample to determine how reliable the data are (relative variances of observation error) and to use these same estimates to determine the values of the model's parameters in the presence of behavioral error. If something were not known about the error variances, there would be a multiplicity of estimates of the parameters. This is the lack of identification. For this problem, statisticians have said that it is like 'eating one's own tail' to use the model and data to determine relative variances and then to use these relative variances to estimate the model's parameters. In the estimation of the linear model with joint normal errors of observation, the likelihood function goes to infinity unless some restrictions are imposed on the error process. In an older era, econometricians quite sensibly gave up this model, unless there was good external information about the error structure. The same problem faces the econometrician in trying to use the model to generate expectations and then to use these expectations to estimate parameters of the model. At some point there must be an infusion of new information; otherwise it is a case of 'eating one's own tail.' The attractive feature of the approach using sample survey data is that new information is actually brought to bear on the process of expectations formation. The rational expectations theorists, on the other hand, must impose arbitrary and presumed restrictions on the probability structure of error in order to deal with the problems of under-identification and non-uniqueness.

Finally, the new school of expectations theorists argue that it is futile to intervene in the economy with policy changes. The futility argument stands apart from the argument that expectations should be consistently generated, *i.e.,* we may have consistent expectations without there being an impossibility of policy implementation. I would argue against both ideas – that expectations are formed as the new school asserts and that policy intervention is futile – but there are many contemporary theorists who subscribe to the consistency hypothesis for expectations formation and not to the futility of policy doctrine.

It is said that people anticipate the moves of policy makers in advance because they have access to the same information and model. This does not seem to be a sensible point of view. There is an extremely large dispersion in people's perceptions of the future. That is what makes a market. In many respects, the fact that people *do* have quite different expectations creates perceived market opportunities for both buyers and sellers. There is little plausibility to the proposition that people, on average, are using the same model that the professional model builders are using, or even implicitly coming to the same conclusions. There are great differences in abilities to get latest information; there are differences among people in what is available; and there are differences in the way information is filtered into a course of economic action.

In recent years we have seen economic policies well advertised in advance, and we have also seen people reacting to these policies just as models have predicted. The present American administration announced tax cuts of given dimension for three years' running. Model builders predicted private spending reactions to these tax cuts *and* large ensuing deficits from the very beginning. That is why Charles Wolf finds that mainstream model builders outperformed others in this period. The policy changes were fully predicted, and the response to them followed model predictions. It is hard to see any substance to the futility argument in these events. Also, after the revelation of the Mexican debt crisis in 1982, the Federal Reserve system pursued an anticipated policy of monetary expansion. There were few surprises, and the reaction was fully as predicted by the models. In fact, this is a period in which Stephen McNees found model projections to be performing reasonably well.

People do change their economic decisions when large policy changes are introduced, but as long as people's decision changes follow the patterns laid out by mainstream macroeconometric models, there is no support for the futility hypothesis. According to that hypothesis, people will make changes when policies change. That is obvious enough, but if these changes are approximately as models predict, then the futility argument is not relevant. Not only would people be expected to change their decisions, but their *behavior* would have to change as well, in order for the futility doctrine to be useful. In some versions, it is asserted that reaction coefficients of econometric equations are functions of exogenous policy variables. This is purely a contrived argument in order to arrive at a conclusion that policy will be ineffective. It is true that models with variable coefficients provide a generalization over the fixed coefficients model, but coefficients can change in many ways. They might be random; they might have trends, but there is no solid evidence that they are functions of policy variables in just such a way as to controvert the intended effects of policies. The variable coefficients model provides a useful generalization, taking us in the direction of nonlinearity. Where the evidence exists, nonlinearities have been introduced, often through having variable coefficients. No doubt research will continue in these two directions to find the best possible specification, but there is no reason to direct research toward models with coefficients that are very special functions of certain exogenous variables. At this stage there is no obvious improvement over the model in which coefficients are fixed parameters, with some proven nonlinearities, and policy effects are felt through changes in exogenous variables that do not cause reaction coefficients to change.

Summary

CARRYING FORWARD THE TINBERGEN INITIATIVE
IN MACROECONOMETRICS

The historical roots of macroeconometric model building go back to the studies of Jan Tinbergen in constructing statistical models of The Netherlands and the United States. His work built on the contributions of J.M. Keynes to macroeconomic theory and Simon Kuznets to the design of accounts to measure national income and product. Wassily Leontief's input-output models helped to extend the effort to many industrial sectors. Other economic theorists and statisticians also made important contributions in the 1930s and 1940s. A breakthrough has been the arrival of the electronic computer. Many seemingly impossible tasks are now quite easy. Among the many approaches to economic forecasting, policy analysis, and cyclical analysis, macroeconometric modeling stands out as the most accurate and insightful. There are many challengers, but none that is demonstrably superior on a replicated basis. The present thrust of model building has extended beyond Professor Tinbergen's original work at the national level. World models of economic inter-dependence are now operational in many international centers.

PROFITABILITY AND FACTOR DEMANDS UNDER UNCERTAINTY **

BY

EDMOND MALINVAUD*

In Paris during the winter 1943–1944 a mathematics student was attracted by economics. Without the guidance of any professor, he was trying to understand various books dealing with this field. One day he entered the little shop of a publisher, *rue de la Sorbonne*, and bought a book with the fascinating title 'Les fondements mathématiques de la stabilisation du mouvement des affaires,'[1] *i.e.* Mathematical foundations of the stabilization of business fluctuations. The author was an 'expert temporairement attaché à la Section Financière et au Service des Etudes Economiques de la Société des Nations,' J. Tinbergen. As he was studying the book very carefully, this young man could not imagine that forty five years later he would be given the honor of delivering the Tinbergen Lecture.

Today then I am paying tribute to one of my best teachers, one whom I did not bother with questions but who with this book played an important role in my economic education. Probably my approach to economic phenomena was to a significant extent shaped by what I then learned from Jan Tinbergen.

The subject of this lecture concerns what has been the main question motivating my research during the last decade, namely the medium-term relationship between wages and employment. This question concerned Tinbergen fifty years ago and was indeed very much discussed at the time. For instance, he writes in his 1938 book that 'wage policy is not very important for business trends because of the double role played by wages as factors of demand on the one hand, and of production costs on the other. However, wages become important when one considers their impact on the output equilibrium level in a country competing on the world market' (pp. 91–92). Similarly, an article published jointly in *Econometrica* in 1939 with Pieter de Wolff provides, as one

---

* Collège de France, Paris.
** Second Tinbergen Lecture, delivered on October 8, 1988, in The Hague for the Royal Netherlands Economic Association.

1 Tinbergen (1938).

of its important results, an estimate of the long-run elasticity of the wage rate on the demand for labor (Tinbergen and De Wolff, 1939).

I am not going to discuss today the full system that determines the medium-term impact of the real wage rate on employment, a system that has in particular to take into account the role of wages with respect to the demand for goods. I shall concentrate my attention on what I believe to be the crucial part of this system, namely the part representing the decisions of firms about their capital equipment, with its two dimensions: productive capacity and capital intensity, *i.e.* the factor proportion implied by its full utilization.

I shall first define the nature and the results of my inquiry. I shall then present the model that I find appropriate for this purpose. The rest of my presentation will be devoted to an outline of a fuller treatment of the model that has been published elsewhere, in French (Malinvaud, 1987).

1 AN OVERVIEW

Attention has been given recently in applied as well as in theoretical economics to the relationship between profitability and investment. Discussions on economic policy, in Western Europe in particular, often concerned the question of whether profitability had to be restored in order for investment to increase again, for new competitive productive capacities to be built up and for the demand for labor to expand. On the other hand, often stimulated by the recent progress of disequilibrium economics, macroeconomic theory also considered this subject, which it had surprisingly neglected for so long. However, much remains to be done in order to fully integrate profitability within investment theory.

This integration is now provided by what is called the q theory of investment. According to this theory the amount of productive capital that firms aim at is related to the ratio q between the present value of future profits, expected to result from production, and the cost of this capital. In order to justify the theory, the initial portfolio argument of J. Tobin (1969) may look somewhat far-fetched and has not been precisely incorporated within the models of producers decisions. The more recent papers by H. Yoshikawa (1980) and F. Hayashi (1982) refer to adjustment costs that have now become the *deus ex machina* in any theoretical model involving investment. But adjustments costs are certainly not very significant when one considers medium-term phenomena. The core of the explanation must be different.

Non-formalized economic literature has for a long time considered that profits were the rewards of risk-taking by entrepreneurs and that some degree of profitability was required in order for this risk-taking to reach the appropriate level. The theory of factor demands under uncertainty should then exhibit this role of profitability. This is the theory I tried to elaborate, taking uncertainty of future demand and irreversibility of investment as the main reasons explaining why profitability matters.

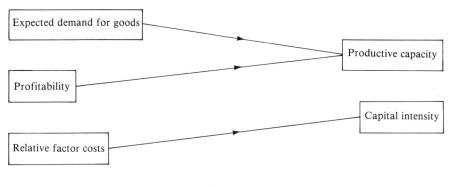

Figure 1

It should be noted at this stage that, being concerned with medium-term phenomena, I shall neglect here whatever limit the availability of owned or borrowed funds may impose on investment. Past profits are then not important as a source of finance but only to the extent that they explain expected profitability.

In order to introduce my results, I shall use a teaching tool that Tinbergen particularly likes, the arrow scheme representing the directions of causation. My discussion will concern the exact meaning and validity of the vision presented by Figure 1, according to which productive capacity would depend on profitability and the expected level of the demand for goods, whereas capital intensity would depend on relative factor costs.

Three main conclusions can be drawn from the analysis of a static partial equilibrium model of a representative firm, a model that I shall precisely define in a moment.

In the first place one must be careful when speaking of the role of probability. The value taken by Tobin's q is endogenous, since it depends not only on exogenous prices and costs but also on capital intensity and on the expected rate of capacity utilization, which varies with productive capacity. Hence, comparative statics properties must take as exogenous not the change in q, but the direct impact that changes in prices and factor costs have on q or, better, an appropriately defined indicator of this impact.

In the second place, the elasticity of productive capacity with respect to profitability varies a great deal, depending on the reference equilibrium. This elasticity increases with uncertainty and would vanish if demand would become sure. It also quickly decreases when profitability in the reference equilibrium improves. Hence, the role of profitability exhibits a strong non-linearity.

In the third place, the two central properties are only approximate. Productive capacity does not depend only on profitability and on the random distribution of demand; it also depends somewhat on relative factor costs. Capital intensity does not depend only on relative factor costs; it also depends somewhat on profitability and on the distribution of demand.

2 THE PRODUCTION FUNCTION[2]

When defining any model of the firm, the first problem is to decide how much to allow for the substitutability between labor and capital. Tinbergen was conscious of the problem in 1942 when in *Weltwirtschaftliches Archiv* he treated in parallel two specifications, one with a Cobb-Douglas production function, the other with strict proportionality between labor and capital. Since then we have had the invention of the concept of a putty-clay technology, which is well known here in Holland. This is essentially the concept I am using.

The irreversibility of productive capital has two dimensions. When capital is built, not only must specific techniques of production be chosen, but also the size of the productive capacity must be selected. The combination of mobile factors and the maximum feasible output with this capital are then strongly determined.

In order to represent these two features, I shall characterize capital by two variables: its intensity k and its capacity $\bar{y}$. The latter is simply the maximum output that can be obtained from this capital, whereas capital intensity is here, by definition, the ratio between the volume K of capital and its capacity:

$$k = \frac{K}{\bar{y}} \tag{1}$$

Labor will be considered as fully mobile and as being the only other factor of production. As soon as the quantity y of output will have been decided, the required labor L will be known and proportional to it, the proportion depending, of course, on capital intensity. I shall represent this relationship by:

$$L = yg(k) \qquad O \leqq y \leqq \bar{y} \tag{2}$$

Hence, the four main variables may be divided into two groups: $\bar{y}$ and k to be chosen in advance, y and L to be decided later for the current productive operations. Similarly, one can speak of two production functions.

The *long term production function* applies at full capacity. It is derived from (1) and (2) when $\bar{y} = y$; it then relates L, K and y in the way traditional production functions do, although perhaps in a somewhat unfamiliar manner. It then assumes constant returns to scale, a hypothesis that will be maintained for simplicity throughout the analysis.

The function g, which characterizes *ex ante* substitutability between capital and labor, is of course decreasing. It will be assumed here to be differentiable. One can easily check the following properties.

---

2   The specification will be fundamentally the same as in L. Johansen (1972).

– the *ex ante* marginal rate of substitution between capital and labor is equal to minus the derivative of *g*, *i.e.* to – *g'*;
– the *ex ante* elasticity of substitution between capital and labor is equal to η given by:

$$\eta = \frac{-g'[g - kg']}{kgg\,''} \tag{3}$$

The *short term production function* takes $\bar{y}$ and k as given, but no longer assumes equality between output and capacity. It is given by (2) and implies constant returns to scale below capacity. On a graph with L and y being measured on the horizontal and vertical axes, respectively, this production function would be represented by two straight line segments, the one from the origin to $(\bar{L} = \bar{y}g\,(k), \bar{y})$; the other being horizontal from this point to the right.

The technology assumed here can be said to be 'putty-clay' since it implies *ex ante* substitutability and *ex post* complementarity. The static nature of the specification, however, simplifies matters up to a point that proponents of the putty-clay technology might perhaps refuse.

3 THE DEMAND FUNCTION

Attention will be focused on the *ex ante* choice of capacity and capital intensity. This choice of course depends on the market conditions confronting the representative firm. They will be assumed to correspond to what is now commonly specified in models of monopolistic competition.

The firm is a price taker for its inputs: the unit costs w of labor and r of capital are then exogenous. No rationing exists on factor markets, which means in particular that labor shortage is not expected. But the firm faces a random demand function for its output. This is specified by a function $S(y,u)$ giving the money value that the sale of output y has when the state of demand is u. As a function of y, S is assumed to be concave. As a function of u, S and its derivative with respect to y are assumed to be non-decreasing.

The *ex ante* probability distribution of u is assumed to be known by the firm. For simplicity it is specified as depending only on two parameters Eu and h:

$$P(a) = Prob\,\{u \leqq a\} = F\left[\frac{a - Eu}{h\,Eu}\right] \tag{4}$$

Eu may be thought to be the expected value of u and h its coefficient of variation, the function F being kept fixed in the whole analysis. The uncertainty about future demand that is exhibited by this probability distribution may of course in part reflect fluctuations of demand during the period of utilization of capital.

Decisions of the firm are assumed to maximize the expected value of profit:

$$W = S(y,u) - wL - rK \tag{5}$$

(E. Malinvaud (1987) also discusses the case of risk aversion and of insolvency risk.) It is noteworthy that, with this criterion, one can as well take the factor costs and the nominal value of the sales function to be random, as long as they are assumed to be stochastically independent of the level of demand u: the notations w and r then refer to the expected values of unit factor costs; similarly $S(y,u)$ refers to the expected value of output y conditional on the state of demand being u.

4 OPTIMAL BEHAVIOR

Ex post, knowing $\bar{y}$, k and u, the firm chooses y so as to maximize

$$S(y,u) - wg(k)y \tag{6}$$

subject to $y \leqq \bar{y}$. Since S is concave as a function of y, the solution is

$$y = \text{Min}\{\hat{y},\bar{y}\} \tag{7}$$

where

$$R(\hat{y},u) \geqq wg(k) \geqq R^+(\hat{y},u) \tag{8}$$

$R(y,u)$ and $R^+(y,u)$ being the left and right partial derivatives of $S(y,u)$ with respect to y, *i.e.* the marginal revenue function. It is assumed that this system (8) has one and only solution $\hat{y}$ (which amounts in practice to assuming that the labor cost w is not too high).

Ex ante maximization of the expected value of profit W takes as given the short term behavior specified by (7) and (8); it then determines capacity $\bar{y}$ and capital intensity k. In order to express the maximization conditions, it is convenient to introduce a new variable $\bar{u}$ characterizing the state of demand for which $\hat{y}$ is just equal to capacity $\bar{y}$. In other words $\bar{u}$ is the solution of:

$$R(\bar{y},\bar{u}) \geqq wg(k) \geqq R^+(\bar{y},\bar{u}) \tag{9}$$

It is assumed to be uniquely determined and is then a function of $\bar{y}$ and k. Equations (7) and (8) then imply that $y = \hat{y}$ when $u < \bar{u}$ and $y = \bar{y}$ when $u \geqq \bar{u}$.

The first-order conditions for maximization can then be written as:

$$\int_{\bar{u}}^{\infty} [R(\bar{y},u) - wg(k)] \, dP(u) = rk \tag{10}$$

$$- T(\bar{y},k)g'(k) = \frac{r}{w} \tag{11}$$

in which $T(\bar{y},k)$ is the expected degree of capacity utilization $Ey/\bar{y}$ and can be computed as:

$$T(\bar{y},k) = 1 - P(\bar{u}) + G(\bar{y},k) \tag{12}$$

with

$$G(\bar{y},k) = \frac{1}{\bar{y}} \int_{0}^{\bar{u}} \hat{y}\, \mathrm{d}\, P(u) \tag{13}$$

Second-order conditions for maximization are not absolutely innocuous, as shown in E. Malinvaud (1987), but will here be assumed to hold.

Equations (10) and (11) have clear economic interpretations. Since $R-wg$ is the marginal gross profit, which according to (8) is essentially zero for $u < \bar{u}$, equation (10) means that the capital cost of a unit of capacity must exactly be covered by the expected value of the marginal gross profit. Equation (11) means that the *ex ante* marginal rate of substitution between capital and labor, corrected for the expected rate of capacity utilization, must be equal to the relative cost of capital with respect to labor.

Equations (10) and (11) determine $\bar{y}$ and k as functions of the parameters, in particular w, r, Eu and h. This determination will be assumed to be unique. The *ex ante* expected demand for labor EL is then easily derived as:

$$EL = \bar{y}\ T(\bar{y}, k)\ g(k) \tag{14}$$

It is again a function of the parameters.

The aim of the model is a precise discussion of comparative statics effects: how do $\bar{y}$, k and EL change as functions of w, r, Eu and h? However, a discussion on the general specification turns out to be too cumbersome to be really illuminating. This is why comparative statics properties will here be studied for two particular specifications, which are analytically simple and may be considered as covering the most relevant cases.

5 COMPARATIVE STATICS: THE KINKED DEMAND CURVE

Let us first concentrate on the case in which:

$$S(y, u) = p \operatorname{Min} \{y, u\} \tag{15}$$

implying

$$R(y, u) = p \ \text{if} \ y \leqq u \\ 0 \ \text{if} \ y > u \tag{16}$$

The firm can sell as much as u at the exogenous price p, but it can sell no more. The demand 'curve' has the form of an extreme kink.

The comparative statics properties that follow do not need the kink to be that extreme; they require only that the solution of (8) be $\hat{y} = u$, which here amounts to assuming $p > wg\ (k)$ but would hold as soon as the marginal revenue would drop at the kink from above $wg\ (k)$ to below it.

Reasons for the kinked demand curve to provide an interesting approximation in macroeconomics have been given for instance by T. Negishi (1979) and J. Drèze (1979) and will not be repeated here. Price rigidity may provide an additional reason in the context of this paper if randomness of demand is viewed as taking the form of random fluctuations of the demands to be served in future periods.

With the specification (15), equations (10) and (11) take simpler forms:

$$[p - wg(k)][1 - P(\bar{y})] = rk \tag{17}$$

$$- T(\bar{y}) \, g'(k) = \frac{r}{w} \tag{18}$$

$\bar{u}$ being replaced by $\bar{y}$ and $\hat{y}$ by u in the definitions of the functions T and G.

Differentiation of these two equations gives the system that provides the basis for the comparative statics properties.[3] Easy interpretation of the properties is found when the exogenous infinitesimal changes δp, δw and δr in price and unit costs are replaced by their impacts on the relative cost of capital with respect to labor $c = r/w$ and on the profitability indicator:

$$q = \frac{\mathrm{E}(py - wL)}{rK} \tag{19}$$

which may be called Tobin's q, even though no reference is made to its evaluation by the stock market. The impacts are then defined by:

$$\frac{\delta c}{c} = \frac{\delta r}{r} - \frac{\delta w}{w} \tag{20}$$

$$\frac{\delta q}{q} = \left[\frac{\delta p}{p} - \frac{\delta r}{r}\right] + \frac{wg(k)}{p - wg(k)} \left[\frac{\delta p}{p} - \frac{\delta w}{w}\right] \tag{21}$$

Notice that (21) does not define the relative change of q, since this indicator also depends on the endogenous variables $\mathrm{E}y$, $\mathrm{E}L$ and K. In classical capital theory the relevant comparative statics properties do not involve the change in the value of capital but rather the impact that changes in quantities have on this

---

3   Comparing (17) and (19) one derives the equation:

$$q = T(\bar{y})/[1 - P(\bar{y})]$$

whose right-hand member involves only one endogenous variable, the productive capacity $\bar{y}$. This equation should not be interpreted as showing that capacity is determined by Tobin's q and nothing else. Indeed, q is also an endogenous variable, as appears clearly from (19). Although using a different explanation, namely the presence of adjustment costs, the literature on the q theory of investment derives similar simple relations between q and investment. Causal interpretations often given to these relations are no more justified than the one considered above.

value. Similarly here, the relevant properties do not involve the change of q but the impact that changes in prices and costs have on q.

For simplicity here we shall also assume $\delta h = 0$, *i.e.* changes in the expected value of demand Eu will be assumed to imply proportional changes in the standard deviation of demand. Differentiation of (17) and (18), F being assumed twice differentiable, then leads to:

$$a \left[\frac{\delta \bar{y}}{\bar{y}} - \frac{\delta Eu}{Eu} \right] + \frac{G}{T} \frac{\delta k}{k} = \frac{\hat{\delta} q}{q} \tag{22}$$

$$\frac{G}{T} \left[\frac{\delta \bar{y}}{\bar{y}} - \frac{\delta Eu}{Eu} \right] + \varepsilon \frac{\delta k}{k} = - \frac{\delta c}{c} \tag{23}$$

in which a and ε are positive coefficients, which depend on the reference situation, and the argument $\bar{y}$ of G and T has not be written.

It is immediately clear from (22) and (23) that changes in expected demand do not react on capital intensity, but imply proportional changes of productive capacity.

Moreover, discussion of the values of the coefficients shows that G^2/T^2 may be taken as small with respect to $a\varepsilon$. It is then an admissible first approximation to say that capital intensity only depends on the relative cost of capital with respect to labor, the elasticity $1/\varepsilon$ being equal to the product of the *ex ante* elasticity of substitution η and the share of the expected cost of labor in the expected total cost. This is the familiar relationship.

It is also an admissible first approximation to say that, for a given state of demand, productive capacity depends only on profitability, or rather on the impact of price and unit costs on profitability. The elasticity then is:

$$\frac{1}{a} = \frac{Eu}{\bar{y}} \cdot \frac{h[1 - P(\bar{y})]}{f(\bar{y})} \tag{24}$$

$f(\bar{y})$ being the derivative of F evaluated at $u = \bar{y}$. This elasticity tends to zero when the degree of uncertainty h decreases to zero. Discussion of equation (24) also shows that the elasticity is likely to quickly decrease as profitability q in the reference situation improves, this property applying for nicely behaved distributions. In other words, one can conclude that, for productive capacity to be sensitive to changes favoring profitability, uncertainty of demand must be significant and profitability low.

6 COMPARATIVE STATICS: THE LINEAR DEMAND CURVE

Let us then take a kind of opposite to the kinked demand curve, namely a linear demand curve, leading to the following linear marginal revenue function:

$$R(y, u) = b \left(1 - \frac{y}{u} \right) \tag{25}$$

b is positive and equal to the price obtained for y close to zero, whereas the quantity demanded at a zero price is equal to $2u$.

The short term decision then is given by (7) and the following form of (8):

$$\hat{y} = t(k) \cdot u \tag{26}$$

where $t(k)$ is the mark-up ratio that would be obtained at $y = 0$:

$$t(k) = \frac{b - wg(k)}{b} \tag{27}$$

Similarly (9) implies

$$\bar{u} = \frac{\bar{y}}{t(k)} \tag{28}$$

It follows that G and T given by (13) and (12) then only depend on $\bar{u}$.

Reflecting on the relevance of this linear case for macroeconomics, it is worth noting that the short-term decision implies the following price for output:

$$
\begin{aligned}
p &= \frac{1}{2}(b + wg) & &\text{if } u \leqq \bar{u} \\
p &= b\left(1 - \frac{\bar{y}}{2u}\right) & &\text{if } u \geqq \bar{u}
\end{aligned} \tag{29}
$$

Either the state of demand, as given by u, is such that there will be excess capacity and the price then depends only on the wage rate and on b, not on the precise level of the state of demand u, for fixed $\bar{y}$ and k. Or this state of demand is so favorable that capacity will be fully used and the price will be 'what the market can bear,' *i.e.* it will not depend on the wage rate. I consider such a short term flexibility of the price charged as unrealistic. This is one of the main reasons why I prefer to concentrate my attention on the case of the kinked demand curve, which is less commonly considered nowadays.

Let us, however, go on and consider the form taken here by the first-order conditions (10) and (11), namely:

$$[b - wg(k)] V(\bar{u}) = rk \tag{30}$$

$$- T(\bar{u}) g'(k) = \frac{r}{w} \tag{31}$$

where the function $V(\bar{u})$ is defined by:

$$V(\bar{u}) = \int_{\bar{u}}^{\infty} \left(1 - \frac{\bar{u}}{u}\right) dP(u) \tag{32}$$

One notes the formal similarities with equations (17) and (18) applying in the case of the kinked demand curve. There is, however, a significant difference.

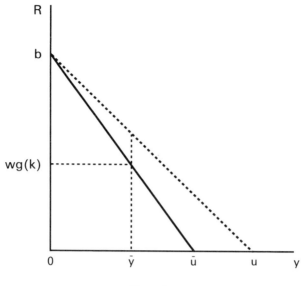

Figure 2

Equations (30) and (31) determine $\bar{u}$ and k rather than $\bar{y}$ and k. Of course the relation (28) shows that one easily goes from $(\bar{u}, k)$ to $(\bar{y}, k)$, but one may suspect that comparative statics properties are less simple. Let us further note in passing that the relation between $\bar{u}$ and $\bar{y}$ is easily visualized (see Figure 2 where the solid straight line and the dotted line respectively represent $R(y, \bar{u})$ and $R(y, u)$ as functions of y).

For comparative statics properties two types of change of the demand curve must be considered. A shift δEu of the expected value of u means a change in 'the size of the market.' On the contrary a positive δb means a proportional increase in the price that can be charged at each level of output. Differentiation of (30) and (31) for a fixed coefficient of variation h eventually leads to:

$$\frac{H}{V}\left[\frac{\delta \bar{y}}{\bar{y}} - \frac{\delta Eu}{Eu}\right] + \frac{G\delta k}{T k} = \left[\frac{\delta b}{b} - \frac{\delta r}{r}\right] + \frac{(1-P)wg}{rk}\left[\frac{\delta b}{b} - \frac{\delta w}{w}\right] \tag{33}$$

$$\frac{G}{T}\left[\frac{d\bar{y}}{\bar{y}} - \frac{\delta Eu}{Eu}\right] + \left[\varepsilon - \frac{GV}{T^2}\right]\frac{\delta k}{k} = \left[\frac{\delta b}{b} - \frac{\delta r}{r}\right] - \left[1 - \frac{GVwg}{Trk}\right]\left[\frac{\delta b}{b} - \frac{\delta w}{w}\right] \tag{34}$$

in which $H(\bar{u}) = 1 - P(\bar{u}) - V(\bar{u})$ and the arguments of the functions have not been written.

Comparison with (22)–(23), applying in the case of the kinked demand curve, is interesting. One first notes that changes in the size of the market act in the same way: they do not react on capital intensity and imply proportional changes of productive capacity.

In the left hand side of the equations, the coefficients outside of the main diagonal are the same in (33)–(34) as in (22)–(23). On this diagonal the coefficient of δk is somewhat reduced, but (32) shows that V should be small, so that the change has little effect. However, the coefficient of $\delta \bar{y}$ has a completely different expression from (24). Like the coefficient a in (22), it is, however, an increasing function of its argument for nicely behaved distributions. Again, the effect of profitability on capacity is small except in cases where uncertainty of demand is significant and profitability is so deteriorated that $\bar{u}/Eu$ is unusually small. Similarly it is found that the product of the coefficients of the main diagonal are likely to dominate G^2/T^2, so that the approximation stating that, for a given state of demand, capacity depends only on profitability and capital intensity only on relative costs may still be considered as valid.

This interpretation, however, takes it for granted that, in the right hand side of the equations, one still finds the impacts of price and unit cost changes, respectively, on profitability and on the relative cost of capital with respect to labor. This is not exactly so. The right hand side of equation (34) is not exactly equal to the change $-\delta c/c$ of the relative cost, as defined by (20). The impact of the change of the wage is somewhat reduced. This is easily explained: when the wage rate increases, $\bar{y}$ and k being kept fixed, the impact is partly transmitted as an increase in the price charged for output, as shown by (29); hence a relative increase in w is a little less inducing to capital–labor substitution than an equal relative decrease of r.

The right hand side of (33) also is less easily interpreted than that of (22). Whereas the latter was clearly the impact on profitability, the coefficient multiplying the relative change of the real wage has no obvious meaning in the present case. We note that, in view of (17), the right side of (33) would be precisely equal to $\delta q/q$ in the case of the kinked demand curve. Indeed, this form of the right hand side applies more generally to any specification of $S(y, u)$, as can be seen by differentiation of (10).

With the linear demand curve, one can compute the value taken by q, as defined by (19), and find:

$$q = \frac{(b - wg)}{rk} \left[T - \frac{1}{2}(G + H) \right] \tag{35}$$

The impact of changes of b, w and r on q, while $\bar{y}$ and k are kept fixed (but the impact on $\bar{u}$ is taken into account), may also be computed as being:

$$\frac{\delta q}{q} = \left[\frac{\delta b}{b} - \frac{\delta r}{r} \right] + \frac{2TV}{T + V} \frac{wg}{rk} \left[\frac{\delta b}{b} - \frac{\delta w}{w} \right] \tag{36}$$

It is easy to see that the coefficient multiplying the last bracket is usually much larger in the right hand side of (33) than in (36). (As long as excess capacity occurs with a high probability, as $\bar{y}$ and k are fixed, changes in w are, to a large extent, transmitted to the price p.) Moreover, trying to define a 'marginal q' does not seem to help. The conclusion then is that, for computation of a relevant indicator of 'the impact of profitability,' one should refer to the expression given by the right hand side of (33) rather than to any direct measure of profitability.

7 CONCLUDING COMMENTS

A summary of the results was given in section 1 of the paper. It will not be repeated here. But one may now be in a better position to reflect on the interest of the model and of its treatment.

Its main purpose was the derivation of some comparative statics properties induced by the behavior of the firms. These properties are relevant within a fuller discussion of the likely impacts of macroeconomic policies, wage policy in particular. But then other elements have to come into play, the formation of the demand for goods being the most important one. Although favorable to profitability, wage restraint is likely to depress demand. Whether it helps to stimulate the creation of new productive capacities or not depends on which of the two effects dominates. Similar remarks would apply to other policy issues. In other words, I see the model as one of the main building blocks of a larger system intended for the study of the medium-term equilibrium. This is the reason why the conclusions of this paper are intermediate products to be used in more embracing theories of the type of those studied by J. Tinbergen in the thirties.

The value of the model of course depends on its realism. To judge it, one may first wonder whether the specification is the proper one: what should one think about the relative importance of the features that it represents and of those that it neglects? Are the hypotheses about technology, markets and behavior satisfactory as a first approximation?

One may also want to confront the model to data. The difficulty then is that expectations are assigned a major role, concerning both the level of demand and the profitability of production. At present we have hardly any data on medium-term expectations of business firms; we have to infer these expectations from past evolutions, an inference that is subject to errors. Two types of tests are nevertheless conceivable and have been applied on French data. The first one directly considers the first-order equations, such as (17)–(18), or more simply the equation deduced from them in the footnote that follows their presentation. I tried to apply this idea in Malinvaud (1986 and 1987). The second type of test was provided by P. Artus (1984) who fitted on macroeconomic time series a dynamic investment model inspired by the static model of this paper. I shall not surprise any econometrician when saying that the tests, although not negative, cannot yet be considered as fully conclusive.

REFERENCES

Artus, P. (1984), 'Capacité de production, demande de facteurs et incertitude sur la demande,' *Annales de l'INSEE*, 1984.

Drèze, J. (1979), 'Demand Estimation, Risk Aversion and Sticky Prices,' *Economic Letters*, 4, pp. 1-6.

Hayashi, F. (1982), 'Tobin's Marginal q and Average q: A Neoclassical Interpretation,' *Econometrica*, 1982.

Johansen, L. (1972), *Production Functions*, Amsterdam, 1972.

Malinvaud, E. (1986), 'Jusqu'où la rigueur salariale devrait-elle aller? Une exploration théorique de la question,' *Revue économique*, 1986.

Malinvaud, E. (1987), 'Capital productif, incertitudes et profitabilité,' *Annales d'économie et de statistique*, 1987.

Negishi, T. (1979), *Microeconomic Foundations of Keynesian Macroeconomics*, Amsterdam, 1979.

Tinbergen, J. (1938), *Les fondements mathématiques de la stabilisation du mouvement des affaires*, Paris.

Tinbergen, J. (1942), 'On the Theory of Trend Movements,' First published in German, to be found in: L.H. Klaassen, L.M. Koyck and H.J. Witteveen (eds.), *Jan Tinbergen - Selected Papers*, Amsterdam, 1959.

Tinbergen, J. and P. de Wolff (1939), 'A Simplified Model of the Causation of Technological Unemployment,' *Econometrica*, 1939.

Tobin, J. (1969), 'A General Equilibrium Approach to Monetary Theory,' *Journal of Money, Credit and Banking*, 1969.

Yoshikawa, H. (1980), 'On the "q" Theory of Investment,' *American Economic Review*, 1980.

Summary

PROFITABILITY AND FACTOR DEMANDS UNDER UNCERTAINTY

The medium term relationship between wages and employment very much concerned Jan Tinbergen in the 30's and is concerning us again today. Precisely analyzing the demands for labor and capital is a prerequisite for understanding this relationship. With this purpose two propositions are here scrutinized: the productive capacity that a firm chooses mainly depends on its expectations about future demand and on the profitability of production; the desired capital intensity mainly depends on the relative cost of capital with respect to labor. In the model uncertainty of future prospects and irreversibility of investment play the major roles.

ON THE THEORY OF MACROECONOMIC POLICY**

BY

JAMES TOBIN*

1 JAN TINBERGEN AND THE THEORY OF POLICY

A great privilege and honor it is for me to speak here today to all of you who are joining me in homage to Jan Tinbergen. I have long regarded Jan Tinbergen as the model economist, the personal example I most hope young economists will follow. He was and is of course a scientist, full of curiosity about how the world works. But his motivation has always been more than curiosity. He wants to know how the world works so that he can make it work better. Knowledge is the foundation of policy. It was natural for Tinbergen to set forth a formal theory of policy nearly fifty years ago (Tinbergen 1952 and 1956), and it was equally natural for him to relate the theory to practical problems of policy in The Netherlands and elsewhere and to implement it and illustrate it with the help of theoretical and econometric models. Thus Tinbergen was the originator of the subject on which I propose to speak to you today.

For many social scientists public policies are phenomena to be described, analyzed, and understood, just like other aspects of individual and social behavior. Those scholars seek to tell how politics and government work, not to try to make them work better. This is certainly a legitimate standpoint, in economics most prominently represented by James Buchanan and other public choice theorists. They regard do-gooders like Tinbergen and me as naive. We think we have an audience, the general public or legislators or government administrators. We assume that to some degree they identify their personal interest with the public interest, wish to promote social welfare, and respect reason and fact. Certainly that is the spirit in which Tinbergen conceived his theory of policy.

Tinbergen embedded policy in a mathematical economic model. Some variables in the model are identified as policy instruments, some as objectives of policy-makers. Policy instruments are 'exogenous' in the sense that policy-

*   Yale University, New Haven.
**   Third Tinbergen Lecture delivered on October 20, 1989, in Utrecht for the Royal Netherlands Economic Association.

makers are free to set their values. There are other exogenous variables, whose values are set by nature or foreigners or other forces external to the model. The model also contains 'endogenous' variables; their values depend on the exogenous variables, policy or non-policy. Target values for some endogenous variables are the objectives of policy. Those objective variables are not the only endogenous variables, but they are the ones that matter.

You can imagine solving such a model so that the solution, or what econometricians call the 'reduced form,' tells directly how the objectives depend on the policy variables. It is easiest to think of this solution for a set of linear equations. The first truth, simple but illuminating, is that the policy-maker cannot hope to hit targets for more objective variables than the number of instrument variables. The second truth is that the availability of N instruments does not guarantee that as many as N objective targets can be hit. There must be N *independent* instruments, in the sense that the effects of any one instrument on the objectives are not proportional to those of any other, or of any combination of others. The third truth is that a redundancy of instruments is conceivable, more instruments than needed to hit all the attainable targets, whether or not some other targets are unattainable.

Very frequently some tradeoffs are ineradicable. For example, we probably don't know how to get more equity from the economy without losing efficiency. The array of policy instruments does not include tools that could overcome this familiar tradeoff. For this reason, instruments are insufficient. Yet at the same time, for a given standard of efficiency we might be able to identify numerous combinations of instruments that would yield the same degree of equity. In that sense, instruments are redundant.

2 APPLICATIONS IN MACROECONOMICS

Rather than pursuing that example, let me turn to my topic of macroeconomics. Tinbergen's framework may seem simple common sense, but it was not obvious beforehand. In the early days of the Keynesian revolution, the idea was to throw everything available at the problem of the moment, depression, unemployment or war-generated inflation. Against unemployment, for example, spend more on public works, cut taxes, print more money, and lower interest rates – all. So undiscriminating and single-minded an attack was perhaps justified during the Great Depression because the target was so remote and so central, and because the constraints on the instruments were so tight that overshooting was not a worry.

After the Second World War, Keynesian economists learned to regard fiscal policy and monetary policy as distinct macroeconomic instruments, substitutes for one another. (It is true that they are not always independent. If printing money is the only way to finance government deficits, then there is no monetary policy independent of fiscal policy. Likewise a small open economy with a fixed foreign exchange rate may not be able to have its own monetary

policy.) Fiscal and monetary policies are both instruments of demand management, of short-run or counter-cyclical economic stabilization.

The two standard objectives of demand management are full employment
and price stability, one a numerical target for an unemployment rate variable,
the other a numerical target for a price inflation variable. Well, we have two
objectives and two instruments. Can't we achieve macroeconomic bliss? At
least one popular American macro textbook misread Tinbergen and said so,
and some economists who should know better have slipped into the same
mistake. The fallacy is an example of the second truth. With respect to the two
targets, fiscal policy and monetary policy are collinear instruments.

That unfortunate fact of life is a consequence of what I call the 'common
funnel theorem.' The theorem says that the consequences of a given volume of
aggregate demand, on the one hand, for output and employment and, on the
other, for money prices and wages are independent of the sources and composition of that volume of demand. Neither fiscal nor monetary instruments affect
the target values directly. Both affect them through the same medium, aggregate demand. The demands generated by fiscal policies and those generated
by monetary policies are poured, along with demands from all other sources,
into a common funnel. How much goes into prices and how much into output
depends on the outflow from the funnel. The output/price or unemploy-
ment/inflation tradeoff is inexorable; that is to say, it can't be eliminated or
mitigated by altering the fiscal/monetary policy mix.

Another way to put the point is this: A certain volume of aggregate demand
will place the economy at a certain point on the aggregate supply (AS) curve
relating output to price level or on the short-run Phillips curve relating unemployment to inflation. Whether that volume is supported by an easy fiscal
policy combined with a tight monetary policy or by a tight fiscal policy combined with an easy monetary policy will not shift the AS curve or the Phillips curve
and, therefore, will not alter the points reached on those curves.

I guess that many of you are busy thinking of exceptions to my common funnel theorem. I recognize that deviations are easy to imagine, but they are
generally unsystematic. For example, the composition of aggregate demand
will usually depend on the mix of the two policies. An easy fiscal/tight money
mix will be expected to result in relatively more private and public consumption
and less investment than the opposite mix. Quite possibly this difference in
composition, in any given economy at any particular time, carries with it some
difference in price behavior. I just don't see that there is any way for a macro
theorist to generalize about that difference or for a macro policy-maker to
count on it.

However, there is one systematic exception I will acknowledge. It applies to
an open economy in a regime of floating exchange rates with free movement of
funds across currencies. An easy fiscal/tight money policy mix means higher
interest rates are associated with any given real GNP. They attract internationally mobile funds and appreciate the local currency. The appreciation

makes prices of internationally tradable goods lower in local currency. The improvement in overall price indexes and their inflation is probably only temporary, because the price declines are borrowed from other countries and are accompanied by deterioration in the home economy's trade balance and current account. This is not a game every country can play at once. It is a 'beggar-thy-neighbor' tactic against inflation in one country, just as policies that lead to exchange depreciation are 'beggar-thy-neighbor' tactics against unemployment.

Most economists nowadays think there is no permanent unemployment-inflation tradeoff. That proposition contains both good and bad news. The good news is that the conquest of inflation entails no cost in unemployment. The bad news is that the amount of irreducible – 'natural' – unemployment may be very high. Anyway the short-run tradeoff is a practical problem in anti-recession or anti-inflation policy-making, and the inability of the two instruments, fiscal and monetary, to overcome the tradeoff is a serious handicap.

Frustrated by the high unemployment rates seemingly necessary for disinflation or for price stability, many macroeconomists have, at various times, stressed the need for additional independent policy tools. The tie between prices and output or wages and employment due to the common funnel might be broken by price and wage controls or incomes policies. It is interesting that both Keynes and Tinbergen viewed money wage rates as a possible policy instrument. Perhaps direct wage/price instruments could lower the natural or inflation-safe rate of unemployment. Perhaps structural reforms – which Tinbergen termed 'qualitative' policies to distinguish them from quantitative instruments – could make the short-run tradeoff less painful or even lower the natural unemployment rate.

The two instruments, fiscal and monetary, should be together capable of hitting some pair of targets. One member of the pair would be a real GNP and employment target, with whatever price outcome is conjoined to it. That would be a target for aggregate demand, most likely the natural or inflation-safe unemployment rate. What would be the second target? It might be a variable connected with external balance, the exchange rate or international reserves or the current account.

More fundamentally, the fiscal/monetary policy mix affects the composition of national output as between investment and consumption. As noted above, a tight-fiscal/easy-money policy mix would favor investment, both domestic and foreign. Those who are concerned for the future standard of living of the society relative to the present would naturally favor that policy mix. The opposite combination of policies in the United States in the 1980s has led to a binge in current consumption at the expense of future Americans.

Although we commonly speak of monetary and fiscal policies each as univariate, as I have been doing here, we know that under each heading fall numerous specific instruments. The monetary authority can set reserve requirements and impose other restrictions on bank portfolios, can set its own discount and lending policies and rates, and can engage in open market operations in a variety of assets, foreign and domestic, short and long. From a macroeconomic viewpoint, most of these monetary instruments are different ways of doing the same thing, and the central bank chooses among them on quite subsidiary considerations. However there might be some gain in the scope of macroeconomic control from using a variety of open market interventions, in foreign exchange and in long-run securities or even equities, not just in the usual very short-term markets.

The variety of fiscal instruments is even greater. In macroeconomics we look mainly at direct impacts on aggregate spending on goods and services. For government purchases, the impacts are obvious. For taxes and transfers, we emphasize the income effects on spending. Traditional fiscal theory, therefore, treats the items in government budgets as collinear instruments. But attention to incentive and substitution effects enriches the policy menu. Although income tax cuts encourage almost exclusively consumption, an investment tax credit, such as was in effect in the United States from 1962 to 1986, mainly stimulates investment. In that respect, the investment tax credit was a substitute for easy monetary policy as an instrument for moving the composition of current GNP in favor of future growth. With respect to that objective, public investment outlays should of course be differentiated from collective consumption.

3 UNCERTAINTY ABOUT THE EFFECTS OF INSTRUMENTS

The theory of policy so far discussed assumes that the effects of policy instruments on endogenous variables, including policy objectives, are known with certainty, or assumes that expected values are all that matter. Things are quite different when considerations of risk are added in an essential way. My Yale colleague and collaborator William Brainard amended Tinbergen's theory in a classic article (Brainard 1967). The essential point is to recognize the errors in the regression coefficients in the macroeconomic model, as well as the additive errors in equations.

In the theory so amended, policy instruments are much less likely to be redundant. For hitting the same targets with smaller variance, more instruments are always helpful, provided their coefficient errors have some statistical independence. The argument is just an application of portfolio theory. The policy-maker is the portfolio manager, and the instruments are the assets. But the objectives of the policy-maker are more complex than those of a wealth-owner. The wealth-owner is trying to maximize expected return for a given amount of risk and then to choose her most desirable efficient combination of return and risk. The policy-maker has a number of incommensurable policy-objective variables, not just one, and has to weigh the expected values and risks of all of them.

Risk aversion imparts some conservatism to policy. In this respect the

Brainard theory is probably realistic. With coefficient uncertainty, big doses of policy medicine enlarge the variance of the outcomes, however much they may improve the expected values. A cautious central banker will not, for example, aim for low unemployment even if the expected value of the associated inflation were acceptable if he thought that the probability of a large inflationary deviation from the mean outcome was also high.

What is important, more precisely, is the standard error of the regression (or reduced-form) forecast of a policy-objective variable. That error, we know, is positively related to the distances of the regressors from their mean values in the sample data on which the model was estimated. Policy-makers do not like to move into *terra incognita*. They do not like to move in big steps. They like to gain observations close to the territory where they are going to operate.

We should, however, not exaggerate the 'take-it-easy' moral of this theory. The warning is against big departures from experience, not against big doses of policy instruments *per se*. Policy instruments often have the same effects on endogenous objectives as some non-policy exogenous variables, and their coefficient errors are likewise highly correlated. Consider, for example, a central bank's increase in the supply of base money and an exogenous decline in the demand for base money, say public's demand for currency or the banking system's demand for excess reserves. Both the policy move and the non-policy events have the same macroeconomic effects. Thus it would not be conservative to withhold a large increase in base money supply if the authorities knew that it would offset a large autonomous decline in demand for base money. Indeed a compensatory injection of base money, even if large, is the conservative thing to do. The same might apply to fiscal policy, where government outlays and taxes have effects equivalent to some exogenous private demands for goods and services. In the Great Depression it was not conservative of governments to try to keep their budgets balanced.

4 PITFALLS IN POLICY EXPLOITATIONS OF EMPIRICAL REGULARITIES

The estimation of policy effects is of course very tricky. Years ago we thought of policy instruments as completely autonomous, exogenous to the economy we were modeling, uninfluenced by the endogenous variables of that economy, insulated from the random disturbances in their values. But if policy-makers themselves were following some rules, even roughly, then their settings of instruments were not exogenous. Observed correlations of instrumental and objective variables may reflect the behavior of the makers of policy, not the behavior of the economy. Those correlations are misleading if they are interpreted as telling how the economy would respond if policy-makers acted differently from the rules they followed in the sample period of observation. 'Goodhart's law' says that in economics any observed regularity will vanish if policy-makers attempt to exploit it.

There are numerous examples in macroeconomics. Before central bankers fell under the sway of monetarism, they followed accommodative, at least partially accommodative, policies. When expansion of the economy increased the demand for bank credit and for deposits and currency, the central bank allowed the supplies to expand as well. In recessions, they allowed money and credit aggregates to shrink along with the economy. Milton Friedman and other monetarists cited the time series correlations of money stocks and nominal national incomes as evidence of the sovereign power of monetary policy, and alleged that stabilizing money supply would stabilize the economy. But when central bankers took the criticisms of the monetarists seriously and ceased to be so accommodative, the correlations became much weaker.

Fiscal policy provides another example of how misleading a guide to policy simple correlations can be. Government deficits have generally been negatively correlated with economic activity, seemingly contradicting the Keynesian view that deficit spending would be expansionary. Of course, the paradox is only superficial. There are two explanations for it. One is the endogenous variation of government finances in response to fluctuations in economic activity. Tax codes and expenditure laws are such that revenues automatically – that is, without new policy decisions or legislation – move procyclically and expenditures countercyclically. Because of this endogeneity, it is a mistake to regard the deficit as an instrument. Tax and expenditure laws and formulas are instruments; given them, budget outcomes are endogenous. The 'full employment budget' and numerous variants of it are an attempt to eliminate these endogenous cyclical effects and to provide a rational quantitative measure of fiscal policy.

A variant of this confusion occurred in the 1980s in the United States. Standard macroeconomic models, both theoretical and econometric, say that deficit spending policies will raise real interest rates. Apologists for the Reagan deficits appealed to the absence of positive simple correlations between deficits and interest rates. The absence of such correlations reflects the fact that the same fluctuations of economic activity that move deficits countercyclically move interest rates procyclically. They don't tell what happens when deficits are massively increased by policy rather than moved endogenously. We found out in the 1980s, when both real interest rates and federal deficits were much higher than in any previous post-1945 recovery.

The second explanation of negative correlations between deficits and economic activity is that governments often reinforce the 'built-in stabilizers' with endogenous changes in fiscal policy: tax cuts, generous transfers, and public works to combat recession, tax increases and expenditure economies and postponements to fight inflation.

Of course the whole purpose of econometrics, as Tinbergen and the other giants of the 1930s, 1940s, and 1950s developed it, was to solve exactly this problem of sorting out causes and effects. The idea was to specify equations that would stand up in the face of changes in policies and policy rules – and in the face of non-policy shocks as well. Yet if observed data record little variation in policies or policy rules, or in non-policy variables equivalent to them, the most sophisticated techniques will be unable to forecast the effects of policy innovations.

The celebrated 'Lucas critique' (Lucas 1976) goes still further, asserting that the structural or behavioral equations of macroeconometric models would not be stable under changes in policy rules, or policy regimes, because private economic agents adapt their own behavior to that of the government. Applied to monetary policy, the argument is that since changes in purely nominal magnitudes cannot make any real difference to rational agents, changed settings of monetary instruments are effective only when they are unexpected or misperceived. Applied to fiscal policy by Robert Barro (1974), the argument is that changes in taxes and transfers can have no macroeconomic effects, specifically no effects on economy-wide spending and saving, because rational agents will know that reverse changes of equivalent present value will occur in the future.

Lucas, Barro, and other exponents of the New Classical Macroeconomics are guilty of the fallacy of misplaced concreteness. They apply to the hurly-burly of short-run adjustments and fluctuations theorems that might under ideal conditions apply to long runs and long horizons. The logical consequence is the 'real business cycle theory' of Kydland and Prescott (1982) and others. This approach is premised on the idea that both individuals and society at large adapt rationally and optimally to all unavoidable natural, technological, and external shocks to which the economy is subject. The observed fluctuations in business activity which we call cycles are, in this view, simply the history of those adaptations. Money matters not at all, and Barro-type intertemporal substitutions nullify fiscal policies – although of course public claims on real resources do make a difference. There is no business cycle problem, in the sense of Keynes, Tinbergen, and the builders and estimators of macro models.

Recent history has not been kind to these approaches. Relative to them, the old-fashioned macroeconometric models have been doing well. Jan Tinbergen is a modest man, and he never thought that econometric equations, his or others', would last forever. I am sure he is now, and was fifty years ago, prepared to believe that clear changes of policy regime, like other changes in the environment of economic activity, alter structural equations and their coefficients. Lucas and company have made us more sensitive to such possibilities, properly so.

5 RELATIONS BETWEEN QUALITATIVE AND QUANTITATIVE POLICIES

Tinbergen distinguished quantitative policies – setting and changing the values of instrument variables – from qualitative policies – alterations in structure by regulation, deregulation, and institutional innovation. In important respects these are substitutes for each other. The more numerous are effective built-in fiscal stabilizers, the less necessary are discretionary changes of fiscal instruments. If one thinks of policy rules as equations of the system, then if other structural equations are altered, whether by deliberate qualitative policies or spontaneously, the policy equations will need to be changed too.

One way to look at policy rules and other structural equations is to regard the model as a whole as a mechanism converting exogenous shocks into fluctuations of endogenous variables, including those which are policy objectives. For example, in a classic article William Poole (1970) showed that, although the same expected value of real national product could in principle be obtained either by setting the money stock or by setting interest rates, the variance of that policy objective around its target mean would depend on the instrument used. This insight can be generalized to policy rules and to the variance–covariance matrix of several objective variables.

In the Poole model, the policy rule in question is the central bank's supply of money in response to a short-term interest rate. The central bank does not know whether an observed increase in the interest rate is the result of strength in the goods market (upward IS shift) or of an increased demand for money (inward LM shift). Accommodation is desirable in the latter case but not in the former. The coefficient of the interest rate in the central bank's supply curve can be chosen so as to minimize the variance of national output. To pursue and generalize the Pool example, now suppose that, as actually has been happening, the government relaxes legal ceilings on the rates banks can pay depositors. This deregulation sharply reduces the built-in accommodation of the monetary system, because a general rise in interest rates no longer induces private agents to economize money holdings. As a result, a more accomodative optimal money-supply rule is now optimal (Tobin 1983).

6 WHAT CAN ECONOMISTS SAY ABOUT POLICY OBJECTIVES?

In his classic 1953 book Tinbergen begins with a brief mention of 'a collective ophelimity function' as the object to be maximized. This function – sometimes called social utility or social welfare – would make commensurable the numerous economic outcomes that matter. It would be something like a weighted average of their values. But after the first page Tinbergen deals only with vectors of quantitative objective outcomes, without trying to rank the vectors, much less summarize them in scalar scores. I have taken the same standpoint throughout this lecture so far.

Yet the pervasiveness of intractable tradeoffs, the lack of sufficient independent instruments to hit several important goals simultaneously, makes ranking and scoring of vectors of policy goals very important. We can wash our hands of the task by assigning both the burden and the privilege to the political process, to public opinion and government policy-makers. After all, we economists have no business imposing our own social values. But economics cannot and should not, I think, dodge these issues completely. Our discipline can at least contribute to clarity and sophistication of thought about social choices. Many practical objectives of policy are not ultimate values but measurable variables somewhere between those values and actual tools of policy. In this sense they are intermediate instruments.

For example, in macroeconomics the two traditional short-run objectives, low unemployment and price stability, are not ends in themselves. Even real national product is not a goal *per se*. We economists are disposed to consider consumption (including leisure, public goods, and other non-market commodities) as the activity that generates utility or ophelimity. We usually score outcomes for individual consumers by the utility attaching to their prospective streams of consumption over time, and over contingent 'states of nature' as well.

Our standard paradigm says that tastes, together with technologies and resource endowments, are the deep fundamental data of an economy, from which all economic behaviors and outcomes are derived. The paradigm is vulnerable to several difficulties, which we occasionally acknowledge but commonly sweep under the rug. Even at an individual level, utility is not clearly and unambiguously formulated; people are often ambivalent or schizophrenic. Tastes are not wholly exogenous and stable. They are transient and inchoate. They are much influenced by changing social and cultural trends, by information and disinformation, by habits and traditions, by advertising and other sales promotion efforts. Utility is a weak reed on which to hang intertemporal choices, especially those involving uncertainty. Although contemporary theory places heavier and heavier weight on utility, it is hard to believe the concept can bear the burden.

Moreover, we know there is no way to aggregate individual preferences into social rankings, let alone to combine individual utilities into a collective ophelimity index. As if this were not obvious, Kenneth Arrow proved it rigorously years ago. The impossibility applies to aggregations across contemporaneous cohorts, *a fortiori* across generations living and unborn. No wonder so many of today's macro theorists purchase mathematical rigor by assuming that society can be represented by a single consumer, if not immortal at least identical in endowments and tastes generation after generation.

A common diagnosis of the current United States economic problem is that my country, in both private and public sectors, is saving too little. The implicit value judgment is that currently living generations are mistreating future generations; we are consuming at their expense. One symptom and vehicle of this misbehavior is the United States current account deficit. (Its counterpart in Japanese and European, mainly German, surpluses might similarly represent excessive saving.) The policy moral is to tighten fiscal policy in the United States (and ease it in the surplus countries).

The contrasting *laissez faire* view is that these payments imbalances, and the differences in saving behavior underlying them, reflect rational personal and national choices. They require and invite no policy moves. Americans want to consume more now and less later; Japanese and Germans want to do the reverse. International and intertemporal markets permit both sides to do what they want. There is no problem.

The *laissez faire* view is mistaken, I think. The current U.S. generation does not realize what it is doing, what the future consequences and costs will be. As voters and consumers, they have been deliberately misinformed – by politicians whose priority was to cripple the civilian public sector of the nation by demagogically exploiting the public's natural distaste for taxes. In this situation, I think Jan Tinbergen would agree in principle, it is the duty of the economist to help the public make informed and rational choices, not to acquiesce in the mindless faith that everything is always for the best.

The big issues of stabilization policy in the last thirty years have, as I already noted, frequently involved the unemployment–inflation nexus. Macroeconomists have not helped the public understand and assess the costs of inflation. Are there indeed costs of inflation *per se*? Or are they costs of any price changes, whether up or down, or of deviations either way of prices from previous expectations? At a more primitive level, the general public and politicians confuse absolute price levels and relative prices, or general across-the-board inflation and changes in specific prices. They also confuse continuing inflationary trends with one-shot changes in prices.

Even economists often charge to inflation the inevitable social costs of phenomena of which inflation is a symptom (like wars and OPECs). The true policy issue presented by an unavoidable adverse shock requires comparing its costs under alternative policy responses, some of which might entail more inflation than others. Policy responses in Europe, North America, and Japan to the oil price shocks of 1973–74 and 1978–79 aimed at disinflation and generated severe recessions in the process. Were these the least-cost responses to those shocks? I do not answer the question. I just say that it is the correct question.

'Time inconsistency' is a popular recent topic in the theory of policy. Typically the government is assumed to have, for some unexplained reason, social objectives different from those of the society it is governing. (This sounds like Buchanan's public choice theory, but here it is not a question of elected officials and bureaucrats who are manipulating the political system in their own interests.) The government deceives the public in order to make the economy come out the government's preferred way. The usual application is to the inflation-unemployment tradeoff, assumed to be absent in the long run. The government makes private agents think that prices will be stable and behave accordingly. Then the government exploits those expectations and behaviors by an inflationary policy, which produces a bulge of employment and output. The people don't really want so much employment and output, so the bulge recedes after they catch on to the government's true strategy. Does this make sense? If the government is rational it knows that the strategy cannot work repeatedly. If the government is benign it doesn't wish a non-optimal outcome anyway.

A common analogy is to the classroom teacher who wants the students to study but does not care to inflict a test on them and on herself. The teacher announces the test but then cancels it at the last minute. But maybe the students really want both the study and the test, and anyway a teacher cannot credibly threaten tests that never take place.

The time inconsistency story is another example of the treatment of the economy as a whole as a single individual. Likewise in the 1970s several macro theorists held forth the prospect of painless disinflation accomplished by credible threat of resolutely restrictive monetary policy. The threat would be that, regardless how severe the recession, how great the unemployment, how widespread the bankruptcies, the government and central bank would persevere until inflation dropped to zero. Workers and unions could not count on macro-policies to save their jobs; they would have to lower their money wage rates. Business managers could not count on macro-policies to save their markets and their solvencies; they would have to lower their prices. According to the theory, under this threat the inflation would melt so fast that the threatened hardships would not occur.

Events under Mrs. Thatcher and Paul Volcker did not confirm the theory. Was Volcker guilty of 'time inconsistency' in declaring premature victory?

The trouble is, I think, that the actual game does not involve just the two players government and private economy. It is an $n + 1$-person game, one government (maybe more actually) and n private sectors, who are playing against each other as well as against the government. Here is a manifestation of the problem of coordination, the central problem of macroeconomics. The typical private player has no incentive to act constructively in response to the government's threat unless he thinks many other players will do likewise. No one can see the spectacle in the theater or stadium if everyone stands, but who has the incentive to obey a general admonition to sit down? When the teacher tells her grade school class there will be no picnic unless all gum-chewing ceases, would any rational child who shares the general liking of gum stop? Threats against everybody in general addressed to nobody in particular rarely work.

In the theory of policy under uncertainty, one objective is a low variance of outcomes. If we had scalar ophelimity, it would be a low variance of that index. What we actually mean by 'low variance' deserves thought. Is fluctuation over time bad in itself? We don't care much about diurnal, weekly, seasonal, or in some cases even year-to-year fluctuations.

Policy plans involve re-settings of the various instruments in order to achieve desirable future paths of the objective variables. The re-settings would not in general be decided in advance, only the rules that relate them to experience. The variances of concern are *ex ante* estimates of measures of deviations of actual realizations from expected paths. Those measures are related to the variances over time of the processes determining the objective variables, but they are not the same thing.

7 CONCLUDING REMARKS

I have spoken of policy 'rules,' but I close by warning against taking the concept too literally. In monetary policy in particular there has been a long debate on rules *versus* discretion. This debate overlaps the argument about blind *versus* feedback rules. 'Discretion' means 'feedback' in practice because policymakers take account of information, rather than setting instruments independently of observations. 'Leaning against the wind' was a Federal Reserve rule throughout the 1950s and much of the 1960s. It means partial but not complete accommodation, but it allows lots of room for discretion, *i.e.* for consideration of circumstances not foreseen or even foreseeable in any formula.

Rules are bound to be pretty simple. It's not possible to formulate rules for policy-makers that cover all contingencies, any more than it is possible to write Arrow-Debreu contracts. In the United States we are fortunate that the Federal Reserve abandoned monetarist rules in 1982. Thanks to some skillful pragmatic fine-tuning by Paul Volcker and now Alan Greenspan, America, unlike Europe, has enjoyed a long and successful recovery. For one thing, the recovery has reduced unemployment by at least one more percentage point than anyone would have thought inflation-safe ten years ago. The Federal Reserve has been willing to learn by experience how far it was possible to go.

Even in the 1950s Jan Tinbergen was acutely aware of the problem of international coordination of national macroeconomic policies. That is a much bigger problem today, because of the massive size, fluidity, and extraordinary technical efficiency of global financial markets. We used to say that it is not possible for every sovereign nation to achieve its goals regardless of events elsewhere. Now, clearly, it is not possible for any nation to do so. By the same token, the policies of each country spill over into outcomes elsewhere. For example, although every government and central bank may aim for price stability within its jurisdiction, it is not feasible to accomplish adjustments to international imbalances in payments without changes in national price levels relative to each other. This is true whether the international monetary regime involves fixed or floating exchange rates.

The Group of Seven creates the shadow of coordination but not the substance. True international coordination is the biggest challenge to the theory and practice of macroeconomic policy for the next decade. It is a political challenge, of course, but also an intellectual one worthy of a Jan Tinbergen.

REFERENCES

Barro, Robert, 1974, 'Are Government Bonds Net Wealth?,' *Journal of Political Economy*, 82, pp. 1095–1117.

Brainard, William C., 1967, 'Uncertainty and the Effectiveness of Policy,' *American Economic Review*, 57, pp. 411–425.

Kydland, F.E. and E.C. Prescott, 1982, 'Time to Build and Aggregate Fluctuations,' *Econometrica*, 50, pp. 1345–1370.

Lucas, Robert E., 1976, 'Econometric Policy Evaluation: A Critique,' in: K. Brunner and A. Meltzer (eds.), *The Phillips Curve and Labor Markets*, Amsterdam.

Poole, William, 1970, 'Optimal Choice of Monetary Policy Instruments in a Simple Stochastic Macro Model,' *Quarterly Journal of Economics*, 84, pp. 197–216.

Tinbergen, Jan, 1952, *On the Theory of Economic Policy*, Amsterdam.

Tinbergen, Jan, 1956, *Economic Policy: Principles and Design*, Amsterdam.

Tobin, James, 1983, 'Financial Structure and Monetary Rules,' *Kredit und Kapital*, 16, pp. 155–171.

Summary

Jan Tinbergen originated the theory of policy in the 1950s. Here I apply it to contemporary macroeconomics. The two standard instruments of short-run demand management cannot achieve the two usual targets, full employment and price stability. With respect to those goals, these two instruments are collinear, except for small and transient effects on foreign exchange rates. But the mix of fiscal and monetary policies, relative to one another, does have important effects on the composition of national output, as between investment and consumption.

I point out that policy-makers, like portfolio managers, should diversify the instruments they use when they are uncertain of their effects. I discuss some pitfalls in the empirical estimation of policy effects, especially possible misinterpretations of simple correlations, and I note that policy rules cannot be invariant to changes in macroeconomic structure. I argue that policy 'rules' should involve responses to new information and in practice allow 'discretion.' Finally, I suggest that Tinbergen's theory of policy needs to be extended to policy coordination among nations.

THE PRINCIPLES OF PRIVATIZATION IN EASTERN EUROPE**

BY

JÁNOS KORNAI*

It is a great privilege for me to deliver a lecture in honor of Jan Tinbergen, and in doing so to express my admiration for him as a scholar and as a person. Along with several generations of economists, I consider myself his disciple. He is an example to us all, not only for his pioneering achievements and the great scholarly value of his life's work, but for the moral purity and uprightness that imbue all his works. I am indebted to him intellectually, but in addition I recall with the deepest gratitude how actively he helped me in the initial stages of my career. It was still rare at that time for someone from the intellectual world of Eastern Europe to appear and try to join the professional currents in the West. Professor Tinbergen smoothed my path in a friendly and tactful way. I was greatly encouraged by the genuine interest with which he approached the problems of Eastern Europe.

1 INTRODUCTION

A wide-ranging debate on privatization in Eastern Europe is taking place, both in the region itself and abroad, among Western experts. The debate, of course, is not confined to men and women of science. Since privatization is among the fundamental issues of the postsocialist transition, governments, parties, international organizations and the business world must take a position on it. A hundred different views have been expressed so far and a hundred different specific programs have been put forward for resolving the problems in practice.[1] I make no attempt here to formulate any hundred-and-first program,

* Professor of Economics, Harvard University, Cambridge, Mass., U.S.A. and Institute of Economics, Hungarian Academy of Sciences, Budapest, Hungary.

** Fourth Tinbergen Lecture, delivered on October 19, 1990 in Utrecht for the Royal Netherlands Economic Association. The Hungarian text of the lecture was translated by Brian McLean, to whom I am grateful for his excellent work. I also thank Mária Kovács and Carla Krüger for their assistance in gathering the literature on the subject.

1 There is a very extensive literature on the subject. I have selected here just a few of the studies in English which deal with Eastern European privatization: Fischer and Gelb (1990), Frydman and Rapaczynski (1990), Lipton and Sachs (1990), Levandowski and Szomburg (1989), and Hinds (1990). An excellent survey of the polemic is provided by Stark (1990). This brief list does not include works concerned with privatization in the capitalist countries.

although I do put forward my own views.[2] My main purpose is to help readers to conduct a methodical analysis of the problem. I outline an intellectual structure allowing people to assemble the body of information they possess and confront the alternative views encountered with each other before formulating a position of their own.

The word 'privatization', which features in the title, is used in two senses. In the narrower sense it means the transfer of assets hitherto owned by the state into private hands. The broader interpretation covers the property relations in the economy *as a whole*, so that privatization of the economy must be understood to mean that the share of the private sector grows until it ultimately becomes the dominant economic sector. This study is concerned with the concept of privatization in that broader sense.

The title mentions Eastern Europe, and in the main the study deals with the group of small countries embarking on the road of postsocialist transition. However, I believe that most of the problems discussed in the study resemble those in the Soviet Union as well.

Section 2 deals with the values fostered during privatization, section 3 with the evolutionary nature of the transformation and the role of the state, and sections 4 and 5 with the main forms of private ownership. Finally, section 6 deals with the pace of privatization.

2 VALUES

Some of those taking part in the international debate put forward their practical proposals on privatization without clearly answering some crucial questions: What purposes do they want the process to serve? What values do they seek to implement? What criteria do they intend to apply to the decision?

I share the philosophy of those who argue that the ends and the means must be clearly distinguished in any analysis of practical tasks.[3] Lucid clarification of the criteria for judgement is also required for any subsequent appraisal of processes after they have taken place. Rather than attempting to detail all the values taken into account, I only mention the ones I consider the most important to the subject. I classify these under four aspects.

1. *The sociological aspect, in longer, historical terms.* What is the new democracy's direction of movement in a society inherited from the socialist system?

---

2   I first formulated my own proposal in a book (1990). This study further develops and expands the ideas I put forward on privatization, in the light of the subsequent debates and practical experience. My earlier proposals on some questions are corrected in this lecture, where I feel this is necessary.

3   This is one of the methodological ideas that run as a *Leitmotif* through Tinbergen's works. See Tinbergen (1952), for instance.

Socialism in its classical, Stalinist form gave rise to a society which was governed bureaucratically and organized hierarchically. Nationalization extended beyond firms in production to cover practically every activity, so that every able-bodied person, with a few exceptions, became an employee of the state.

In countries like my own – Hungary – where reforms had begun many years ago, there had been a movement away from that ultimate form of *etatism* before democracy arrived in 1989–1990. I shall not deal here with such transitional states, but turn straight away to the longer-term prospects offered by the process.

1-a. It would be desirable for the structure of society to resemble in its main features the structure in the most highly developed capitalist countries. A broad stratum of independent, autonomous business people and entrepreneurs should emerge. Rather than the vast majority of the property being concentrated in the hands of just a small group, there should also be a broad middle class that includes the masses of owners of small and medium-sized enterprises. Society should undergo *embourgeoisement*.[4] The bureaucratic, hierarchical stratification of society should be widely superseded by stratification according to property. In other words, the hyperactive, overgrown role of the state in the economy should be reduced, even though the economic activity of the state will remain considerable.

All this transformation in the structure of society should be coupled with the modernization of production and the other activities of society, through the spread of up-to-date technologies and lifestyles.

This 'Western-style' image of society is seen as an attainable goal by many Eastern Europeans who think about the prospects of transforming society, but it is not, of course, the sole course envisaged, even among those opposed to the concept of society espoused by the earlier socialist system.

1-b. Some people are put off by modern day Western Europe and North America, with their business mentality, commercialism, profit-mongering, and oversized and overcrowded modern cities, the environmental damage caused by industrial civilization, and many other drawbacks. So instead they tend towards an image of another, romantically 'unsullied' society. Those subscribing to this kind of 'third-road' *Weltanschauung* are attracted by the proximity of nature in a village, by the peace of a small town, and by the simplicity of small-scale agricultural and industrial economies.

1-c. There is another 'third-road' image of society where the intention is to blend capitalism with plebeian-*cum*-socialistic ideas. The goal becomes a 'people's capitalism' that would turn all citizens into proprietors.

All these images of future society have direct implications for the way the process of privatization is judged. For my part, I favor an orientation towards the 'Western-style' social structure 1-a, even though I am aware that it has

4   See Szelényi (1988).

many bad features. I am ready to condemn these and advocate efforts to diminish them, but I am also aware that these bad features will inevitably appear. Those who subscribe to 'Western-style' social development must accept it warts and all. I do not consider the 'third-road' images of the future just mentioned either practically attainable or desirable.

2. *The economic aspects.* This does not form a single criterion; a variety of economic interests can be taken into account.

2-a. The most important economic criterion in my view is to arrive at forms of ownership that induce efficient production. One of the most damaging features of bureaucratic state ownership prevailing under the socialist system was that it gave little incentive to efficiency, and in fact frequently encouraged waste. One of privatization's missions must be to bring about a close and overt linkage between the direct financial interest of owners on the one hand and market performance and profit on the other.

Let me pick out three other economic requirements which are also worth taking into consideration.

2-b. The privatization process should help to reinforce the security of private property.

2-c. The fiscal motive: privatization can help to increase state revenue through the proceeds from the sale of state-owned property, in addition, the relief of budgetary expenditure of subsidizing loss-making state-owned firms, and the opportunities of finding new sources of tax revenue.

2-d. The monetary motive: the effects of some forms of privatization are anti-inflationary; they help to eliminate the 'monetary overhang' of unspent purchasing power. Other forms have the precisely opposite effect of increasing inflationary pressure.

3. *The aspect of political power.* Though scholars concerned with criteria of economic rationality or ethics may be averse to considering this aspect, the fact must be faced that privatization of any kind is a political issue. Governing political parties and groups want to reinforce and preserve their power, while those in opposition see the issue through the lens of their aspirations to form a government. So one cannot ignore the problem of how popular, deservedly or undeservedly, any privatization program will be.

3-a. Among the factors considered by those who want to return property confiscated by the state to its earlier owners is the political weight of the group it benefits, or: how many votes can be won at the next election.

3-b. Those who support employee ownership would like to win the political support of this broad stratum in society.

3-c. Finally, advocates of giving free shares or vouchers to all citizens count on the idea being popular with the public as a whole.

I will return to this question later. Let me confine myself here to a single observation. Those who seek political popularity through some scheme or other often forget to examine carefully and critically whether those whose approval they expect really *are* enthusiastic about the idea. I could hardly find a convincing public-opinion survey on the subject. For my part I still have doubts, although I must admit that my skepticism is based on insufficiently reliable impressions. Those who receive the property may be disillusioned and angry, not politically grateful, to find what they receive is less than they expected and were promised, and that the process is slow and cumbersome.

4. *The aspect of distributive ethics.* This system of criteria is another highly complex one, full of inner contradictions. The ethical principles considered here are confined to those connected directly with the distribution of income and wealth.

4-a. Those who suffered losses under the previous system must be wholly or partly *compensated* during privatization. Some take the view that, where possible, the actual items of property confiscated should be returned if they still exist in their original physical form. Others support the idea that the compensation should merely be in money or securities. Several versions of the latter approach are conceivable, with various restrictions on redemption and the degree of transferability.

A range of difficult questions arises in this respect. What kind of injuries deserves redress? Should compensation be confined to the economic damage sustained through confiscation, or should it cover losses of other kinds as well, ranging from cases of unjust imprisonment or execution to those who lost their jobs or were denied the chance to continue their education or to travel abroad? And what should be the earliest qualifying date? Should it be when the communists came to power, or has the time now come to redress the injuries of those who received no compensation under the socialist system for losses sustained in the Second World War and the period of fascist rule, for instance?

Ultimately, those who espouse the ethical arguments for reprivatization want to apply the ethical principle of just recompensing. An economic argument, listed under 2-b, can also be brought forward in support of reprivatization: restoring the old property relations is a tangible demonstration of the idea that private property is sacrosanct. But this argument can be countered with another that likewise rests on criterion 2-b: the protracted process of reprivatization may undermine the security of property relations based on the *status quo*. A building or business claimed by a former owner may already be in private ownership.

Reprivatization can also conflict with other economic criteria. It robs the treasury of income or actually involves extra public expenditure (criterion 2-c). If those entitled to compensation are given securities and these can be traded, many will sell them in order to spend the proceeds straight away on the consumer goods market. That means this procedure will increase the inflationary pressure (criterion 2-d).

A further comment is needed on the programs for compensation through reprivatization. An attempt is made by their supporters to give the impression that the *state* is granting the compensation to a certain section of the public. But what is the state in this context but the sum of all the taxpayers? Compensation by way of reprivatization is a *redistributive* action that transfers wealth to the beneficiaries of the compensation from the pockets of non-beneficiary, tax-paying citizens. There is no question of those who gained at the time from confiscation now recompensing those who suffered losses from it. The members of the *present* generation receiving no compensation have also lost, suffering like everyone else from all the consequences of the economic losses and backwardness caused by the previous system.

4-b. It can be argued on grounds of *moral entitlement* that a specific group has a right to some part of the state or other communal wealth in view of their social position. 'Let the land belong to those who till it.' 'Let factories belong to those who work there.' 'Let state-owned flats belong to those who live in them.' Even if the debate is confined to the ethical plane, it can be objected that the rest of society also contributed to creating these assets. Do today's tillers of good land, today's workers in a profitable factory, or today's tenants of attractive, spacious apartments really deserve more valuable property than those less fortunate? In the last resort, the slogans quoted are redistributive principles that favor some groups in society at the expense of the rest.

4-c. There are demands for *fairness* and *equality*. This principle is voiced chiefly by those who want to divide part of the property of the state among all citizens. The question of whether this program clashes with the other criteria is discussed later on. Let us remain for the time being within the logic of ethical arguments.

The old system failed to fullfil its egalitarian promises: democracy inherits a society marked by unequal distribution of material wealth and intellectual capital. Compared with these initial conditions, little is changed if rich and poor, well educated and unschooled, healthy and sick alike receive a modest free gift. Moreover, the free gift will soon be sold by those in need and bought cheaply by those who are clever and have the capital to buy it. Sincere advocates of a more equal distribution of income and wealth should campaign in the field of fiscal policy, welfare policy and education, health and housing policy, where the scope for furthering their objectives is greater.

Privatization is intended to introduce a capitalist market economy. Although the market and capitalist properties have many useful qualities, above all the stimulation to efficient economic activity, fairness and equality are not among their virtues. They not only reward good work but also good fortune, and they penalize not just bad work but also ill-fortune. While they are useful to society as a whole by encouraging exploitation of good fortune and resistance to ill-fortune, they are not 'just.' I think it is ethically paradoxical to mix slogans of fairness and equality into a program of capitalist privatization.

Mention has been made of a range of criteria whose appraisal can serve as a basis for arriving at a position on the question of privatization. Some of these are compatible and complement one another. But there are also values which conflict with each other in this particular context. Short-term economic interests may clash with the long-term interests behind the transformation of society. Ethical considerations may run up against sociological or economic requirements.

The value judgements on which my own view rests have emerged to some extent in what I have said already, but I will summarize them here briefly. Even though I am an economist, it is aspect 1, the long-term sociological criterion, that I rate as decisive, and I also opt for alternative 1-a, as I consider the emergence of a broad stratum of entrepreneurs and business people and widespread *embourgeoisement* to be of paramount importance. I accordingly place the strongest emphasis of the economic arguments on 2-a: privatization must be accomplished in a way that gives the strongest incentive to efficient production. Although the other economic criteria are also important, I rate them as subordinate to the ones I have mentioned. I acknowledge the fact that aspects of political power also apply, but they do not influence me in my choice of values. I am not indifferent to the moral aspects of distribution, but I would refrain from applying them in the context of privatization.

Naturally I respect the right of others to choose values different from my own. What I would like to recommend to statesmen, legislators, the specialists who suggest legislation and the journalists who monitor and criticize the plans and their execution is this: let them analyze and make public the choice of values that justify the privatization programs they support. Let them face up to the conflicts of values and the 'trade-offs' between conflicting requirements, and admit it openly if they jettison one value in favor of another. Let them refrain from pretending that the practical proposal they prefer is a neutral one that would further all the values for consideration equally well.

3 THE TRANSFORMATION'S EVOLUTIONARY NATURE AND THE ROLE OF THE STATE

A view widely spread is that state institutions should play a very large part in privatization. Such a view can be found in governmental circles. In Hungary, for instance, a central authority called the State Property Agency tried for a long time to concentrate almost every act of privatization in its own hands. A similar kind of centralization could be observed in Germany.

There is also strong emphasis on the role of the state in the views put forward by many foreign experts, who certainly cannot be accused of wanting to increase their own power. I myself have heard the following proposal: the Soviet Union should quickly establish 20 investment funds by state decree. The managers to head them should be appointed by government, with the advice of experts from abroad. The funds should be assigned the shares in the firms formerly owned by the state, and the stock in the investment companies should then be distributed free to all citizens.

I think the inordinate state centralization of Hungary's privatization and the notion of forming investment funds by state decree to manage private property are good illustrations of what Hayek termed a 'constructivist' approach.[5] They are artificially created, whereas the vitality of capitalist development is a result from the fact that its viable institutions arise naturally, without being forced.

During the period of Stalinist collectivization in the Soviet Union, it was possible to eliminate the class of well-to-do farmers, the *kulaks*, by state decree. But no state decree can create a class of well-to-do farmers; that will emerge only by a process of historical development. The state can decide to implement confiscation, but no state resolution can appoint a Ford, a Rockefeller or a DuPont. The selection of the class of owners in a capitalist economy takes place by a process of evolution. And it is an evolutionary process that selects among the institutions and organizations that emerge, causing the ones that are not functioning well under the prevailing circumstances to wither away, and choosing as survivors the one truly fit for their task.[6]

The Polish economist J. Kowalik coined the ironic term 'etatist liberalism' for the curious school of thought that suggests pursuing liberal objectives (private property, individual autonomy, consumer sovereignty) by artificially creating organizations contrived by officialdom, and aims at controlling the transformation of society by bureaucratic state coercion and administrative measures.

What the state should primarily be expected to do is to stand aside from the development of the private sector and ensure that its own agencies remove the bureaucratic obstacles. There are a number of feasible state measures that go beyond this and actively assist in the privatization process, and these are discussed later. But governments should not be expected to replace the spontaneous, decentralized, organic growth process of the private economy by a web of bureaucratic, excessively regulatory measures and a hive of zealous activity by state officials.

4 TYPES OF OWNERS

A. *Personal owners*. First let me give a few examples, to make this concept clear.

1. A family farm or a family undertaking in another branch of the economy, which does not employ outside labor apart from family members more than occasionally.

---

5   See Hayek (1960) and (1973), chapter 1.

6   The idea that the market performs a natural selection among organizations already appeared in Schumpeter [1911] (1968) and was later elaborated upon in more detail by Alchian (1974). Schumpeter's idea of selection is strongly emphasized in connection with the transformation of the socialist countries in the works of Murrell (1990a, 1990b).

2. A small or medium-sized firm where ownership and management have not been separated and the owner remains in charge.

3. A newly founded firm in Schumpeter's sense, managed by the entrepreneur establishing it and normally employing borrowed capital, not the entrepreneur's own.[7]

4. A joint-stock company of any size in which an individual or group of individuals has a dominant share-holding. This need not necessarily be a majority of the shares; a holding of 20-30% is often sufficient to give the dominant owner (or group of owners) a decisive say in the choice and supervision of management and in major financial matters and investment decisions.[8] Dominance of this kind can emerge so long as the other shareholders are sufficiently passive, which can be the case, for instance, if ownership of the shares is fragmented. The situation may be similar if the rest of the shares are held by the state, and the state refrains voluntarily from active intervention in the firm's affairs.

5. A firm in which the former chief executive officer or a group of managers have become owner's, or at least dominant shareholders, through a management buy-out.

I have not conducted a rigorous classification of mutually exclusive cases, merely listed examples, and these may overlap in some feature or other. The examples can cover small, medium-sized and large firms alike. They may take legal forms that entail unlimited liability or liability limited to various degrees, and range from a family farm to modern joint-stock companies. So what, in the end, do these cases have in common? The presence of a live, 'visible,' 'tangible' person or group of persons at the head of the firm. This individual, family or group has a strong and direct proprietorial interest, so that the size of the firm's profits or losses affects the owner's pocket. In addition, the owner either runs the firm directly or plays a dominant role in hiring and firing the managers and overseeing what they do.

A *personal owner* can enter the stage of the postsocialist economy in two ways. One is by setting up a brand new undertaking. The other is by buying part or all of an existing state-owned firm. The two methods are often combined: a state asset is bought by an existing private firm.

I believe this personal owner to be the key figure in Eastern European

---

7   'The original nucleus of means has been but rarely acquired by the entrepreneur's own saving activity...' writes Schumpeter [1949] (1989, p. 266), and goes on to catalogue the various sources of finance, including the credit system. One of the sources 'was tapping the savings of other people and 'created credit'... 'Credit creation' introduces banks and quasi-banking activities...' In this study and several others, Schumpeter analyses the connection between the credit system and entrepreneurs in detail.

8   The term *noyau stable* (stable core) has become widespread, following French literature. See Friedmann (1989).

privatization. Let me recall the previous section of this study, which I ended by outlining my own selection of values. It is compatible with this selection to assert that the appearance of personal owners on a mass scale will ensure to the greatest extent the desired transformation of society, the *embourgeoisement* (criterion 1-a), and the incentive towards efficiency (criterion 2-a). Moreover, if one constituent of this process is the purchase of state assets, it will also satisfy the fiscal and monetary criteria (2-c and 2-d). It can be stated, therefore, that the vaster the area in which ownership and control pass into the hands of personal owners, the more successfully privatization will proceed. One of the most encouraging features of the transformation in Eastern Europe is the perceptible advance of this evolution.[9]

There is a widespread notion that an upper limit on privatization by purchase is set by the amount of savings accumulated by the general public. Comparisons of the savings at the public's disposal with the value of the state's wealth are used to arrive at alarming forecasts. The conclusion reached is that it could be 50 or a 100 years before the public has managed to buy up the state's wealth. So there is no other solution: the property of the state can only be reduced quickly by distributing state assets free of charge.

In my view this line of argument relies on false premises. The purchasing power intended by the public for investment (including the purchase of state property) can be multiplied several times by suitable credit and deferred-payment schemes.[10] The proportion of the down-payment to the credit or deferred payments can be as little as 1:10 or 1:20. This proportion is what determines right from the start how much of the state's wealth can be bought by those wanting to go into business with the savings they initially possess. In addition, the process can speed up as soon as some of the businesses start to show a profit and a greater propensity to invest. Above all, it depends on the domestic and foreign banks and other financial intermediaries what range of attractive credit and deferred-payment schemes they offer. Moreover, the main way foreign governments and international financial and economic organizations ready to help can contribute to building up the private sector in Eastern

---

9   Statistics in the Eastern European countries have reached a critical situation. All previous statistics were based on detailed information provided by the large state-owned firms. Their proportion is shrinking. At the same time, the statistical offices are not equipped, neither organizationally nor methodologically, to observe and measure the activity of the private sector, least of all under circumstances in which the private sector tries to disguise as much of its activities as possible in order to escape taxation. So it is impossible to give reliable estimates for the scales of expansion of various types of private ownership as a whole.

10   Here again I draw attention to Schumpeter's statement on the relation between the entrepreneur and the credit system, quoted in note 7. Schumpeter attributed such importance to this that he incorporated it into the *definition* of capitalism he formulated: 'Capitalism is that form of private property economy in which innovations are carried out by means of borrowed money.' (Schumpeter (1939), Vol. I, p. 223.)

Europe is by setting up financing and backing schemes of this kind. To some extent special 'venture-capital' institutions will have to be established, for there is no denying that special risks are attached to lending money to new private businesses in a postsocialist economy. But these risks can be reduced by an appropriate mortgage system to ensure that the property reverts to the lender if there is a default on the payments. Alternatively, the lender can be a co-owner from the outset. And if the state really wants to be active, it should go about it by offering at least partial credit guarantees that lessen the lender's risk. The majority of private entrepreneurs will, in any case, be more reliable borrowers than many inviable state-owned firms which repeatedly bailed out even though they defaulted on their loans.

As long as the credit and deferred-payment schemes are devised with sufficient caution, they will not entail a risk of inflation. In fact, the debt repayments and interest will siphon some of the potential consumer spending away from the entrepreneurs (criterion 2-d).

It is worth drawing particular attention to the question of management buy-outs. The public is ambivalent towards them. It is pleased that experts, rather than dilettantes, take over the factory, but displeased to see members of the 'nomenclatura' under the old regime transmuted into born-again capitalists. In my view it is not worth legally prohibiting something that will inevitably occur. It is more expedient to bring the occurrence into the open and place it under the supervision of the public, the law and the appropriate authorities. Clarification of the moral and business rules for management buy-outs is needed, including the normal credit terms. Let a manager or group of managers capable of buying a business property from the state according to these rules do so by legal means.

Special attention should be paid to the question of peasants wanting to farm privately, private small-scale industry and trading, and small business as a whole. It is quite common in the developed market economies for these groups to receive credit on favorable terms, and possibly longer or shorter-term tax reductions. This is appropriate in Eastern Europe as well, particularly now, when the aim is to set these groups on their feet and encourage new small businesses on a mass scale. One factor in criterion 1-a is the creation of a broad middle class; an important ingredient in that process is the speeding up of the development of small and medium-sized firms.

This ties in with another range of problems: how to overcome the distortion in the size distribution of firms. Excessive concentration took place in the socialist economy. Whereas the larger proportion of employment in most Western and Southern European countries is in firms with less than 500 employees, small and medium-sized firms in most Eastern European countries were wound up on a mass scale or artificially merged.[11] The need for a

11   Ehrlich (1985), using data for 1970, made a comparison between the size distributions of industrial firms in a group of Western European capitalist and Eastern European socialist countries. According to her calculation, only 32% of those employed in capitalist industry worked in firms with more than 500 employees, while 66% of those in socialist industry did.

healthier size distribution is among the reasons for giving favorable considera-tion to credit applications from small and medium-sized businesses.

B. *Employee ownership.* I am thinking here of the form in which the shares in a state-owned firm which has been converted into a joint-stock company are taken up by its employees. The most commonly used term for this in Anglo-Saxon writings is employee stock-ownership plan (ESOP). The idea comes in a number of variants; in some the employees receive all the shares, and in others only a smaller proportion. The proposals also vary on the conditions under which the employees receive the shares, ranging from entirely free distribution to price and payment conditions that are more favorable than the market terms. Finally, various suggestions have been put forward on what limits to place on the sale of the shares, for instance restricting transferability either temporarily or permanently.

The decision makers are influenced primarily by the political criteria when they consider this form of ownership. So long as the politicians have convinced themselves through reliable research into public opinion that there is a real call for employee stock ownership, and that employees actually demand it, I see no particular danger in accepting some moderate version of it, *i.e.* in offering the employees, on favorable terms, a fairly small proportion, say 10-20% of the shares in a firm due to be privatized. In my view it is more expedient to offer the shares for sale to the employees at a large discount than to give them away for nothing.

In the case of a smaller firm, it is also conceivable for all the shares to pass into the hands of the employees, in other words for the form of ownership of the firm in question to come close to a partnership or a true cooperative.

The consistent (or perhaps I should say extreme) advocates of employee ownership go much further. They would like all state-owned firms (or as many as possible) to assume this form of ownership entirely, irrespective of their size. Many of them couple this proposal with the idea of transfer free of charge. They put forward two main arguments for their position. One is criterion 2-a: an employee who is also an owner will have a stronger incentive to produce effi-ciently. For my part I do not see proof of this. On the contrary, if employees choose their own managers, the managers become dependent on their own subordinates, which can undermine wage and labor discipline. Sufficient evidence for this assumption is provided by the experience with workers' self-management in Eastern Europe, particularly Yugoslavia.

The other argument advanced for comprehensive employee ownership is to choose criterion 4-b from the aspect of distributive ethics: let the factory belong to those who work in it. My counterarguments have been expressed in the sec-tion on value criteria.

I would expect the various forms of employee ownership to gain a similar position to the one they have in the developed Western European and North American countries sooner or later, in other words that they will represent a respectable proportion, but they will fall far short of becoming the dominant form.

C. *Institutional ownership.* This large group of property ownership needs dividing into sub-groups before I can comment properly on the alternative ideas put forward.

C-1. Banks and other banking institutions. Some of the postsocialist economies inherited from the socialist economy a two-tier banking system in which there were already commercial banks alongside the central bank. Certain postsocialist countries, which entered the postsocialist period directly, skipping the period of reform within socialism, still inherited the monobank system, and are now obliged to set up a network of commercial banks. But whichever of the starting positions pertains, the banking sector has the following characteristics at the beginning of postsocialist transition.

The sole owner of the banks is the state. There may have developed what is known as 'cross-ownership', under which state-owned firms outside the banking sector are shareholders in the banks, sharing ownership with the institutions nominated for the task by the state administration, and contrary, a bank may hold shares in a state-owned firm which has been converted into a joint-stock company.[12] But cross-ownership remains merely an indirect form of state ownership, and is no substitute for privatization.

The various organizations making up the banking sector of Eastern Europe are engaged in a quite narrow range of activities. Developed market economies possess a great many financial institutions that do not qualify as 'banks' according to the strict legal and economic criteria in force, such as credit-card companies, venture-capital companies, investment funds, mutual funds, saving-and-loan associations, exchange bureaus and so on. There are strong reasons why postsocialist economies need to develop a banking sector with a similarly varied and multiple profile.

Some of these bank-like financial intermediaries (which cannot be called 'banks' in the strict sense) may appear in private-ownership form from the outset. A major role in the development of the new quasi-banking institutions can be played by foreign capital.

The development of genuine private banks, particularly large private banks, seems more difficult, even though their activity is clearly essential to a modern market economy. On the one hand, foreign banks can be expected to open branches in the Eastern European countries, and of course these will be real private banks. It is possible that one or two institutions performing quasi-banking functions that were privately-owned from the start may be converted into true banks. Smaller banks performing local functions could be formed by domestic entrepreneurs. Alongside all these developments, the privatization of the currently state-owned commercial banks will take place. Particularly in the

12 Cross-ownership was discussed in my book (1990). Detailed descriptions of the phenomenon, based on experiences in Hungary, can be found in the studies of Móra (1990) and Voszka (1991); these had not yet reached me at the time this lecture was delivered.

beginning, this will presumably mean only partial private ownership and main-ly foreign involvement.

Privatization of the banking sector in the broad sense will not take place all at once. It will take some time before private property becomes the dominant ownership form. Several factors will play a part in this.

One bottleneck is shortage of expertise, experience and up-to-date technical equipment. One only has to remember that these are countries where even pay-ment by check has yet to spread among the population and in trade and ser-vices. Another example of backwardness is that consumer credit is used only sporadically in these economies.

Another requirement for development is the creation of requisite legislation, and, beside that, success in building up a system of state regulation and super-vision of the banking sector. It would be desirable if state intervention were not on a scale as to stifle individual initiative, but at the same time the sector cannot be left to its own devices. The security of depositors and the financial stability of the country both require legal, insurance and supervisory guarantees.

The subject so far has been privatization of the banking sector itself. However, this ties in closely with the privatization of other parts of the economy. Reference is often made by debaters on the subject to the German (erstwhile West German) and Japanese examples, where a sizeable proportion of industrial shares is in the hands of large banks. On these grounds the recom-mendation is presented that a considerable proportion of the shares in the state-owned firms should already have been handed over to the Eastern European banks.

Not much will be achieved, in my view, if this idea is applied prematurely and hastily; it will be ineffective chiefly in terms of criteria 1-a and 2-a, which I con-sider the most important. It will not produce a true owner with a strong interest in increasing efficiency. There are many cases at present where a large state-owned firm making heavy losses is closely tied up with a large state-owned bank, which may be a shareholder and is usually its main creditor. If that is the case, the bank and the firm share an interest in seeing the firm bailed out and artificially sustained. The danger is that if a bank, under the present property relations, is also a shareholder in large joint-stock companies, it will fail to ap-ply business criteria adequately.

Another danger is that the state-owned banks will remain the 'politicized' in-stitutions they were before. The parties in government will, at any time, treat them as their own backyard, and try to plant their own people in leading posi-tions. This is also a warning against the plan to turn the banks in their present state into factory owners, through a deed of gift by the state, even though the banks themselves are owned by the state.

My view is that it will become desirable at a later stage for the ownership rela-tions to develop along the lines just mentioned in connection with the Japanese and German examples. As the weight of domestic and foreign private ownership increases among the owners of a bank or a quasi-banking institution,[13] they can become partial owners of formerly state-owned non-financial firms. The more a bank or other bank-like financial institution operates on a truly commercial basis and is dominated by private ownership, the more it can be expected to satisfy criterion 2-a: to exercise strict control over the firm it owns and take a truly proprietorial attitude. In other words, as privatization of the banking sector advances as an organic process, so, at the same rate, can whole blocks of shares and portfolios of holdings in various firms previously owned by the state pass into the ownership of the banks. For instance, such blocks and portfolios could form part of the state's capital contribution to joint ventures established in the banking sector.

C-2. Pension funds. The pension funds have become one of the main holders of corporate shares in several developed capitalist countries. Notable in this respect is Britain, where more than half the shares are in the hands of the pension system.[14] Many participants in the privatization debate recommend that the pension funds in Eastern Europe assume a similar ownership role. So the problem must be discussed in a little more detail.

The provision of pensions was a task of the state under the socialist system. Pension contributions were paid as tax and pensions were a liability on the state budget. Even where pension provision was in the hands of a separate institution and the sum received in pension contributions was nominally treated as a separate fund, any surplus in the fund was utilized in practice by the state and the state covered any deficit. Although the real value of pensions was always quite low, and further reduced by the effects of inflation, the nominal sum was guaranteed by law. No other decentralized pension system operated in the socialist economy.

Radical alteration of the pension system came on the agenda during the post-socialist transition, but the final forms it will take have yet to be developed in many Eastern European countries. The pension systems of the developed capitalist countries are not uniform in any case, and no consensus has emerged in Eastern Europe on which Western country's pattern to follow. Although it is not a task for this study to take a position on this, the role of pension funds cannot be avoided in connection with institutional shareholdings. I therefore start out from the following assumptions.

Sooner or later a mixed system emerges. One of its segments is a state scheme

---

13   Let me repeat something underlined earlier: the key issue is not the percentage of the shares in some private owner's hands, but whether or not the private owner has a decisive say. It is possible that a reputed foreign bank might become the dominant owner of a Hungarian bank even though it is only a minority shareholder.

14   According to Schaffer (1990), 32% of British shares were in the hands of pension funds in 1987 and 25% in the hands of insurance companies. As for the role of pension funds and insurance companies, Schaffer's proposals resemble in many respects the idea put forward in this study.

with the task of guaranteeing a pension on at least a subsistence level for those qualifying for it. Of course a guaranteed state pension above this minimum level can be laid down by law, but this must only be done in the knowledge that the ultimate financial source is taxation, or social security contributions collected in the same way as taxation.

The other segment of the pension system is private in nature, and its primary source of funding is the payment of voluntary contributions. Their cost is shared between employers and employees according to legal stipulations and labor contracts. The network of pension funds is decentralized, and it can be joined by both non-profit organizations, whose sole task is to provide their members with pensions, and profit-oriented insurance companies, which undertake to pay annuities similar to pensions.

The revenue and expenditure of the state segment rest on compulsory legal stipulations. Membership of the private segment, on the other hand, is voluntary. Employers and employees are free to decide whether to join or not. In the case of a developed decentralized pension system, every employer or employee can choose between several kinds of private pension schemes.

There is no way of telling beforehand exactly what the future pension system in Eastern Europe will be like, but it seems quite realistic to assume that it will resemble the system just outlined. It is also clear that the transition to a mixed system (containing a private segment) can only be gradual, for the starting point differs among generations. Those already on pension or approaching pensionable age no longer have a choice; they must be provided with a guaranteed pension. The longer the life expectancy for individuals, the more possible it becomes, in this respect as well, to offer them freedom of choice. They may decide at their own risk whether or not to devote part of their savings to some private pension scheme or other. It will clearly be a long time before a mature, responsible, decentralized private pension-fund sector develops. This also belongs to the type of process I termed organic development.

Let us now return to the question of shares. Numerous private pension funds in the West invest the capital accumulated from contributions in shares and other securities.[15] The funds employ professional managers who try to build up the most favorable portfolios, paying close attention to the interests of their members. Although they are able to control all purchases and sales of this enormous fortune, they can only assert their influence indirectly, by buying certain securities and selling others. Their transactions influence market prices, which are then reflected in the valuation of the companies. This ultimately has a disciplinary effect on company managers, as a sharp drop in the valuation of their company sheds a bad light on them, while a conspicuous rise in valuation is evidence, of varying accuracy, of their success. In all events, this kind of

---

15   Many pension funds in the United States, for instance, leave it to the contributors to decide what proportions of their contributions are to be invested on the stock market, the bond market and the money market.

ownership only partially satisfies criterion 2-a: to provide an inducement to company managers and effective control over them.

Starting out from the value premises put forward in the first section, the conclusions in relation to privatization are obvious: it is worth aiming to turn the decentralized pension funds into shareholders. There is no need to rely exclusively on them investing part of their accumulated contributions in shares at some future date. The establishment of non-profit, private pension funds could be helped in the first place if each were assigned a portfolio of previously state-owned shares as a constituent of their initial capital. The transfer can even be free of charge, for there is an implicit offset: they are taking over some of the pension commitments which have hitherto been borne exclusively by the state budget.

Legislation is needed, of course, to lay down the conditions for such transfers. Care must also be taken to provide them with portfolios of shares which can be expected to have a positive yield. Otherwise the transaction will be fraudulent, for the ones who suffer will be the pensioners whose pension expectations include the prospective yield from the fund's shareholdings.

Moreover, the difference between pensions from the state and pensions from the private segment must be made clear to the voluntary members of the decentralized pension systems. There is a degree of exposure in either case. Pensioners in the state segment are at the mercy of those who devise and apply the legislation on pensions provisions, while pensioners in the private segment are exposed to the fluctuations of the security market and to the degree of success with which the private pension fund manages its securities.

The value premises also show what plans should be rejected. The idea has come up that the state pension system should receive shares before any decentralization and privatization of the pension system takes place. In Hungary, for instance, the transfer has actually begun. This, in my opinion, is a pretence move, from which no particular benefit can be expected. The centralized, state pension system is a branch of the state bureaucracy, and so it should be. But if its function is to provide pensions guaranteed by law, its sources of income should not be exposed to the fluctuations of the stock market or the fortunate or unfortunate trends in corporate profits.

C-3. Insurance companies. Here the situation is very similar to the case of the pension system, and so the conclusions can be drawn straight away by referring to the previous point.

So long as the insurance companies are large, oligopolistic institutions exclusively owned by the state, it is only a pretence measure to transfer shares to them. The result is just another form of 'cross-ownership' discussed earlier, since one state-owned institution becomes an owner of another.

The value premises I have made suggest that it is worth supporting a partial privatization of the insurance system. The system might contain state and private segments operating side by side, and the latter include both non-profit and profit-oriented insurers. The private insurance companies should be encouraged to invest some of their accumulated capital in shares. With suitable legal guarantees and supervision, the state could hand share portfolios over to non-profit private insurers, even free of charge, as a way of encouraging their establishment and consolidation. This again is a kind of ownership transfer where there is an implicit offset: the private insurance sector which emerges by a process of organic development can steadily take over some of the commitments of the guaranteed state insurance system.[16]

C-4. Cultural and educational institutions, charitable societies and foundations, churches. The list contains the kind of institutions which in a developed market economy may invest some of their accumulated savings in shares or other securities. The same will no doubt apply in Eastern Europe. The tighter the bonds tying the leaders of such an institution to the institution itself, the stronger its traditions, and the greater the responsibility they feel for the performance of its functions and for its financial position, the more they can be relied upon to be good custodians of the wealth placed in their charge. For that to happen, of course, such institutions must find financial managers who can perform the task of handling their securities professionally.

Here again one has a group of potential buyers of state property: these institutions can be expected to purchase shares. But the process can be speeded up as well. My value premises do not advance any argument against such institutions receiving share portfolios even free of charge. The only requirements are suitable legislative and supervisory guarantees. And one must ascertain, of course, that there are the vital social conditions to ensure that the institution receiving the gift of state property will really be a good custodian, because those running it have the institution's interests at heart.

C-5. Local governments. Some of the wealth of the state previously managed centrally is likely to be transferred into the hands of local government authorities. This is a necessary and desirable trend, since it promotes the decentralization of power, but it clearly does not mean privatization. A municipality is part of the state, and so once again, the property is passing from one arm of the state to another. It is worth mentioning this because the cases covered by C-1 to C-4, which can really imply privatization are frequently confused in

---

16 Let me draw special attention to the need for this transfer of commitments to be conducted fairly. Under no circumstances should the individual citizen (in case C-2 the pensioner and in case C-3 the sick or other insured person) suffer losses. Nor should it happen that the state segment hastens to shed its commitments, arguing that the private segment has now received free shares, if in fact such shares do not yet ensure enough income to cover the outgoing pensions and insurance claims. In this respect particular attention, foresight and caution are required to guard private citizens, already troubled by uncertainties, from further worry.

debate with case C-5, which is merely decentralization within the state, not privatization at all.[17]

Having come to the end of the discussion of institutional forms of ownership, there are some further general observations to be made. It is inadvisable to create the institutional forms of truly private ownership in a bureaucratic way, by state decree, all at once. And apart from being inexpedient, it is not usually possible in any case. Such institutions will arise through processes of evolution. The speed with which they develop depends on several factors, for instance the inclination of domestic and foreign capital to invest in them (C-1, C-3), and the availability of domestic and foreign professional staff capable of managing institutional share portfolios (C-1, C-2, C-3, and C-4). But it also depends on the activities of the state's legislators and executive apparatus: on how fast the right legal frameworks and supervisory institutions develop, how much initiative the bureaucracy shows in bringing the requisite new institutions into being, and finally to what extent there is a free transfer of state property to create the initial capital for the organizations serving as institutional owners.

D. *Anonymous shareholders.* An important part in modern, mature capitalism is played by anonymous shareholders who do not themselves possess enough capital to make them heard directly at the general meeting of a joint-stock company, but are able to vote with their feet. If they do not have enough confidence in the future profitability of a firm in comparison with the profitability of alternate investments, they sell their shares, or in the opposite case, they buy shares. The trend in the demand, supply and price of the shares then exerts indirect influence on both the major shareholders represented at the general meeting and the management of the company. This indirect influence is applied through a broad network of intermediaries: the stock exchange, the brokers, and the banks or other financial institutions dealing with the purchase and sale of shares.

These institutions of ownership are beginning to appear in the Eastern European economies as well. Stock exchanges already function in the capitals of a few countries and they issue reports on the turnover and daily prices of the publicly traded shares. But all this is still in its infancy. It will take time before this form of ownership, along with the primary and secondary markets for securities, becomes widespread by a process of organic development. A great many things are needed for this to happen: expertise and routine, confidence, a large corpus of competent staff, the right legal regulations, effective state supervision, and so on.

---

17   It is another matter that the transfer of some of the state wealth previously handled centrally to the ownership of local authorities may speed up the privatization. This effect only ensues, of course, if the local authority is legally authorized to place property in its possession in private hands, and if it has an economic incentive to do so as well. Also important may be whether the elected local authority officers and councillors think their assistance to privatization will be popular with their voters.

Let us take a look into the more distant future. One can expect the role of joint-stock companies and the distribution of their ownership to develop in a similar direction to the one in the developed capitalist countries. So what are the characteristics of the situation there?

In a range of European countries where the capitalist market economy has operated continuously, without the interruption of the socialist system, only part of the total productive wealth operates in the corporate sector, composed of joint-stock companies, and only a proportion of the corporate sector is accounted for by companies whose shares are publicly traded.[18] This proportion is smaller in continental Europe than in the U.S.A. or the U.K.

Some people are prepared to invest their savings in shares voluntarily. But others will not take the associated risk and prefer other kinds of investment. That is one explanation for the concentration in the distribution of share ownership. In the United States, for instance, the Securities and Exchange Commission has demonstrated that 87% of the population on the lower level of income distribution owns only 1% of the shares, while those in higher income brackets own 99%. Within this group, the richest 1% own 80% of the shares, and the very richest 0.1% own 40% of the shares.[19]

So real capitalism is not 'people's capitalism.' In the light of the American figures, it seems a curious idea to turn all citizens into shareholders overnight by a free distribution of shares. To use Hayek's terminology again, this is a 'constructivist' idea, artificial, contrived, and therefore quite alien to the real development of capitalism. I do not think the whole population treasures an inward desire to own a little piece of share capital. Moreover, there is a danger that the expert, honest and adequately supervised institutions and staff required for a primary and a secondary market in shares of such a giant extent will be absent.

For my part I expect only one benefit to come from mass share-distribution campaigns, and that is a drastic reduction in the proportion of state ownership. That may facilitate the expansion of a dominant group inside a joint-stock company, because it will no longer be confronted with a predominant state owner. This advantage in itself should not be underestimated, but one cannot expect too much of it either. Ownership of share or voucher allocations for every citizen will do little to further the two purposes to which I gave particular emphasis in the section on value criteria: development of broad strata of entrepreneurs and business people (objective 1-a), and strengthening of the incentive towards efficiency (objective 2-a). At the same time, I fear there will be negative effects for the other economic criteria. The state treasury, hard-pressed in any case, loses the potential income from sales (criterion 2-c). Some

---

18   This should be understood to mean the shares which are quoted and traded on the stock exchange.
19   The figures are from Light and White (1979), p. 338.

recipients of the gift soon pass on their shares or vouchers and appear on the consumer market with the proceeds, which raises the inflationary pressure (criterion 2-d). In all events, this is a trade-off in which the advantages of speeding up privatization are opposed by drawbacks which merit serious consideration.

It seems there will not be a general, free distribution of shares or vouchers in East Germany or Hungary, but implementation of such ideas are quite far advanced in Poland and Czechoslovakia. Experience may refute the skepticism expressed above, in which case I am prepared to review my position.

As mentioned before, the justifications given for schemes which distribute shares or vouchers to all citizens free of charge include arguments based on distributive ethics as well: this is considered to be a start for the new capitalism that is fair and offers equal opportunities (objective 4-c). I have put forward some of my counter-arguments already. I would now like to add a further observation after the survey of institutional forms of ownership. Those who really want to improve the equality of opportunity and approve of distributing state property free of charge should press for the donation of truly profit-yielding shares to charities, health and educational institutes, foundations offering scholarships and other similar, non-state, autonomous institutions. This would really help to improve the position of those way down on the distribution scale of income and wealth, and would do so more effectively than a handout of shares or vouchers to rich and poor alike.

At this point it is worth summing up briefly my point of view on free distribution, which has been touched upon at several points in this study. There is, in my opinion, a case for a gratuitous transfer of part of the wealth formerly owned by the state to new private owners. The following can be included among them: private, non-profit pension and insurance institutions, cultural and educational institutions, charitable societies, foundations, and churches. In effect, the discount price of shares purchased by employees also contains a gift element. These transfers should only be made under specified conditions. (The conditions have been mentioned in this study.) I do not see a justification for any distribution of gifts beyond that.[20]

5 DOMESTIC AND FOREIGN OWNERSHIP

The question arises with all forms of ownership and institutions discussed so far as to whether the owner is domestic or foreign. Let me first put forward two extreme points of view. One is a position of narrowminded nationalism and xenophobia, whose exponents want to exclude all foreign imports of capital,

---

20 In my book (1990), I rejected the idea of granting all citizens free shares or other securities, and did not touch on other forms of free transfer at all. So my present position corrects my earlier one on an important point, because I now support a few forms of free transfer indicated to be both feasible and desirable.

seeing in them a threat to national independence and the specific national character of the emerging economy.

This position, in my view, causes serious damage. Eastern Europe has a huge need for foreign support in all forms. It is particularly important to have direct foreign investment of capital in all sectors of the economy, but most of all in the financial sector. It is desirable that foreign capital should take part in the purchase of the firms formerly owned by the state. Where the property is bought by a serious foreign firm, it enters as a real owner, fulfilling the requirements of criterion 2-a, that there should be an incentive towards efficiency and strict control over management.

I also do not agree with the other extreme: the position that the proportion of foreign capital in any sector is quite immaterial. The economy contains key positions which are expedient to keep in national hands, because they are indispensable to sovereignty. It is worth ensuring, through a circumspect policy, that the source of all capital investments from abroad should not be concentrated in a single country, but spread among various countries. This gives the recipient country more scope for manoeuvre and so reinforces its independence. Apart from those considerations, there is a need for the country's own citizens to take part in the forming of a large business class, as that will strengthen the domestic base for a market economy founded on private property. Among the requirements of criterion 1-a, the transformation of society in the direction of *embourgeoisement*, is that capitalism should strike root primarily in domestic soil.

6 THE PACE OF PRIVATIZATION

Those who take part in the debates on privatization are frequently asked whether they recommend fast or slow privatization. I think the question is phrased in the wrong way. No one would call himself an advocate of slowness. If I may add a subjective comment here, I myself am particularly put out if people call me an advocate of slow privatization.

What the debate should be about is not the speed but the choice of values, the role assigned to the state, and the assessment of the importance of the various forms of ownership and types of owner. Once anyone takes a position on these points at issue, the speed to be expected arises *as a result* of that decision.

I would like to declare that I am a believer in the process of privatization proceeding as fast as possible. But I do not think that it can be accelerated by some artful trick. I do not believe that finding some clever organizational form plus bureaucratic aggressiveness in enforcement are sufficient conditions for fast privatization.

The key issue, in my view, is not the pace at which the wealth hitherto owned by the state is transferred into private hands. The most important thing is the pace at which the private sector grows, (i) in the form of newly established firms, or (ii) through the transfer of state wealth, or by combinations of both these forms.

The following calculation is easy to check. Let us assume that at the start of the privatization process, the state sector accounts for 75% of the actual GDP and the private sector for 25%.[21] Production by the private sector then rises by 25% a year and production by the state-owned sector falls by 10% a year. Under those conditions, the private sector will dominate production at the end of the fourth year. Privatization in the broader sense depends on the difference in pace between the two processes, and above all on the vitality of the private sector, not on how cunning a way can be found of transferring state-owned shares into private hands.

There are grounds for optimism in that. The course of privatization is not ultimately set by the wisdom or stupidity, the strength or weakness of Eastern European governments, opposition forces, foreign governments, international organizations, or advisers at home or abroad. At most, they may slow down or speed up the events. The process is directed by an irresistible inner force: the inherent motivation of the present and future private owners.

REFERENCES

Alchian, A.A., 'Uncertainty, Evolution, and Economic Theory,' *Journal of Political Economy*, 58 (1950), pp. 211-221.

Ehrlich, É., 'The Size Structure of Manufacturing Establishments and Enterprises: An International Comparison,' *Journal of Comparative Economics*, 9 (1985), pp. 267-295.

Fischer, S. and A. Gelb, *Issues in Socialist Economy Reform*, Mimeo, MIT, Cambridge, Mass., 1990.

Friedmann, J., 'Sur l'expérience de privatization et sur les noyaux stables,' *Commentaire*, 1989, pp. 11-18.

Frydman, R. and A. Rapaczynski, *Markets and Institutions in Large Scale Privatizations*, Mimeo, New York University, New York, 1990.

Hayek, F.A., *The Constitution of Liberty*, London and Chicago, 1960.

Hayek, F.A., *Legislation and Liberty*, Chicago, 1973.

Hinds, M., *Issues in the Introduction of Market Forces in Eastern European Socialist Countries*, Mimeo, World Bank, Washington D.C., 1990.

Kornai, J., *The Road to a Free Economy: Shifting from a Socialist System. The Example of Hungary*, New York, 1990.

Lewandowski, J. and J. Szomburg, 'Property Reform as a Basis for Social and Economic Reform,' *Communist Economies,* 1 (1989), pp. 257-268.

Light, J.O. and W.L. White, *The Financial System*, Homewood, Ill., 1979.

Lipton, D. and J. Sachs, 'Privatization in Eastern Europe: The Case of Poland,' *Brookings Papers*, (1990), pp. 293-333.

Móra, M., 'The (Pseudo)-Privatization of State-Owned Enterprises,' *Acta Oeconomica*, 43 (1991), pp. 37-58.

Murrell, P., *The Nature of Socialist Economies: Lessons from Eastern European Foreign Trade*, Princeton, 1990a.

21   This includes the second economy not considered in the official statistics.

Murrell, P., *An Evolutionary Perspective on Reform of the Eastern European Economies*, Mimeo, University of Maryland, College Park, 1990b.

Schaffer, M.E., *On the Use of Pension Funds in the Privatization of Polish State-Owned Enterprises*, Mimeo, London School of Economics, London, 1990.

Schumpeter, J.A., *The Theory of Economic Development. An Inquiry into Profits, Capital, Credit, Interest and Business Cycles*, Cambridge, Mass., [1911], 1968.

Schumpeter, J.A., *Business Cycles: A Theoretical, Historical and Statistical Analysis of the Capitalist Process*, New York, 1939.

Schumpeter, J.A., 'Economic Theory and Entrepreneurial History,' in: *Change and the Entrepreneur*, Research Center in Entrepreneurial History, Harvard University, Cambridge, Mass. 1949, pp. 63–84. Reprinted in: J.A. Schumpeter, *Essays*, New Brunswich and Oxford, R.V. Clemence, 1989, pp. 253–271.

Stark, D., 'Privatization in Hungary: From Plan to Market or From Plan to Clan?,' *East European Politics and Societies*, 4 (1990), pp. 351–392.

Szelényi, I., *Socialist Entrepreneurs: Embourgeoisement in Rural Hungary*, Madison, 1988.

Tinbergen, J., *On the Theory of Economic Policy*, Amsterdam, 1952.

Voszka, É., 'Tulajdonreform vagy privatizáció?,' (Reform of Ownership or Privatization?), *Közgazdasági Szemle*, 38 (1991), pp. 117–133.

Summary

THE PRINCIPLES OF PRIVATIZATION IN EASTERN EUROPE

The paper surveys the choice criteria in selecting the mode of privatization. The main aspects are: 1. the sociological aspect with a longer time horizon, and in particular the objective to create a large class of business people; 2. economic aspects, and in particular the objective to increase efficiency and improve management; 3. political aspects and, 4. distributional-ethical aspects, including considerations of restitution and compensation for the loss of confiscated property. The paper discusses the role of the state and the evolutionary character of the privatization process, and analyzes various property forms. The significance of the evolution of personal owners gets special emphasis. Further subjects of the discussion are employee ownership, various forms of institutional ownership, give-away schemes of privatization and property rights of foreigners. Finally, the author explains his position concerning the speed of privatization.

POLICIES FOR ECONOMIC GROWTH **

BY

ROBERT M. SOLOW *

The last time I visited The Netherlands was in the early 1960s. Naturally I checked to see what has happened to the economy since then. Between 1960 and 1973 real GDP per worker rose at an annual rate of 3.6 percent and real GDP per person in the population at 3.9 percent. Between 1973 and 1980 the corresponding figures were 1.4 and 2.1 percent, and between 1980 and 1988 they were slower still, 0.2 and 1.0 percent. During the 1980s the rate of growth in The Netherlands was the slowest in western Europe except for Ireland.

In 1960–1973 The Netherlands grew faster than Denmark or Sweden and almost as fast as West Germany. In the last decade, GDP per worker rose appreciably less in The Netherlands than in any of the other three countries.

I do not have to remind you that these dry numbers have a social meaning. At the pace of 1960–1973, GDP per person doubles in 18–19 years, less than a generation. The normal expectation is that each generation will be much better off than its parents. At the 1973–1980 pace the doubling time is 35 years, closer to two generations. At the 1980–1988 rate it is 72 years or almost three generations. The experience of my own country could be described similarly and I believe that this has left traces in the temper of politics and social life.

The question then arises: what does economics have to say about such facts and about the policies that might be called upon by a nation that is unhappy with its performance. I want to discuss these questions in general, not in the particular context of The Netherlands. This is a very appropriate subject for a lecture dedicated to Jan Tinbergen.

I became a serious student of economics just after the Second World War. Looking back one can see that this was just the time when the main teaching centers in the United States were beginning, but only beginning, to break away from the old 'literary' way of doing economics and to acquire a new style of thought that I will describe as 'model-building.' The pioneers of the new approach had already taken the first self-conscious steps about ten years earlier.

* Professor of Economics, Massachusetts Institute of Technology, Cambridge, Mass.
** Fifth Tinbergen Lecture delivered on October 4, 1991, in Amersfoort for the Royal Netherlands Economic Association.

But the reorientation they had launched was delayed by the war itself. Provincial English-speaking economics lagged still further behind, and there was a lot of active resistance to new ideas.

For us provincials, the main books we studied were John Hicks's *Value and Capital* and, a little later, Paul Samuelson's *Foundations of Economic Analysis.* For me, personally, Jan Tinbergen was already an important presence, pointing the way to a new kind of economics. I think that the first original paper I wrote as a graduate student was an attempt to generalize his model of a ship-building cycle, and apply it to other markets.

There was another Tinbergen paper that I did not read then, and only heard about much later. That was called 'On the Theory of Long-run Economic Development,' and was published in German in 1942. If I had known about it my own work of the 1950s might have taken a slightly different form. In that article Tinbergen took as his object of study an economy that was not subject to business cycles or other short-term fluctuations. Instead he tried to understand what forces determined its trend behavior, and how those forces were related to one another. It was an article about the theory of economic growth.

Tinbergen's paper already contained many of the building-blocks that entered the modern theory of economic growth in the 1950s. In particular he is able to decompose the aggregate growth rates of Germany, Great Britain, France and the United States into the part explained by the increase in population and the stock of capital and the residual explained by 'increased efficiency' or 'technical development.' As you will see, this is exactly along the lines I propose to speak about today, so this will be a very Tinbergenian Tinbergen Lecture.

What I will not do today is provide numbers for you. Tinbergen did that in his 1942 paper (and of course I have done it also, on other occasions). I want to speak more qualitatively than quantitatively. It is possible that Tinbergen's early contribution would have been more influential if he had pursued the discussion of growth in a more qualitative, though exact, way.

Discussion about economic growth is not just a game for economists. Citizens, government officials and party politicians talk about it too, often making demands and promises. Nation-states compare themselves with one another and debate how to do better. 'Doing better' seems naturally to translate itself in terms of economic growth. In this field as in others, policy debate is often carried on in vague and ambiguous language. The participants in those debates sometimes seem to prefer it that way. But ambiguity is not good enough for the model-building economist. We will have to begin by clarifying the concepts before we can discuss intelligently what might be done about them.

When we discuss economic growth, just what is it that is supposed to grow? I have nothing special to say about population growth, which is not much of an issue in Europe anyway. So we will be thinking about growth per capita. That still leaves it open whether it is growth of output per person in the population, or per person employed, or per hour worked, or even per unit of all factors of production, including capital and natural resources. For most purposes any one of these measures of productivity will do, so long as we are conscious of the specific choice that has been made. One would look differently upon increases in national output per person that come about by increasing the length of the work-week or by attracting people from school, home or retirement into the active work force or by 'pure' increase in productivity. Generally, unless I say something to the contrary, I will mean growth of output per hour worked.

There is a second ambiguity that is potentially more confusing. It is not a good idea to mix up economic growth and business-cycle upswings. Journalistic writing and political debate often describe any year-to-year or quarter-to-quarter increase in national output as 'growth.' Some increases in output come from the activation of idle capital and idle – even if employed – labor. Sometimes, of course, it works in reverse and output falls. These fluctuations are quite different from the changes that occur in the course of economic growth. They have different causes and also different consequences. They call for different policies. When I speak of economic growth I mean to refer to increases in the *capacity* to produce output, not in production itself. Sometimes it is possible to distinguish between the *potential* output of an economy and its *actual* output. The business cycle consists in fluctuations of actual output around a given trend of potential output. The story of growth is the story of the trend of potential; and growth-oriented policy is policy aimed at affecting the potential trend.

Finally there is a more subtle distinction; it has to do with the phrase 'long run.' When model-building economists talk technically about economic growth they are usually thinking about a 'steady state' or about growth that continues at a more or less steady rate for a very long time. They know it cannot go on forever but for some interesting questions there is not much difference between 'forever' and 'for a long time.' But now think of a quite different situation: imagine an economy that has a constant, unchanging level of productivity. Then something happens – the invention of the computer, for instance – and productivity begins to rise. We know that it is going to reach a new plateau and level off there. Then it will become constant again, higher than it was before but no longer changing. Such a process might take twenty years or even longer for a major invention. If you look at the annual growth rate, it will start at zero, build up to a positive value, perhaps quite suddenly, then start to fall back and reach zero again after twenty years have passed. How shall we describe that episode? Of course I have just described it quite accurately. Perhaps nothing more is needed. But should we classify it as an episode of temporary growth or as something else? It is surely not a steady state and steady-state theory should not be applied. I do not object to classifying this story as an interval of temporary growth. Such one-time gains in productivity are very valuable achievements. If growth is glamorous, then maybe it is useful propaganda to talk about a temporary burst of growth. If we do that, however, we must remember that it is not an occasion for blame, when the annual growth rate starts to fall toward zero. The fall in the growth rate is not necessarily some kind of failure; it is a natural and inevitable part of the process of getting from one productivity plateau to a higher one. Of course achieving a new plateau is to be distinguished from achieving a higher growth rate that can be counted on for a long time. A careful vocabulary will preserve that distinction.

The modern theory of economic growth as developed in the 1950s and 1960s had implications for policy that were generally felt to be rather pessimistic. It may have been a misguided evaluation but that is how it seemed at the time. The essential conclusion was that the long-run steady-state growth rate for a national economy could be expressed as the sum of two numbers. The first was the rate of growth of employment, measured in total hours worked or better still in the combined utilization of labor hours and capital services. The second was described as the rate of 'technological progress,' but it was well understood that this had to be interpreted very broadly to include changes in the health, educational level and motivation of workers and changes in the efficiency with which markets allocated resources of labor and capital to production. (It was a sign of the times that natural resources played no role in the theory. But that was taken care of in the 1970s when OPEC served as a reminder.) According to this scheme, growth of output per hour worked has its only permanent source in this generalized sort of technological progress.

The point may be clearer if I state it another way. We can construct a more or less complete list of all the inputs into national production, including as a species of input the level of technology achieved. Then sustained growth can be generated only by sustained growth of some or all of these inputs. Sustained growth of output per hour worked can be generated only by sustained growth of some or all of the inputs when they too are expressed per hour worked, except for the level of technology. The reason for the difference is the natural presumption that technology is not 'used up' by being spread over a larger number of workers or hours as ordinary inputs are.

Growth in the level of technology is exactly what is meant by technological progress. To the extent that changes in the quality of labor and in the efficiency of resource-allocation can be measured separately and included in the list of inputs, the index of technological progress can be purified of those elements and restricted to narrowly technological factors; but it is probably essential that we include improvements in the organization of production as well as traditional engineering-based improvements in machine operation, process control and materials.

The same sort of argument leads to the conclusion that sustained productivity growth can also come from growth in the stock of human capital per worker and from growth in the stock of ordinary plant and equipment per worker. It follows then that policies to accelerate growth must aim at *increasing* the sustained growth of human or physical capital. This is where the theory's pessimism enters, if that is the right name for it.

It turns out to be no easy matter to create a permanent increase in the *rate of growth* of the stock of physical capital. Suppose there are diminishing returns to capital. That is an economist's phrase, but it has an everyday meaning. Imagine imposing more and more plant and equipment on a fixed base of labor and natural resources, so that production becomes steadily more capital-intensive. If the profitability of successive doses of investment get smaller and smaller under those circumstances, then the famous law of diminishing returns applies. And then it turns out to be essentially impossible to make the stock of capital grow any faster than the rate of technological progress. There is a natural upper limit to the growth of capital per worker, and that limit is the rate of technological progress. The limit shows itself in the following way: a national economy that tries to keep its stock of capital growing any faster will find itself forced to invest a larger and larger fraction of its national product. But it cannot invest more than all of its output, except by temporary borrowing, and long before that stage the reduced profitability of investment will surely call a halt to the process of increasing capital intensity. There is no hope of accelerating growth beyond that 'natural' limit for more than a relatively short time.

This is an important point so I will put it in yet another way. An economy dissatisfied with its rate of growth might propose to do better by devoting a larger fraction of its national product to investment. If it had previously been investing about 20 percent of GNP it might try to invest 25 percent from now on. This could be accomplished by any policy that increased the profitability of investment, by lowering taxes on business profit or by direct subsidization of private investment accompanied perhaps by increased public investment. What the theory says, and what most economists believed (at least until very recently) is that such an increase in the national investment share would create only a temporary episode of faster growth of the sort I described earlier. The growth-promoting policy would indeed bring about an immediate acceleration of the overall growth rate but eventually the growth rate would fall back to where it was before. The economy would be richer for having invested more; the gain would take the form of a *higher* income per worker or per person, but not a more rapidly *growing* income per person. I want to emphasize that it could be very worthwhile to exchange a higher fraction of income saved for a higher level of income. The result could be higher consumption per person, growing as before. It is only the rash demands of citizens and the even rasher promises of candidates that make this reward seem minor compared with the impossible wish for a higher growth rate.

It appears at first obvious that whatever is true about physical capital should be true of human capital. They seem quite analogous. That may be the case, and then the same proposition holds: acceleration of the permanent growth rate cannot be achieved by accelerating the growth of the stock of human capital. An attempt to do so would be frustrated by the increasing cost, in labor time and other resources, of 'producing' additional human capital. But one must admit that the analogy may not be so close. The accumulation of human capital appears to be much more a matter of quality than of quantity. People acquire new skills rather than more of the old skill. Of course we speak all the time of more education or more training, but then we seem to be measuring input into the education or training process rather than what comes out of it. I am not sure about any of this; I only want to mention the possibility that the accumulation of human capital obeys rather different laws from those governing physical capital, in terms of its own production and perhaps in terms of its use in the production of goods. It is possible, then, that sustaining faster economic growth through accelerated accumulation of human capital is a feasible proposition. One should not just assume this to be so; uncertainty is not a license for optimism. It might be the prudent course to adopt the pessimistic view with respect to human capital too.

Having said this I should point out that the same reasoning also suggests a little uncertainty about physical capital as well. The increase of capital intensity is usually accompanied by changes in the quality of capital goods and not merely their quantity. So perhaps the presumption of diminishing returns is not so plausible even there. Economic theory tries to handle this difficulty by treating the improved quality or different character of capital goods as an aspect of technological change. When old machinery is replaced by new machinery that costs more, the higher cost is added to the 'stock of capital' and the effects of their 'newness' is somehow incorporated in a higher level of technology. I do not want to pretend that this is a straightforward or exact procedure. It has been much argued about. But it is an approximate way – and so far the only way – to get on with the job. If it is fair to deal with physical capital in this way, the same method might be applied to human capital, to make a separation into 'more' and 'better.' Unfortunately there is little or no experience to guide us. Even if human capital is subject to diminishing returns, its importance in the growth process offers some scope for policies that can increase the level of income permanently even if not the growth rate.

With all these qualifications, the conclusion from post-war growth theory was that the only source of sustained acceleration of growth is somehow a faster rate of technological progress. A policy aimed at faster growth for a very long period must then be aimed at steady improvement in the level of technology that is available to be applied to industrial production. Some of this can come from faster imitation of technological leaders elsewhere in the world and some of it can come from faster application of known technology from laboratory to factory. But eventually it will have to come from the faster accumulation of technological knowledge.

We all know that there is a chance element in the process of innovation. Lightning strikes. It strikes where the ground has been prepared, but it does not automatically strike just because the ground has been prepared. We also know that the chance element is only a part of the process. The rest is deliberate, and costly. Resources have to be mobilized and spent, in the form of people and of objects. When more is spent, more is likely to be achieved even if one cannot be sure exactly what will be achieved. So there is something for growth-oriented policy to do. Governments play a direct part in organizing and financing research; and governments can make research more profitable for the private sector, just as with other forms of investment.

Nevertheless, it has to be said that we understand very little about the process of technological innovation and not much more about the process of translating new technology into higher productivity. No one doubts that spending more people and resources on innovation will produce more innovation. But the quantitative links are another matter. What would it take to raise the rate of technological progress by one percent per year and sustain it? Anyone who will give an answer to that question is living dangerously. Is there a basis for policy here? I think there is. Private enterprise almost certainly invests less in research and development than society at large would and should wish. More would be better, and there would certainly be a payoff in higher productivity, whose benefits are very widely diffused. But exactness in this kind of calculation is not attainable. I doubt that anyone will ever be able to say accurately that this program of research and development will add x percent to national product per worker or that another sustained program of research and development will add y percent per year to the pre-existing rate of productivity increase.

I do not know whether that is a discouraging conclusion. From the economist's point of view it is; of course one would like to be the Tinbergen of this field, to replace vagueness by precision or the hope of precision. From the point of view of the policy-maker, however, it is not so discouraging. Intelligent policy can still be made, and modesty is after all a virtue.

So far I have been describing what the 'older' growth theory, the growth theory of the 1950s and 1960s, had to say about policies for economic growth. Let me try to summarize, without the nuances. To do so I will go back to the idea of a trend of potential output, an index of what the economy can achieve if it operates always at some normal or desirable rate of capacity utilization or some acceptable unemployment rate. There is no harm in expressing the potential in terms of output per worker or per hour worked. The theory differentiated sharply between policies that could *lift* the potential trend curve from those that could *tilt* the curve, *i.e.* change the rate of growth. The conclusion was that the conventional range of fiscal or regulatory policies, those aimed at increasing the rate of capital formation, or even the rate of human capital formation, could lift the potential trend but not tilt it. A sustained increase in the share of GNP invested would create only a temporary episode of accelerated growth. The payoff to a reduction in current consumption would be a permanent increase in the level of consumption beginning some time in the future. To tilt the potential curve would require a rise in the rate of technological progress. There are policies that might accomplish that goal: promotion of research and development, encouragement of entrepreneurial behavior. The benefit of such policies can be very great but their degree of success is uncertain and probably intrinsically uncertain. The response to policy will be in the right direction, but whether the resulting acceleration of growth will be large or small, permanent or temporary, is beyond knowing.

In this picture there are two options for growth-oriented policy. One is to aim for temporary increases in the growth rate, to accept that lifting the potential trend is ambitious and important. Then there are several policy directions, all of which lead in the right direction. Increases in investment will do the trick and the menu includes increases in plant-and-equipment investment, increases in human-capital investment through education and training, increases in public investment in the infrastructure of transportation, communication and information flow, and, of course, investment in research and development. The second option is to seek higher growth rates on a long-term basis. Then the theory says that only the research-and-development-and-entrepreneurship path is a candidate and one cannot know exactly – or even approximately – what will be required to achieve a measurable acceleration of steady-state growth.

In the modern world there are some problems that the older theory never dealt with and for that reason I only want to mention them here. Skilled people can migrate, and new technology can migrate even faster. So investment paid for in one country can benefit primarily other countries – in the case of brain drain – or can benefit other countries as well as the originating country – in the case of technological imitation. The globalization of economic activity means that even a whole nation may be too small to 'internalize the externality' and capture a large fraction of the return on its own investment. That is why, for example, disputes over 'intellectual property rights' are now as prominent as disputes over conventional trade barriers. One can imagine three sorts of outcomes: either there will be satisfactory agreement on intellectual property rights, or ways will be found to internationalize the costs of all but the most proprietary research and development, or there will be serious attempts at secrecy and protection in the field of technology. Either of the first two outcomes would be preferable to the third; but there is no guarantee that the world will evolve in that direction.

I have been careful to talk about the growth theory of the 1950s and 1960s, the 'old' growth theory. (Tinbergen's article of 1942 was in that tradition.) More recently, since the mid 1980s, there has emerged a 'new' growth theory which comes to more-than-slightly different conclusions. The pioneers, as all economists know, were Paul Romer and Robert Lucas but there is now a long list of contributors. The usual name for what is new about the new theory is that the growth rate is 'endogenous,' which only means that it is determined within the theory rather than taken as a given. The reference is to the fact that in the older growth theory the steady-state rate of growth is always essentially given by the rate of technological progress which is not further explained. I think that puts the emphasis in the wrong place. None of the old growth theorists ever believed the rate of technological progress to be independent of economic decisions and events. But, having nothing very specific to say about how it is determined, they simply took it as given. The sorts of things I said earlier about research and development decisions could have been said any time, and no doubt were.

The real novelty in the new growth theory is that each version – and there are several – rests on a strong assumption about production that gives investment decisions very great leverage on growth rates. Almost always the key assumption suspends the operation of diminishing returns on some factor of production that can be accumulated.

Sometimes this is done quite directly: in some models it is just assumed that there are increasing returns to physical capital. That means that increasing capital intensity, instead of using up the most productive and profitable opportunities for investment, actually creates more productive and profitable ones although only a fraction of the return can be captured by the investor. Sometimes it is done indirectly: in some models it is assumed that there are increasing returns in the production of human capital (or knowledge), though not in its use. For instance, it may be asserted that a maintained increase in the *number* of hours per week devoted by the typical worker to education or training will permanently increase the *rate of growth* of the human capital thus generated. Sometimes the key assumption is quite subtle: in some models the source of increasing returns is not the quantity but the variety of productive inputs. For instance, it has been assumed that final output can be made to grow to infinity just by subdividing a fixed 'amount' of intermediate inputs into an ever greater variety. In all the instances that I have seen, the operative assumption is quite powerful.

From powerful assumptions come powerful conclusions. And the results of the new growth theory offer wide scope for growth-oriented policy. Two sorts of results emerge. In the first place it is shown that a sustained rise in the share of national income invested – in physical capital, say – can create a permanent increase in the economy's growth rate. This is just what the older theory denied. The difference is that in one story the grip of diminishing returns eventually prevails and in the other it does not. If the newer view is correct – and that remains to be discussed – the promotion of investment by tax or public expenditure policy gives a direct and *permanent* push to the growth rate.

The second sort of result is very striking too. It was a characteristic of the older growth theory that any sort of favorable or unfavorable event, as long as it was temporary, would have no effect on the ultimate long-run path of the economy. A temporary tax increase on the profits of capital would depress investment and growth as long as it stayed in place; but when it is removed the economy gradually goes back to where it would have been if the tax change had never occurred. Similarly the sudden destruction of part of the stock of capital, by war or natural disaster, would of course make the economy poorer. But once again the economy would gradually return to the very same steady state it would have achieved if the flood had never occurred. In the newer models that is no longer true. Even a temporary adverse shock to investment or a one-time loss of capital (or human capital) leaves major scars that never heal and may even get worse. If you imagine two identical island economies, one of which loses a quarter of its stock of capital to a storm that the other escapes, the fortunate island may have a permanent and widening advantage in income per head over its unlucky twin. One should always keep in mind that leverage for good is always accompanied by leverage for bad.

These models make policy both very powerful and very dangerous. Even if we remember firmly that words like 'permanent' and 'sustained' only mean 'lasting a long time,' the leverage of policy (and chance) on economic outcomes is great if the new ideas are true. It is even more significant that the range of policies with strong leverage is far broader than in the older sort of model. Depending on how the new-style model is formulated, it may be that investment in physical capital, or in human capital, or an easily achievable increase in the level of innovative activity can mean the difference between slower and faster growth in the long run. No one needs to be reminded that any noticeable difference in growth rates, sustained for a long time, cumulates to enormous differences in the level of income.

The new growth theory has achieved extraordinary popularity among analytical economists. By itself that only means that it is intellectually exciting. New sorts of models can be investigated; and they explain or try to explain parts of economic life that were formerly felt to be outside the scope of economic analysis. The power of the new results makes it all the more important to decide whether the powerful assumptions that lead to them are true. Before jumping to the policy conclusions we must decide whether to accept them or to accept their foundations. Now in fact it is very hard to imagine how those assumptions can be tested directly.

As I have emphasized, the key assumptions all seem to require that some economic activity be exempt for diminishing returns. That is hard enough to test for a single industry or process; and even that would be far from settling the relevant question. Of course some processes exhibit diminishing returns and some increasing returns. The problem is to know which is a better approximate representation for the economy as a whole. Another obstacle to empirical knowledge is that some of the activities whose nature we need to understand are intrinsically hard to define and to measure. This is especially true of activities that are meant to create human capital or usable technological knowledge, or variety in productive inputs or consumer goods. I do not know of any serious attempts to make such tests and I do not know of any convincing evidence that would compel a normally skeptical person to accept – or confidently to reject – those powerful assumptions and their implications. The tendency within economics has been to try something indirect and, as we shall see, tricky. In the meanwhile, skepticism seems like the right attitude, genuine open-minded skepticism.

A combination of circumstances has led to a new sort of research aimed at uncovering the effective sources of growth. One of the circumstances is precisely the emergence of the new sort of theory that I have just been discussing. If you suspect that the growth rate responds sensitively to economic decisions, public and private, then it should be relatively easy to find traces of these effects in the record of economic growth. Of course you need a record in which to search.

That is the second circumstance. There is now available a large body of data, covering the experience of many countries over three or four decades. The advantage of using data from many countries is that they are surely not all alike. The variety of policies and circumstances observed will be greater than any single country will experience during its statistical history. The same is true of such non-policy differences as changes in private behavior, international influences and chance events. So looking across countries is useful for the same reason that the effects of differences in rainfall on crop yields will be easier to discern if you can observe both arid countries and rainy countries.

The disadvantage of such bodies of data is that different countries may not be comparable in some important respect. The experience of relatively poor countries may not be relevant for relatively rich countries, or the experience of agricultural countries may not be relevant for industrial countries. The experience of open economies may not be relevant to relatively self-contained economies. The experience of countries with strongly 'corporatist' institutions may not be relevant to the experience of economies without such organizations. The only answer one can give to that sort of question is to try and see whether consistent and meaningful results can be achieved. Every one of those possible differences can be converted into an explicit hypothesis and tested.

The other potential source of international incomparability is purely statistical. There are different methods of collecting data, different sorts of price indexes, sometimes even different definitions. If the effects we are trying to detect are fairly subtle, these statistical difficulties can easily obscure them. The good news is that there are two collections of international income and product statistics that have been prepared for comparability, one from the World Bank and one from two American scholars, Robert Summers and Alan Heston, who provide data for as many as 138 countries for 30 years, even to the point of grading the quality of the data on a scale from A to D. The bad news is that the two bodies of data sometimes give inconsistent results. They are, however, our only source of extensive empirical knowledge. What do they show?

First let me describe what is done in order to find out. Suppose you had a list of dietary habits, environmental characteristics, genetic factors and perhaps other things, all of which might be expected to have an influence on the incidence of a disease like cancer. You want to find some way to assess their relative importance. One thing you might do is to collect information for a number of countries in the world on the incidence of cancer during some com-

mon period of time, as well as on each of the other characteristics: proportion
of mean in the diet, use of tobacco, amount of direct sunshine, skin pigmenta-
tion and so on. Then there are well known statistical techniques for calculating
how closely the incidence of cancer by country is correlated with this group of
national characteristics, and for estimating how important each of them seems
to be. Usually, of course, you do not get a complete 'explanation' of the incidence of cancer in this way; there remains some unexplained noise. But you
learn quite a lot.

The typical procedure is the same when the thing to be explained is national
differences in rates of economic growth. One starts with growth rates of GDP
or GDP per worker for many countries, averaged over a long enough period to
eliminate the effects of short-term fluctuations. The other variables are taken
from the list suggested by growth theory: rates of investment in plant and
equipment and infrastructure, rates of investment in human capital – usually
measured rather imperfectly by figures on school enrollment, because that is
what is available – and perhaps some figures on the industrial composition of
GDP. Usually one includes the initial level of income, on the old-growth-
theory presumption that the poorer countries at the start have further to go
than the others and will find it easier to make progress for that reason. (You
may be surprised by that, but it almost always turns out to be so.)

It is interesting that many of the studies include descriptive characteristics
that have little or no theoretical connection with the growth rate achieved, but
measure the orderliness and coherence of economic policy: the average rate of
inflation during the period, the size of a country's external debt, its budget
deficit or surplus, even direct measures of political stability/instability. The
range of countries in these studies usually goes all the way from very poor less-
developed countries to very rich industrialized countries, and I suspect that
these political characteristics play a role primarily for that reason. A high rate
of inflation – generally negatively correlated with real growth – is as much an
indicator of a government out of control as it is a reflection of the fact that
rapid (and therefore variable) inflation interferes with the performance of the
price mechanism in allocating resources, and also creates risks that reduce the
volume and efficiency of investment.

The first thing that must be said is that these statistical analyses do not con-
clusively settle the contest between the old growth theory and the new. To my
eye – which may not be neutral, because after all I am an old growth theorist
– the international record suggests that there is no compelling need to invoke
the new ideas. The data can be accounted for in a satisfactory way without
them. (There is one very interesting amendment: something like half of the con-
ventionally measured contribution of labor to the growth of output may be
more specifically the contribution of human capital, the other half belonging
to some sort of 'standard' labor.) But the data are also reasonably compatible
with new-growth-theory ideas, though not with the more explosive versions of
them. It should not be surprising that the historical cross-country record is in-

conclusive. In the first place, some fraction of international differences in growth rates stems from idiosyncratic, unsystematic factors, pieces of good or bad luck, and the like, exactly as with international differences in the incidence of cancer. In the second place, the contrast between new and old in growth theory is not necessarily like the difference between black and white; there is a range of gray and, within the gray area, it is hard to discriminate.

Whichever way the theoretical question is eventually decided, the studies leave no doubt at all that investment, physical, human and intellectual, matters for growth on a time-scale of two or three decades. The issues are only matters of degree and duration. Even 30 years is not a long enough time to distinguish between temporary episodes of accelerated growth and increases in the growth rate itself. A society that wants to accelerate its growth must increase its stock of tangible and human capital faster and accelerate the entry of new technology into production. The payoff is not terribly dramatic and it is uncertain, but it is there. I think it would be good for the accuracy and integrity of policy discussion if promises to raise the growth rate were replaced by promises to lift the trend. I have not been able to think of a catchy phrase, but one would be welcome. Talk about growth rates should wait until it has a more reliable foundation. (Perhaps this is the place for me to say that all such promises should pay more respect to environmental and resource constraints than in the past. I do not want to be misunderstood: I think those constraints are of great importance, especially in a world characterized by enormous inequality as between rich countries and poor. I have not emphasized environmental and resource constraints because I have nothing new or different to say about them.)

The international cross-section studies typically show that fiscal and monetary orderlines – low inflation, limited external debt, a reasonable budgetary stance – are also positively associated with economic growth. This sounds like a more significant conclusion than it is. It does not mean that The Netherlands would grow faster – or lift its trend – if its fiscal policy were a little tighter. What it seems to mean is that the growth performance of African and Latin American countries has been worse than the fundamentals would indicate; and those continents, more than others, have experienced inflation, indebtedness and fiscal extravagance. Modesty is a virtue in reading this evidence, not only because its scope is limited but because the statistical results themselves are fragile. This means that quite small changes in the model, so small that no one could treat them as a matter of principle, often lead to substantial changes in the story told by statistical analysis. It is not possible to be confident about what really lies behind the observed correlations.

For the developed economies, a reasonable interpretation is that the favorable effects of sound macroeconomic policy work mainly *through* investment. That is to say, inflation is bad for growth because inflation is bad for investment, macroeconomic stability is good for growth because macroeconomic stability is good for investment. That is what vaguer notions like 'confidence' come down to. Conscience requires me to repeat that all such inferences from international comparisons are shaky. What does stand out is the importance of physical, human and technological investment, and the old-growth-theory conclusion that, when account is taken of investment and technology, there remains some tendency within the group of industrial nations, for the slightly poorer ones to catch up with the slightly richer ones.

Those conclusions are an adequate foundation for growth-oriented policy as long as one does not ask for too much. I mean two separate things under the heading of 'asking too much.' The first is to demand or to promise too much precision. In the fifty years since Tinbergen's article economists have learned how to think about economic growth and have even been able to achieve some serious quantitative results. But the links between policy and action and between action and growth are uncertain and will probably remain uncertain, not because economists are stupid but because life is like that. A mature democracy should learn that it can pursue growth through investment and technological development. But it cannot be sure exactly when the benefits will arrive and exactly how large they will be. Excessive demands and rash promises are not a good basis for a commitment to a high growth policy.

The other way of asking too much or promising too much is to focus too exclusively on tilting the potential trend instead of lifting it. The new growth theory may turn out to be right in its main contentions. In that case it may point the way to powerful policy initiatives. But we are still a long way from any confidence that this is the case. For the present a mature democracy should learn that the forces governing the slope of the potential trend, the sustainable rate of growth, are complex, mostly technological, and even a little mysterious. What we do know how to do is to lift the potential trend by a few percent. Even if the slope remains as before, that is a fine achievement. Its absolute significance, measured in constant dollars or constant guilders, gets bigger as time goes on. According to Summers and Heston, real GDP per worker in Mexico is half of what it is in The Netherlands. Closing that gap, or even half of that gap, would be a historic change for the Mexican people and a worthy goal for thirty years. It is an interesting question whether realistic policy goals can become viable political platforms.

Summary
POLICIES FOR ECONOMIC GROWTH

The 'old' growth theory of the 1950s led to certain conclusions about the sorts of economic policies that would promote economic growth, and also about their limitations. The 'new' growth theory of the 1980s makes much stronger assumptions and leads to correspondingly stronger conclusions about the scope of growth-promoting policy. This article argues that: (1) empirical work so far has neither confirmed nor denied the strong assumptions underlying the new theory; (2) the theory is worth pursuing because of its intrinsic interest and the possibilities it opens up; (3) whatever the final verdict on the new theory, both theory and evidence support the belief that significant long-run gains, even if not permanent changes in the growth rate, can be achieved by increased investment in the broadest sense, including human capital, technological knowledge, and industrial plant and equipment.

THE RECENT FAILURE OF U.S. MONETARY POLICY**

BY

MARTIN FELDSTEIN*

Thank you. I am delighted to be here in The Hague and honored by the invitation to deliver this 6th annual Tinbergen Lecture. I have been an admirer of Professor Tinbergen since my days as a graduate student when I first studied his theory of economic policy.

The subject of my lecture is the recent failure of monetary policy in the United States. Since the spring of 1990, the rates of growth of real income, of nominal income, and of the broad monetary aggregate have been substantially less than the Federal Reserve had set as targets and than most observers regarded as appropriate. In the language that Professor Tinbergen taught the economics profession, the link between the instrument of economic policy (the Federal Reserve's open market operations) and these targets of economic policy have not operated recently in the way they did in the past. Moreover, the Federal Reserve did not respond by changing the instrument values (the extent of open market operations) sufficiently to compensate for the decline in its potency in affecting the monetary aggregates and total GDP.

It is important to stress that the breakdown of the traditional economic relation has not been between the broad money supply (*M2*) and nominal GDP but between the increase in reserves caused by open market operations and the subsequent change in the broad money supply. The velocity link between the *M2* money stock and the subsequent level of the nominal GDP has not declined; if anything, it has been slightly higher in the past two years than previous experience would have implied. But changes in bank reserves brought about by open market operations have had much less effect on the money supply than the Federal Reserve had anticipated.

* Professor of Economics, Harvard University, and President of the National Bureau of Economic Research.
** Sixth Tinbergen Lecture delivered on October 2, 1992, in The Hague for the Royal Netherlands Economic Association.

Reprinted from "De Economist" vol. 141/1 (1993), pp. 29-42

Two fundamental conditions have caused a reduction in the impact of open market operations on the broad *M2* money stock: the lack of reserve requirements on all but a small fraction of total *M2* and the recent imposition of bank capital requirements that limit the banks' ability to lend. The Federal Reserve failed to appreciate the importance of these conditions and misjudged the strength of the monetary policy stimulus that it was providing.

In this lecture I will discuss these ideas in more detail, will consider why the Fed did not react more aggressively when it became clear that the money supply and the economy were stagnating, and will indicate how the link between open market operations and the broad monetary aggregate could be reestablished by a change in Federal Reserve rules.

My comments focus exclusively on the role of monetary policy in the management of aggregate demand, ignoring the potential use of fiscal policy. This may seem particularly surprising in a lecture in honor of Professor Tinbergen since one of the general lessons that the economics profession learned from Professor Tinbergen's early work is that it is usually incorrect to assign particular policy instruments to particular targets. Each of the instruments should depend in principle on all of the policy targets.

In practice, however, we have come to recognize that fiscal policy is a very blunt tool to use for macroeconomic stabilization and that monetary policy should therefore bear primary responsibility, indeed generally sole responsibility, for guiding the level of aggregate demand. Particularly with the American Congressional form of government, changes in taxes and government spending take a long time to enact and are difficult to modify.

At the present time, the very high level of the U.S. government budget deficit relative to our private saving also hampers the use of stimulative fiscal policy. Because of the large projected future budget deficits, a fiscal policy that seeks to stimulate the economy by increased spending or lower taxes could actually be counterproductive. If financial markets interpret policies that increase the current deficit as evidence that there will be even larger deficits in the future, long-term interest rates might rise by so much that current aggregate demand is actually reduced. Only the politically elusive fiscal package that combines an increased short-run deficit with a reliable decrease in future deficits would unambiguously raise near-term economic activity.

American economists therefore generally look to the Federal Reserve to manage short-run variations in nominal GDP. The Federal Reserve itself, like other central banks, does not literally announce a nominal GDP target but takes price stability as its medium-term goal while at least implicitly selecting a short-run target for nominal GDP that is designed to combine reduced inflation with acceptable changes in unemployment.

Unfortunately, in attempting to implement this goal during the past 18 months, the Federal Reserve has produced increases in nominal and real GDP that have been far smaller than the Fed anticipated and than would have been expected at this stage in the business cycle.

1 TARGETS FOR NOMINAL GDP AND THE MONEY STOCK

Before looking at experience in 1991 and 1992, let me say a few words about the Fed's actions in the years immediately before 1991. A useful place to begin such an analysis is in 1987 when Alan Greenspan became chairman of the Federal Reserve. Greenspan made it clear that his goal would be to carry on the work begun by Paul Volcker by reducing the rate of consumer price inflation from the then prevailing level of about 4.5 percent to 'virtual price stability.' Such 'price stability' was generally interpreted to be about two percent inflation (at least in part because of the overstatement of inflation in traditional price indices).

The Fed's aim was to lower the rate of growth of nominal GDP slowly so that inflation would come down without causing an actual downturn in economic activity. The October 1987 collapse of the stock market caused a temporary shift in Fed policy to meet the increased short-run demand for liquidity. But by early 1988 the Fed was withdrawing the excess liquidity that it had created in prior months and returning to its goal of gradually slowing the rate of increase of nominal GDP.

The growth of the broad monetary aggregate *M2* – which includes currency, checkable deposits, bank savings accounts, time deposits of less than $100,000, and the money market mutual funds issued by brokerage firms – was reduced from 5.5 percent in 1988 to 5.1 percent in 1989 and 3.5 percent in 1990. The rate of increase of nominal GDP fell from 7.7 percent in 1988 to 6.0 percent in 1989. As usual, the initial effect was to reduce real GDP growth (from 3.3 percent in 1988 to 1.6 percent in 1989) with no progress on inflation.

Although 1990 began with nominal GDP growth and inflation very similar to 1989, many observers at the time expected that the second half of 1990 or the beginning of 1991 would see the long-awaited decline in inflation.

The Fed's goal of reducing inflation without an economic downturn was however undermined by Saddam Hussein's invasion of Kuwait in August 1990. The resulting rise in oil prices caused a jump in consumer inflation and a decline in real economic activity. The Fed tightened monetary policy, slowing the growth of *M2* to only 2 percent between August 1990 and the end of the Mideast conflict in January 1991. Real GDP declined at an annual rate of nearly 3 percent in the second half of 1990 and the first quarter of 1991.

Fortunately, the Iraqi invasion was repulsed quickly and the price of oil fell sharply in early 1991. The Fed eased, short-term interest rates fell, and *M2* rose at a rate of nearly 4.5 percent from December 1990 to June 1991. Real GDP increased at a 1.7 percent annual rate between the first and second quarters of the year.

Most analysts expected that the second quarter of 1991 would be the beginning of a healthy recovery. That it was not, I blame on the Federal Reserve and, more specifically, on the Fed's failure to increase *M2* sufficiently rapidly, at least as rapidly as the Fed itself had set as its target.

I emphasize the monetary aggregates because nominal GDP growth has paralleled *M2* growth about two quarters earlier. Over the past 25 years, nominal GDP has grown at an annual rate of 8.3 percent while the stock of *M2* has grown at 8.2 percent. And while there are significant year to year variations in velocity, the normal fluctuations of velocity are small enough that the change in nominal GDP does not differ very much from the change in *M2* two quarters earlier. Thus, during the past quarter century, the annual changes in lagged *M2* velocity (measured as the ratio of nominal GDP to *M2* two quarters earlier) were less than 1.5 percent in more than half of the years and less than 2.5 percent in three fourths of those observations. In only four of the 50 observations did the lagged *M2* velocity rise or fall by more than 3 percent.

This point is worth emphasizing because, as already noted, the broad *M2* money stock grew by much less in the past two years than the Federal Reserve had set as its target. The Fed lacks the ability to control *M2* precisely and did not take strong steps to make *M2* grow more quickly when it was seen to be increasing below the targeted rate. The reasons for this will be discussed below. But first a review of the experience with the money stock and nominal GDP in 1991 and 1992.

1.1 *Monetary Policy in 1991*

During 1990, the Federal Reserve announced that its 1991 target range for the rise of the broad *M2* monetary aggregate would be centered at 4.5 percent from the fourth quarter of 1990 until the fourth quarter of 1991 (with a plus-or-minus two percent allowable margin above and below this target rate). Based on the lack of trend in *M2* velocity over the past quarter century, a 4.5 percent growth of *M2* implied as a first approximation that nominal GDP would grow at a rate of about 4.5 percent after a lag of about six months.

Such a slow growth of nominal GDP would prevent a full recovery from the downturn caused by the Iraqi invasion. Even if a fall in energy prices cut the rate of inflation (as measured by the GDP implicit price deflator) to only three percent, a nominal GDP rise of only 4.5 percent would leave room for real GDP growth of only 1.5 percent. Since the rise in U.S. labor productivity implies that it takes nearly 2.5 percent real GDP growth just to absorb the normal increase in the labor force, the unemployment rate would continue to rise.

There was, however, reason to be more optimistic about the economic outlook implied by the Federal Reserve's monetary target. Although the historic experience showed no *M2* velocity change over the long run, the evidence also implied that during the first four quarters of economic recoveries the 'lagged-velocity' (relating nominal GDP to *M2* two quarters earlier) rose by an average of about one percentage point. With this cyclical rise in velocity, a 4.5 percent increase in *M2* would lead to a 5.5 percent rise in nominal GDP. If the rise in the GDP price deflator did decline to 3.0 percent, real GDP growth would be 2.5 percent and therefore enough to achieve a slow decline in the unemployment rate. Such a slow decline in unemployment would provide a favorable environment for continuing progress in lowering the inflation rate. In other words, the Fed's money target for 1991 was a risky strategy but one that, on the basis of historic experience with cyclical changes in velocity, looked like a way to have declines in both unemployment and inflation in the year ahead.

Unfortunately, the actual increase in the *M2* money stock in 1991 was substantially below the Fed's 4.5 percent target rate. From the fourth quarter of 1990 until the fourth quarter of 1991, the money stock rose only 2.8 percent. The corresponding increase in nominal GDP – from the second quarter of 1991 until the second quarter of 1992 – was 4.3 percent. Thus velocity did rise cyclically in line with historic experience but not enough to compensate for the shortfall of *M2* growth below its target. Even though inflation fell to 2.7 percent, the real GDP growth rate was only 1.5 percent and the unemployment rate rose a full percentage point.

The very slow growth of the money stock was therefore a serious problem for the economy. Despite an above average rate of growth of velocity, nominal GDP grew too slowly to be consistent with a normal recovery. Before looking at the reasons why the Fed failed to provide the stimulus needed for the short-term growth of aggregate demand, it is useful to take a brief look at the evolution of monetary policy in 1992.

1.2 Monetary Policy in 1992

Despite the substantial shortfall of *M2* growth in 1991 and the weakness of the economy, the Federal Reserve decided to aim at an unchanged 4.5 percent growth of *M2* from the fourth quarter of 1991 to the fourth quarter of 1992. It set that target tentatively in the summer of 1991 and then reconfirmed it in February 1992.

In the summer of 1991, setting such a target for 1992 money growth did not seem unreasonable. The money supply had grown at four percent from its fourth quarter 1990 base and looked like it could achieve the 4.5 percent target for the 1991 year. Nominal GDP rose at 5.2 percent in the second quarter of 1991 and the associated rise in real activity seemed to signal an end to the recession.

But reconfirming that target in February of 1992 looked much less appropriate. The *M2* stock had increased at an annual rate of only 2.8 percent in 1991. Nominal GDP growth had slipped to 3.4 percent in the second half of 1991 and real GDP growth to less than one percent.

The primary reason that the Fed did not increase the *M2* target growth for 1992 was a fear that any increase in *M2* would cause market participants to conclude that the Fed was no longer interested in reducing inflation. If financial markets did reach that conclusion, long-term interest rates would rise, hurting housing and other components of demand and therefore reducing the prospects for a solid recovery. Moreover, businesses and workers might seek greater increases in prices and wages to protect themselves from the anticipated rise in inflation.

I argued at the time (in a February 3, 1992 article in the *Wall Street Journal*) that that fear of increased inflationary expectations was exaggerated, and that the Fed could raise its 1992 target for *M2* without increasing fears of inflation by explaining that the faster *M2* growth in 1992 would merely offset the short-fall of actual *M2* growth in 1991.

Since the 1991 *M2* growth had been only 2.8 percent instead of the originally sought 4.5 percent, the 1992 target could be raised by 1.7 percentage points (to 6.2 percent) and still have the originally targeted 9 percent two-year growth of the money stock. Alternatively, the shortfall could be made up over a period of more than one year, implying a 1992 *M2* target between 4.5 percent and 6.2 percent.

More generally, as I argued at the time, the most appropriate rate of growth of *M2* for 1992 would not have been based on an arbitrary catch-up rule but on a calculation of what would be most likely to be consistent with the desired rate of growth of GDP during the period from mid 1992 through mid 1993. I thought a reasonable goal would be six percent nominal GDP growth, a level that would probably involve a 3 percent rate of increase of real GDP and a 3 percent rate of inflation. Achieving that 6 percent nominal GDP growth would most plausibly require a 6 percent rise in *M2* in 1992.

The Federal Reserve's Open Market Committee voted to stay with the original 4.5 percent target for *M2*, but emphasized in discussions with outsiders that this was just the center of a range stretching up to 6.5 percent and let it be known that they expected actual *M2* growth to be in the upper half of the range.

If they had achieved such money growth, the resulting rise in nominal GDP would probably have implied declining unemployment and an inflation rate of about three percent. But once again, as in 1991, the actual growth of *M2* slipped well below the target. The most recently available data show that *M2* has grown at an annual rate of only 1.4 percent from the fourth quarter of 1991 through August 1992. The level in August was no higher than in the first quarter of the year and was actually lower than in February, March, April, and May.

Although an increase in velocity could in theory lead to an acceptable rate of nominal GDP growth, such a large increase would be extremely unlikely based on past experience. For the most recent four quarters, the two-quarter lagged velocity grew at only 1.4 percent. If that rate of growth of velocity continues for the rest of 1992, nominal GDP will increase at a rate of only 3.6 percent from the second quarter of 1992 until the final quarter of the year. Since the implicit price deflator has been rising at 2.9 percent in the first half of the year (and 2.4 percent in the final half of last year), it is very unlikely that a 3.6 percent rise in nominal GDP will provide much scope for real economic growth. The most likely outlook is for a continued increase in unemployment.

While these figures may be too pessimistic, there is little reason to doubt that the Federal Reserve's policies have left actual *M2* growth too low to support declining unemployment. I turn therefore to the question of why this was allowed to happen.

2 WHY THE FED WAS NOT AGGRESSIVE ENOUGH: MANAGING SHORT-TERM INTEREST RATES

Although the Fed sets *M2* targets, the Fed's operational policy instrument is open market purchases and sales of Treasury securities. More specifically, the Fed decides on short-run targets for the federal funds rate at which banks lend to each other and uses open market operations to achieve the desired level of this rate. Because the fed funds rate responds immediately to such open market operations, the Fed has *de facto* control over the fed funds rate and the fed funds rate can therefore be regarded as an instrument of Federal Reserve policy.

For some Federal Reserve officials, short-term interest rates are the essence of monetary policy. For others, changing the Fed funds rate is seen as the best way of affecting the amount of *M2* that the banks create. Whatever the reason, since short-term Fed policy is made in terms of the Fed funds rate and the discount rate, any attempt to understand Federal Reserve policy must begin with a review of the changes that it made in these two rates.

Although the Fed has set cautious targets for *M2* since the end of 1990 and then allowed actual *M2* growth to fall far short of these targets, the Fed was in fact driving short-term interest rates down very sharply by increasing bank reserves aggressively through open market operations. The Fed funds rate fell from 7.3 percent at the end of 1990 to 4.4 percent at the end of 1991 and 3.2 percent in August/September 1992. The fall in the Fed funds rate was parallelled in the Treasury bill market, with 3-month Treasury bill rates falling from 6.8 percent at the end of 1990 to 4.1 percent at the end of 1991 and 3.1 percent in September 1992. Thus short-term interest rates were reduced to their lowest level in about 30 years.

Judged by such interest rates, monetary policy during that period looked very expansionary. Moreover, there is no doubt that the lower interest rates did help to achieve stronger economic activity than would have prevailed without the interest rate reductions. The lower cost of funds raised residential construction and business investment. Lower interest rates raised share prices which increased the wealth and spending of shareowners and encouraged businesses to invest more. Lower monthly payments on existing adjustable rate mortgages increased the spendable funds of cash-constrained households. And the dollar decline that resulted from lower interest rates helped to stimulate exports and the substitution of U.S. goods for imports at home.

Nevertheless, the aggregate level of demand and of economic activity remained depressed. The Fed did not achieve its own *M2* targets and, more generally, failed to provide enough stimulus to achieve its desired level of nominal GDP growth. What went wrong? Looked at from the Federal Reserve's point of view, the economic slump at the end of 1990 and the conclusion of the Mideast hostilities caused the Fed to expand aggressively for several months. The Federal Reserve discount rate was cut from 7 percent to 6.5 percent in December 1990, to 6.0 percent in February 1991, and to 5.5 percent in April. The Fed funds rate came down from 7.3 percent to 5.9 percent during these same months.

But then the interest rate decline ended. The discount rate and the Fed funds rate remained essentially unchanged until September 1991 when they were reduced another half a point. The *M2* stock remained frozen during this period, bringing the cumulative rise in *M2* between the fourth quarter of 1990 and September 1991 to only 2.2 percent.

Although the Fed then moved more aggressively for a few months – cutting the discount rate three times in four months to only 3.5 percent – it was too late to rescue the growth of *M2* for 1991 and the year ended with *M2* growth of only 2.8 percent. The growth of nominal GDP declined to 2.8 percent in the final quarter of the year with real GDP growth of only 0.6 percent.

The interest rate reductions and associated increases in reserves at the end of 1991 appear to have given a temporary boost to *M2* in early 1992 and to have raised the pace of activity in 1992 above the year-end 1991 low. Between October 1991 and February 1992, *M2* rose at an annual rate above 5 percent. Nominal GDP rose at a 6.2 percent rate in the first quarter of the year and real GDP at 2.9 percent.

But the Fed then became complacent again. Short-term rates were kept unchanged between January and June. The stock of *M2* actually declined from February until July (when another discount rate cut caused a small increase in *M2* between July and August).

Why did the Federal Reserve's Open Market Committee (the FOMC) not move more aggressively throughout the period? Why did it stop lowering interest rates even though that would have led to faster growth of *M2* during long periods when *M2* was frozen? There were, I believe, three different reasons.

2.1 *Money in the Pipeline*

During much of 1991, many Fed officials believed that *M2* was about to increase more rapidly without the need for further stimulus. They were convinced by the Fed staff's statistical studies that the previous reductions in interest rates would soon lead to faster *M2* growth. When key Fed officials were pressed on why they were not doing something to increase the money supply, they replied that the additional money was already 'in the pipeline' and would soon be visible. When they began to have doubts in September 1991, they cut the discount rate and the fed funds rate. And when in December they abandoned all hope of seeing the money that they had thought was in the pipeline, they cut the discount rate by a full percentage point.

2.2 *Misleading Indicators*

A much more fundamental reason for the FOMC's reluctance to be more aggressive is that they judged the ease of monetary policy by looking at the federal funds rate and other short-term nominal interest rates. This was misleading in several ways.

First, short rates fell much more than longer-term rates. For example, between December 1990 and December 1991, the rate on 6-month commercial paper fell 300 basis points (from 7.49 percent to 4.49 percent) but the corresponding rate on high-grade corporate bonds only fell 75 basis points (from 9.05 percent to 8.31 percent). The yield curve became quite steep even at relatively short maturities. A business borrower might be able to borrow shortterm funds much more cheaply than a year before but his decisions would have to take into account the likelihood, implied by the yield curve, that rolling over those loans in the future would be possible only at substantially higher rates.

Second, although nominal rates were down, real rates were down substantially less. For example, the interest rate on fixed-rate mortgages with an expected maturity of about 7 years fell from 9.8 percent in December 1990 to 8.4 percent in June of 1992, a fall of 1.4 percentage points. It is, of course, difficult to judge how much expected inflation rates fell during this same period. In December 1990, the GDP deflator was 4.4 percentage points higher than it had been a year earlier. By June 1992 this had dropped to 2.7 percent, a decline of 1.7 percentage points. The decline in the rate of CPI inflation was even greater. But even if expected inflation had fallen by only 1.2 percentage points, the implied decline in the real interest rate during the 18-month period was only 0.2 percentage points rather than the 1.4 percentage point decline of the nominal rate. Moreover, since the yield on long-term bonds fell only 75 basis points, the implied real interest rate on such bonds may actually have risen. Moreover, even the real interest rate is often not the relevant measure. In general, it is appropriate to look at real *net-of-tax* interest rates. Because our tax system taxes nominal interest income and allows deductions for nominal interest costs, real net-of-tax interest rates may actually move in a different direction from real pretax interest rates. Consider for example a prospective home buyer with a marginal tax rate of 28 percent who reduced his expected inflation rate by 1.2 percentage points between December 1990 and June 1992 from 4.5 percent to 3.3 percent. If taxes are ignored, the expected real interest rate declined from 5.3 percent to 5.1 percent.

But the real after-tax interest rate perceived by such an individual actually rose. The original 9.8 percent pretax interest rate corresponded to a net borrowing cost of 7.1 percent and therefore a real net cost of 2.6 percent. Eighteen months later, the 8.4 percent interest rates corresponded to an aftertax rate of 6.0 percent and a real after tax rate of 2.7 percent. Thus, in this case, the real net-of-tax rate actually rose despite the fall in the real pretax rate. As this analysis shows, by focusing on short-term nominal interest rates the FOMC members could convince themselves that they were being very aggressive in easing money even though the relevant real after-tax cost of funds to borrowers changed very little and may actually have increased.

Interest rates were not the only misleading indicator of monetary policy. Some analysts, both inside the Federal Reserve and outside, place substantial weight on the rapid growth of the narrow $M1$ monetary aggregate that consists of only currency and checkable deposits. In contrast to the lethargic movement of $M2$, $M1$ rose rapidly, increasing 8.0 percent between the end of 1990 and the end of 1991 and then rising at a rate of over 10 percent in 1992. Those analysts who focused on $M1$ concluded that monetary policy was very easy.

Experience has shown, however, that $M1$ has a much less stable relation to nominal GDP than $M2$. This has been particularly true since the introduction of interest-bearing checkable deposits. Deposits now move easily between $M1$ and the other parts of $M2$, making it difficult to establish a relation between $M1$ and nominal GDP. Although the Federal Reserve continues to publish $M1$ statistics, it no longer has a target range for $M1$.

The same problem exists with respect to the monetary base, a measure that includes only currency and bank reserves and that is therefore favored as an analytical tool by those who want a measure of monetary policy that is directly controlled by the Federal Reserve. The monetary base also grew very rapidly during this period, rising at a rate of more than 8 percent in 1990 and again in the first half of 1991. However, although the monetary base may seem conceptually useful as a truly exogenous instrument of monetary policy, it has a very unstable relation to GDP. Moreover, more than 80 percent of the increase in the monetary base during this period was due to the rise in currency, much of it held abroad. Thus the monetary base was another misleading indicator of the state of monetary policy.

A further misleading indicator of monetary ease was the decline of the dollar. The dollar, which stood at 1.73 marks and 138 yen in the spring of 1991, fell approximately 10 percent during the following year. Although a falling dollar can be evidence of an easy monetary policy, in 1991-92 it was driven by more fundamental factors, including the persistent and indeed rising U.S. merchandise trade deficit and the return of the U.S. current account to deficit after the brief period in which international payments for U.S. expenses in Desert Storm created a current account surplus.

2.3 *FOMC Attitudes*

Although I have emphasized relatively technical reasons why the FOMC members did not pursue a more aggressive monetary policy, these technical factors only reinforced the more basic attitudes of some of the members.

For some members, the desire to crush inflation quickly was dominant. Despite declines in both nominal and real GDP from 1988 to 1990, there had been no progress in lowering inflation. The GDP price indices showed inflation rates of over 4 percent, as high or higher than they had been at any time since 1983. These FOMC members were ready to accept the risk, indeed the likelihood, of a continued recession as the price to be paid for making progress in breaking inflation. The argument that a gradual recovery after the downturn in late 1990 would be compatible with falling inflation was not persuasive to those who wanted to reduce inflation with greater speed and certainty.

The other relatively common attitude among FOMC members that caused complacency about the failure to meet the Fed's targeted growth of $M2$ was a sense that the monetary aggregates as such are not important. These Fed members emphasize the short-run volatility of velocity. They regard the setting of $M2$ targets as something imposed on them by Congress rather than as a useful guide to monetary policy. Although, all other things equal, they would have preferred to be closer to the targeted $M2$ levels, they were not willing to drive interest rates down faster during 1991 and early 1992 in order to achieve that.

3 THE FED'S LACK OF DIRECT CONTROL OF $M2$

An important reason why the Fed did not achieve its $M2$ targets is that it does not have the ability to control $M2$ directly. In the language of the Tinbergen analysis, $M2$ is not an instrument of policy controlled by the monetary authority. The link between Federal Reserve policy and the $M2$ money stock has thus become very different from the standard textbook picture.

In the textbook world, banks must keep reserves in proportion to the stock of money. The Federal Reserve's open market purchases of Treasury bills increases bank reserves and thus automatically raises the money stock in proportion to the increase in reserves.

In reality, however, banks are now only required to hold reserves against a portion of checkable deposits. No reserves are required for about 80 percent of $M2$. Open market purchases of securities by the Fed automatically lead to a rise in $M1$ but do not necessarily lead to an increase in $M2$.

In practice, the banks have responded to increases in reserves by substituting low cost $M1$ funds (checkable deposits) for the more expensive $M2$ funds (certificates of deposit and money market deposit accounts).

Since the Fed does not have an automatic or precise way of changing $M2$, it must rely on a statistically estimated relation between the short-term federal funds rate (which it can control directly and precisely by open market operations) and subsequent movements of $M2$. On the basis of this relation, the Fed selected the level of the fed funds rate that it thought would produce its desired levels of $M2$ in 1991 and 1992. But when the equation turned out to be wrong, the Fed acted only slowly to reduce the fed funds rate further.

Reserve requirements, which are set by the Federal Reserve, used to be applied to most types of deposits. Since the Fed pays no interest on the funds that the banks deposit as required reserves, the reserve requirements act as a tax on bank deposits. This tax was particularly heavy in the 1970s and early 1980s when inflation caused short-term rates to be very high. This 'reserve requirement tax' made it more difficult for banks to attract deposits after the creation of money market mutual funds. Since the Fed is precluded by law from paying interest on deposits, it has chosen to reduce and eliminate reserve requirements.

If Congress had responded to the increase in the competitive environment of banks by permitting the Fed to pay interest on required reserves, the Fed would have been able to maintain reserve requirements on all types of bank deposits that are in $M2$ and would therefore be able to control $M2$ directly. (This proposal to reassert the Fed's control over $M2$ is discussed more fully in my June 10, 1991 *Wall Street Journal* article.)

Without that mechanical link between open market operations and $M2$, the Fed can reduce interest rates but it cannot control the stock of $M2$. That apparently put too much of a burden on the Fed in trying to judge just how low interest rates had to go to give the stimulus equivalent to the targeted increase in $M2$.

4 THE NEW BANK CAPITAL REQUIREMENTS

The ability of the Federal Reserve to influence the growth of $M2$ and bank credit has also been impaired by the new capital standards. The Basel Accord of 1988 provided that banks engaged in international finance should, by the end of 1992, have capital equal to 8 percent of a risk-weighted measure of total assets. For this purpose, business and personal loans other than mortgages are fully weighted, individual household mortgages are weighted by 50 percent and government bonds are not counted at all. These new bank capital requirements that are now being phased in have significantly reduced the ability and willingness of banks to raise funds and make loans.

The regulatory authorities in the United States decided to apply the risk-weighted capital standards to all U.S. banks, not just those engaged in international finance. They also imposed a separate capital requirement (the 'leverage capital ratio') that applies to all bank assets without any risk weighting. (On the importance of the leverage ratio, see my March 6, 1992 *Wall Street Journal* article and the article by Richard Syron, President of the Federal Reserve Bank of Boston in its 1992 *Annual Report*. For additional comments on the issue of bank capital requirements, see my *Wall Street Journal* articles of February 6th and 21st 1991.)

Many banks did not have enough capital to meet these standards, especially those banks which had suffered losses on real estate and developing country loans. Tough supervisory standards required substantial write-downs of bank capital and a narrow definition of bank assets that ignored the value of the bank as an operating business further depressed the measured value of bank capital. Raising additional capital by issuing new shares was often either impossible or very expensive.

Banks with inadequate or barely adequate capital therefore chose instead to reduce their total risk-weighted assets. They did this in part by substituting low-weight securities (government bonds and home mortgages) for commercial loans and in part by reducing their total assets. Between December 1990 and July 1992, commercial banks added $160 billion of government securities to their portfolios while reducing other loans and investments by $20 billion.

Since the total assets of a bank are equal to its liabilities plus its equity capital, banks that reduced total assets had to reduce their liabilities (*i.e.*, deposits and other borrowing) as well. To shrink their liabilities, banks cut the interest rates that they paid for different types of deposits relative to the yields available on money market funds, bond funds and other substitutes. Since these bank deposits are the components of *M2*, the need to shrink assets to conform to the capital standards led banks to reduce *M2*. The leverage capital requirement was particularly powerful in this regard since banks could not meet the leverage capital standard by substituting government bonds for commercial loans; total assets and liabilities had to be reduced.

For those banks whose total assets are constrained by their available capital, open market operations obviously cannot lead to an increase in *M2*. But even banks that are not literally capital-constrained are reluctant to make loans and investments that will bring them close to their capital limits. They want a reservoir of additional capital as protection against losses that might drive them to or below the required capital level. They want extra capital to meet uncertain loan demands from good customers. And they are now being encouraged by the regulators to accumulate even higher capital ratios by new rules that permit 'well capitalized' institutions to undertake new lines of business, to make acquisitions and to pay less for their deposit insurance. It is not surprising that banks are reluctant to bid for funds with which to increase their assets and prefer to purchase government bonds than to make loans. Because they are focusing on improving their capital ratios, they are less likely to respond to open market operations by increasing their total assets and liabilities and more likely to use the additional reserves to shift to lower cost *M1* deposits while leaving *M2* unchanged.

There is no doubt that increased capital requirements improve the soundness of the banking system and reduce the risk to the government as provider of deposit insurance and lender of last resort. But the timing of the introduction of the Basel Accord capital standards and the addition of domestic leverage capital standards have been a barrier to the current economic recovery. These capital requirements do not make monetary policy impotent but they do make it less powerful than it would be if open market operations could cause a general expansion of bank lending.

5 CONCLUDING THOUGHTS

The weakness of the American economy in 1991 and 1992 is a serious problem not only for the United States but also for other countries around the world that are linked to the United States through trade. The failure of monetary policy to stimulate the American economy is therefore a problem of interest to us all.

In this paper I have explored the reasons why the Federal Reserve did not pursue a more expansionary policy in 1991 and most of 1992. Because reserve requirements apply to only about one-fifth of *M2*, the Fed lacks a reliable way of predicting the effect of open market operations on the subsequent change in *M2*. The Fed has therefore emphasized the statistical relation between changes in the fed funds rate and subsequent changes in *M2* and economic activity. During the past two years, however, the changes in the Fed funds rate have failed to have the effects on *M2* and nominal GDP that previous experience had suggested.

The new bank capital standards may be the primary reason for the reduced sensitivity of *M2*, of commercial bank lending and of total nominal spending to changes in open market operations and interest rates. In this uncertain environment, the FOMC acted in an overly cautious way, in part because of their reliance on a variety of misleading indicators of the stance of monetary policy.

Avoiding future failures of U.S. monetary policy, both in stimulating expansion and in preventing inflation, requires more accurate indicators of the condition of monetary policy and alternative reserve requirement rules that permit tighter links between open market operations and subsequent movements of the broad monetary aggregate.

Summary

THE RECENT FAILURE OF U.S. MONETARY POLICY

The very slow growth of the broad money supply has been a primary source of U.S. economic weakness in 1990 through 1992. The velocity link between *M2* and the subsequent level of nominal GDP has not declined. But changes in bank reserves brought about by open market operations have had much less effect on *M2* than the Fed anticipated for two reasons: (1) reserve requirements now apply to only a small fraction of total *M2*; and (2) the new bank capital requirements limit some banks' ability to lend. The Federal Reserve failed to appreciate the importance of these conditions and misjudged the strength of the monetary policy stimulus that it was providing.

NAME INDEX